# American Institute of Parliamentarians Study Manual

A Study Guide for those
Preparing for an
AIP Accrediting Exam

American Institute of Parliamentarians
2012

# American Institute of Parliamentarians Study Manual

Referenced to
*American Institute of Parliamentarians Standard Code of Parliamentary Procedure*
*Robert's Rules of Order Newly Revised*, 11th Edition
*Parliamentary Law*

© 2012
By American Institute of Parliamentarians
(888) 664-0428
www.aipparl.org
aip@aipparl.org

**All rights reserved**
No part of this book shall be recorded, reproduced by photocopying, or stored in a retrieval system by any means electronic, mechanical, or otherwise without written permission from the publisher.

Students of parliamentary procedure may reproduce portions of the book for use in their education and training sessions.

Produced in the United States of America.

Third Printing, ISBN 978-0-942736-17-5
Printed July 2015
**3** 4 5 6 7 8 9 10

## ACKNOWLEDGMENTS

The Education Department of the American Institute of Parliamentarians thanks the following 2011-2012 AIP Accrediting Department members for development of this manual:

James N. Jones, PRP, CPP-T, Accrediting Director
Mary L. Randolph, PRP, CPP-T, Assistant Accrediting Director
Linda A. Juteau, PRP, CPP-T, Chair, CP Examiners Division
and
Dominic Holzhaus, CP, for providing the appendix materials.

# FOREWORD

This book is designed to help the student of parliamentary procedure recognize similarities and differences in two of the most commonly used parliamentary authorities.

The question and answer sections of this manual are limited to material pertaining to *American Institute of Parliamentarians Standard Code of Parliamentary Procedure* (AIPSC) and *Robert's Rules of Order Newly Revised*, 11th edition (RONR). The appendix provides a study based on the question section of *Parliamentary Law* (PL).

If you are using this manual as a study guide in preparation for certification be aware that additional parliamentary authorities will also be included in any AIP examination at either the Certified Parliamentarian (CP) or Certified Professional Parliamentarian (CPP) level. You should become familiar with other materials and the charts included in both authorities. Keep in mind that the references included in the materials are only a few of the many references that pertain to the questions asked and should be used as a starting point for further study.

> The study questions and answers in this book are intended only for general parliamentary study. The manual is intended to give examples of the types of questions that may be included in a written exam and not intended to be ones on a specific exam. The exam will also include parliamentary authorities not included in this manual.

# PARLIAMENTARY STUDY MANUAL
# CONTENTS

## Questions Section

Multiple Choice ..................................................................................................................7

Short Response ..................................................................................................................30

Essay ..................................................................................................................................39

Scripts ................................................................................................................................43

## Answers Section

Multiple Choice ..................................................................................................................47

Short Response ..................................................................................................................67

Essay ..................................................................................................................................85

Scripts ................................................................................................................................94

## Appendix A ..................................................................................................................98

References:
*Robert's Rules of Order Newly Revised*, 11th Edition (**RONR**)
*American Institute of Parliamentarians Standard Code of Parliamentary Procedure* (**AIPSC**)
*Parliamentary Law* (**PL**)

# Multiple Choice Questions

# Multiple Choice Questions

1. When a society adopts a parliamentary manual—such as **RONR** or **AIPSC**—the rules of that manual are _____ upon it in all cases where they are not inconsistent with the bylaws, any special rules that have been adopted, or any provisions of local, state, or national law applying to that particular organization.
   A. persuasive
   B. pervasive
   C. instructive
   D. binding
   E. suggestive

2. Assume that the society has adopted **AIPSC** as its authority. The chair or parliamentarian consults **RONR** and finds an answer given. **RONR**'s rule is _____.
   A. persuasive
   B. pervasive
   C. instructive
   D. binding
   E. suggestive

3. A state chapter of the American Civil Liberties Union (ACLU) holds a regular convention bringing together its several local chapters. The state ACLU bylaws should
   A. establish a quorum for the convention.
   B. authorize a periodic convention (e.g., yearly).
   C. specify who will be authorized to vote.
   D. prescribe the qualifications of delegates and alternates.
   E. include all of the above.

4. Which one of the following statements about a point of order is accurate?
   A. It is debatable.
   B. It can be reconsidered.
   C. It requires a second.
   D. It is normally decided by the entire assembly.
   E. It can be applied to any breach of the assembly's rules.

5. According to **RONR**, a motion to adjourn is always privileged except
   A. when the motion is qualified, as in a motion to adjourn at a particular time.
   B. when a time for adjournment has already been established.
   C. when there is no provision for another meeting and adoption of the motion to adjourn would have the effect of dissolving the assembly.
   D. A is the only correct answer.
   E. A, B, and C are all cases in which the motion loses its privileged status.

6. According to **AIPSC**, the rank of a motion (or its order of precedence) is determined by
   A. whether or not it requires a second.
   B. the position or status of the mover.
   C. its timing: when it is offered during a meeting.
   D. the motion's urgency.
   E. experience in the British Parliament.

© American Institute of Parliamentarians. All rights reserved.

7. An appeal from the decision of the chair
   A. is given the unusual right to interrupt a speaker, since it must be made immediately or not at all.
   B. must be stated by the chair as an unbiased question: "Those in favor of sustaining the ruling of the chair ...."
   C. is generally debatable; the presiding officer does not need to leave the chair while offering his reasons for the ruling.
   D. majority or tie vote sustains the chair's decision.
   E. all of the above are accurate statements.

8. The assembly authorized the presiding officer to appoint members of a special committee. How does **AIPSC** say the chair of that committee is determined?
   A. In naming committee members, the presiding officer names the chairman first.
   B. Since the assembly authorized the committee, it should name the chair.
   C. The chair calls for nominations and has the assembly elect the chair.
   D. The presiding officer uses a "fill in the blank" procedure to determine the committee chair.
   E. If not elected or appointed, the committee elects its own chair.

9. All but one of the following are advantages of committees. Which does not fit the set?
   A. Greater freedom of discussion is possible.
   B. Domination by the chair is unlikely since he must remain neutral.
   C. Procedure in the comparatively small group can be quite informal.
   D. Hearings may be held to allow members to express their opinions.
   E. Delicate questions can be discussed away from the glare of publicity.

10. What best describes an ex officio member of a committee?
    A. An ex officio member is elected by the assembly or appointed by the chair.
    B. An ex officio member has the same rights as any other member except the right to vote.
    C. An ex officio member is best identified as a consulting or advisory member.
    D. It is desirable to make the president an ex officio member of all committees.
    E. An ex officio member has the same rights, responsibilities, and duties as any committee member including the right to vote.

11. **AIPSC** finds that all but one of the following are little used motions best ignored in most societies. Which does not fit the set?
    A. Object to consideration.
    B. Postpone indefinitely.
    C. Expunge.
    D. Consider informally.
    E. Reconsider and enter on the minutes.

12. Only one of the following motions is subject to amendment. Which is it?
    A. Close debate (previous question, impose cloture, vote immediately).
    B. Question of privilege.
    C. Division of the assembly.
    D. Refer to committee.
    E. Postpone temporarily (Lay on the table).

© American Institute of Parliamentarians. All rights reserved.

13. In the absence of any special rule in the bylaws or standing rules, a majority vote means
    A. a majority of the votes cast by legal voters.
    B. a majority of a quorum.
    C. a majority of the total membership.
    D. a majority of those present.
    E. a majority of those voting, including abstentions and blank ballots.

14. **AIPSC** uses a different term for "I move the previous question." In **AIPSC**, what language is preferred?
    A. Postpone temporarily.
    B. Vote immediately.
    C. Close debate and vote immediately.
    D. I move we vote now.
    E. None of these fairly represents **AIPSC**.

15. **RONR** uses what motion to dispose of a question without a direct vote?
    A. Postpone definitely.
    B. Postpone temporarily.
    C. Lay on the table.
    D. Postpone indefinitely.
    E. Suspend the rules.

16. Which of the following can legally interrupt a speaker who has the floor?
    A. Point of order.
    B. Rescind.
    C. Recess.
    D. Division of the question.
    E. Motion that the rules be suspended.

17. All but one of the following are advantages of the nominating committee. Which does **not** fit the set? Nominating committees can
    A. study the qualifications of candidates for office.
    B. review the leadership needs of the organization.
    C. secure prior consent to serve from candidates.
    D. prevent unnecessary and undesirable nominations from reaching the floor.
    E. interview candidates and prepare summaries of qualifications of candidates.

18. A voice vote seems indecisive to you. The chair listens carefully, and then announces that the ayes have it. As a member of the assembly opposed to the proposal, you are skeptical. Your best course of action is to:
    A. appeal from the decision of the chair.
    B. rise to a parliamentary inquiry.
    C. rise to a point of order.
    D. call for a Division of the Assembly.
    E. throw up your hands in despair because the chair and the supporters of that particular motion have obviously won the day.

19. The chair calls for a rising majority vote on the motion before the assembly. It is obvious to everyone that the motion has carried by an overwhelming majority. The chair fails to call for the negative vote. You, as one of the opponents wishing to register your opposition, should
   A. appeal from the decision of the chair.
   B. move to reconsider the vote by which the motion "passed."
   C. call for a division of the assembly.
   D. rise to a point of order that the negative vote must be called for.
   E. throw up your hands in despair, because nothing will help.

20. Only one of the following motions is legal. Which is the correct one?
    A. I move that we declare unanimous the election of Mr. X for President.
    B. I move that we suspend our rules to allow our distinguished visitor from national headquarters to address us for ten minutes.
    C. Even though our quorum requirement is twenty, and only fifteen are in attendance, I move that we suspend the rules and proceed with business.
    D. I move that we instruct the secretary to turn in a fire alarm to test the response speed of our fire department.
    E. I move that we suspend the bylaws and elect our president by roll call vote.

21. Which one of the following motions permits full debate on the merits of the main question before the assembly?
    A. Withdraw.
    B. Postpone definitely.
    C. Rescind.
    D. Refer (Commit).
    E. Resume consideration.

22. According to **RONR**, what vote is required to take the unusual step of expunging something from the record?
    A. Unanimous (general) agreement by those present and voting.
    B. A two-thirds vote of those present and voting.
    C. A two-thirds vote of all those present.
    D. An affirmative vote of a majority of the entire membership.
    E. **RONR** requires advance notice and calls the action inadvisable.

23. A debatable appeal from the decision of the chair has been made. Which one of the following statements is accurate?
    A. As with all other motions, the chair may not participate in debate unless he leaves the chair and allows the vice president to preside.
    B. Motions to limit or close debate may not be applied to the appeal.
    C. The chair must give those making and seconding the appeal priority in stating their case to the assembly.
    D. The presiding officer, without leaving the chair, may open and close debate.
    E. The presiding officer should state the question this way: "Shall the decision of the chair be reversed by the assembly?"

© American Institute of Parliamentarians. All rights reserved.

24. When the mover of a motion wishes to withdraw his motion,
    A. he can do so freely until the motion has been stated for debate by the chair.
    B. after such statement by the chair, he may withdraw with unanimous (general) consent.
    C. when anyone objects to the request to withdraw, a motion to withdraw can be made by anyone and passed by a majority vote.
    D. the seconder has no special right to object to withdrawal.
    E. all of these statements are accurate.

25. Which one of these statements about the motion to reconsider is **not** correct?
    A. According to **RONR**, but not **AIPSC**, the motion may be made only by one who voted with the prevailing side.
    B. Except in a continuing convention, it may be made only on the same day that the original motion was acted upon.
    C. If made while other business is pending, it is recorded by the secretary but not taken up until pending business is handled.
    D. Action taken under authorization of the original motion cannot be reversed.
    E. The motion requires either advance notice or a two-thirds vote.

26. Which of the following motions may **not** be made on the demand of a single member?
    A. Raise a question of privilege.
    B. Division of the assembly.
    C. Create a blank.
    D. Orders of the day.
    E. Point of order.

27. Which of the following procedures may interrupt a speaker?
    A. Point of order.
    B. Questions of privilege (personal or of the assembly).
    C. Parliamentary inquiry.
    D. Division of the assembly.
    E. Any of the above may interrupt the speaker.

28. The motion to limit or extend debate may do which of the following?
    A. Specify a certain number of speakers to be heard on either side.
    B. Specify the length of time to be assigned to proponents and opponents.
    C. Fix the time at which a final vote will take place on the motion.
    D. Limit the amount of time any speaker may use.
    E. Any of the above may be included.

29. To which of the following can the motion to suspend the rules be applied?
    A. The organization's bylaws.
    B. The organization's charter.
    C. Rules requiring a secret ballot.
    D. Rules protecting absentees.
    E. None of the above may be suspended by any vote.

30. According to **AIPSC**, which of the following does **not** describe a minority committee report?
    A. When any members disagree with a report submitted by a majority of committee members, they submit a report signed by all who agree.
    B. The minority report is presented immediately after the majority report.
    C. The minority report is voted on before the majority committee report.
    D. If a motion to submit the minority report for the committee report is adopted, the majority report is filed for reference.
    E. More than one minority report may be presented.

31. Who prepared the 2012 *American Institute of Parliamentarians Standard Code of Parliamentary Procedure*?
    A. Alice Sturgis, not long before her death.
    B. Sally Sturgis, granddaughter of Alice Sturgis.
    C. Committee of the National Association of Parliamentarians.
    D. Committee appointed by McGraw Hill, publisher of the volume.
    E. Authorship team appointed by the American Institute of Parliamentarians.

32. Procedures in small boards or committees are much less formal than in large parliamentary bodies. Even so, which of the following is essential?
    A. Official actions require a formal decision by those present and voting.
    B. A quorum consists of those who attend a formally called meeting.
    C. The chair should rise when putting a motion to vote.
    D. No formal motion should be entertained unless it is seconded.
    E. The chair presides, but does not argue for or against any proposal.

33. For an organization meeting annually or semi-annually, how should approval of the minutes be handled?
    A. They should be mailed promptly to all members and approval sought at the next meeting of the organization.
    B. The secretary and president should get together and both sign the minutes as a symbol of their mutual approval.
    C. There is no special rule or advice. Handle them just as though the organization met weekly.
    D. The executive committee, or a minutes committee appointed especially for that purpose, should review the minutes as soon as possible and report their approval (with or without corrections) at the next meeting.
    E. No problem! Let the secretary report at the next meeting.

34. **AIPSC** discusses a "Consent Agenda." This unit includes items of business
    A. that are likely to attract many questions.
    B. that will not be controversial.
    C. that must be voted on without change as a whole ("en bloc").
    D. to which members have agreed beforehand.
    E. that require unanimous (general) consent from the membership.

35. Which of following may be suspended by two-thirds vote?
    A. Quorum provision in a constitution or bylaws.
    B. Standing rule requiring advance notice of intent to amend the Constitution.

C. Rules protecting minorities, certainly larger than one third.
D. Standing rules permitting only members to speak during debate.
E. None of these may be suspended under any circumstances by any vote.

36. The opening paragraph of the minutes should include all but one of the following. Which does **not** fit the set?
    A. Date, hour, place of the meeting.
    B. Names of all guests present.
    C. Name of the presiding officer (and secretary, or secretary pro-tem).
    D. Name of the society or assembly.
    E. Type of meeting.

37. The motion to adjourn is privileged in only one of the following cases. Which one does **not** fit the set?
    A. When the motion is qualified to set adjournment at a future time.
    B. When a main motion is pending.
    C. When a time for adjournment has been established by a previously adopted motion or program.
    D. When the effect of the motion to adjourn would be to dissolve the assembly with no provision for a future meeting.
    E. When the assembly is engaged in voting or verifying the results of a vote.

38. **RONR** uses Object to Consideration "to enable the assembly to avoid a particular original main motion altogether …" Which of the following is **not** a characteristic of this motion?
    A. It must be made before any debate has taken place.
    B. It can be applied only to an original main motion.
    C. It requires a second.
    D. It requires a two-thirds vote against consideration.
    E. All of the above are accurate.

39. All but one of the following accurately describes an appeal from the decision of the chair. Which does **not** fit the set?
    A. Its purpose is to enable a member to challenge the chair's ruling.
    B. Since it is the right of any member, it does not require a second.
    C. Permits debate on the merits of the chair's ruling.
    D. **RONR** permits each member to speak only once in debate.
    E. Can have motions to limit or close debate applied to it.

40. All but one of the following statements accurately describes ex officio members of a committee. Which one does **not** fit the set?
    A. Ex officio members hold membership on certain boards and committees "by reason of office."
    B. In order to provide continuity, ex officio members continue membership after expiration of their term of office.
    C. Unless otherwise prescribed in the bylaws, ex officio members have all the rights, including the right to vote, of other committee members.
    D. If the president is made a member of all committees, he should be an advisory or consulting

member and not an ex officio member.
E. The bylaws identify officers who are designated as ex officio members of boards or committees.

41. When one proposes an "amendment by substitution" to a main motion, he is offering
    A. a primary amendment.
    B. a secondary amendment.
    C. an incidental motion.
    D. an incidental main motion.
    E. none of the above accurately describes a substitute motion.

42. Presiding officers frequently hear a member propose a "friendly amendment" during debate. How should this be handled?
    A. There is no such thing. The member is out of order.
    B. It must be handled exactly as any other proposed amendment.
    C. If the proposal seems useful, the chair may ask if there is any objection, and if not, declare the motion as amended before the assembly.
    D. In all cases, a majority vote is required to adopt any amendment.
    E. None of these procedures are helpful.

43. The subsidiary motion to limit debate can be
    A. applied to all main motions.
    B. applied to all debatable motions of any type.
    C. postponed to a certain time in the same meeting.
    D. used to block debate on a touchy subject.
    E. it is not subject to amendment.

44. At a large convention, members of a particular delegation or group may hold a caucus. According to **RONR,** a caucus
    A. restricts the right of other groups to debate.
    B. permits partisans of a particular view to plot strategy.
    C. serves political purposes only.
    D. requires members to vote as the caucus instructs.
    E. serves only uninstructed delegates.

45. How should a nominating committee be constituted?
    A. The best committee consists of present officers and members of the Executive Committee (Board) since they know who has been active.
    B. For speed and efficiency, the president should appoint members to the nominating committee.
    C. Election of the nominating committee by the membership is preferred.
    D. The Executive Board should simply serve as the nominating committee.
    E. The president should serve ex officio with those elected by the members.

46. Which of the following statements apply to consideration on presenting a single slate?
    A. If the bylaws require, the committee presents a single slate.
    B. A single slate does not promote competition for office in organized bodies.

C. A single slate may discourage qualified members to run for office from the floor.
D. A multiple slate may discourage competent candidates who do not relish the prospect of campaigning for office.
E. All are accurate statements.

47. If the motion to limit debate is unqualified (does **not** specify on which motion or motions debate is to be so limited), the motion applies to
    A. the immediately pending question only.
    B. all pending debatable motions of any type or rank.
    C. the main motion and adhering amendments.
    D. all pending incidental, privileged, or subsidiary motions.
    E. the decision of the chair.

48. The motion to refer (commit) can be applied to
    A. any pending main motion only.
    B. any main motion with pending amendments.
    C. everything that is before the assembly at the time.
    D. all main and subsidiary motions.
    E. all are accurate statements.

49. The motion to rescind (or repeal) can be applied to
    A. any motion that was passed, no matter how long ago.
    B. only to motions passed by less than a two-thirds vote.
    C. fines paid by members under regulations in effect at the time.
    D. an appeal from the decision of the chair.
    E. a motion that can be reached by the motion to reconsider.

50. Which of the following motions has the highest precedence?
    A. Commit or Refer.
    B. Repeal or Rescind.
    C. Suspend the rules.
    D. Question of privilege.
    E. Adjourn.

51. Under **RONR**, a call for the orders of the day
    A. stops all proceedings in their tracks.
    B. demands that the predetermined agenda be followed.
    C. is not permitted to interrupt a person who has the floor.
    D. even if accurate, can be rejected by a majority vote.
    E. must be seconded, to avoid frivolous and dilatory tactics.

52. In which of the following cases is a second required?
    A. Nominations made from the floor.
    B. Resolutions brought forward from a committee.
    C. The motion to object to consideration.
    D. The motion to consider seriatim (or by paragraph or section).
    E. The motion for division of the assembly.

53. With one exception, these rules govern the request to withdraw a motion. Which one does **not** fit the set and is **not** an accurate statement?
    A. The initial request must be made by the original mover.
    B. Until the motion has been stated by the chair, the mover may withdraw or amend his motion on his own initiative.
    C. Once the motion has been stated by the chair, it is the property of the assembly and may be withdrawn only with its consent.
    D. The seconder must concur in the request to withdraw the motion.
    E. Once the request has been made and objection offered, anyone may move that the motion be withdrawn, despite the objection.

54. If your parliamentary authority is **RONR**, which one of the following motions opens the main motion to debate?
    A. Object to consideration.
    B. Lay on the table.
    C. Postpone indefinitely.
    D. Refer (Commit).
    E. Division of the question.

55. According to **AIPSC**, to recess when a main motion is **not** pending is classified as a (an)
    A. incidental main motion.
    B. privileged motion.
    C. incidental motion.
    D. request.
    E. main motion.

56. A proposal has been referred to a committee. The committee has failed to report either favorably or unfavorably. Supporters worry. What is their most obvious procedure?
    A. Fret and stew, since once assigned to the committee, it is the exclusive possession of that committee and the organization is helpless.
    B. Order the committee to report at the next meeting of the organization.
    C. Withdraw the proposal from committee and bring it back to the floor by two-thirds or majority vote, depending on circumstances.
    D. Transfer it to another committee.
    E. The presiding officer should talk privately with the committee chair.

57. An amendment to an amendment
    A. is not subject to further debate but only to a final vote.
    B. may itself be amended provided the original mover agrees.
    C. may not be amended.
    D. opens the main motion to further discussion.
    E. requires a two-thirds vote for adoption.

58. The motion to Refer (Commit) in **RONR**
    A. is a privileged motion.
    B. may be applied to any main motion along with any pending amendments.
    C. is a demand to be decided by the chair.

D. is amendable only as to the number of members of the committee.
E. may interrupt a speaker who has been assigned the floor.

59. Which one of the following motions or procedures may be made without securing recognition from the presiding officer?
    A. Previous question (Close debate).
    B. Adjourn.
    C. Lay on the table (Postpone temporarily).
    D. Division of the assembly.
    E. Division of the question.

60. The motion to reconsider may be applied
    A. to any decision made earlier in the same session.
    B. only to motions that were adopted at an earlier session.
    C. only to motions that were defeated at an earlier session.
    D. to motions that were withdrawn earlier in the day.
    E. to any decision made at the last regular session, if it occurred no less than a month earlier.

61. Under **RONR**, on those rare occasions when the organization agrees to rescind and expunge from the minutes, the secretary should:
    A. record the fact that the motion was adopted and the exact material affected.
    B. cover the expunged item with a black marker so that it cannot be read.
    C. draw a line around the offending language and write "rescinded and ordered expunged."
    D. blot out or cut out the expunged material so that it cannot be read in the minutes, but keep a separate record of the action taken.
    E. be sure to include the expunged material, and the notation, in any publication of the records.

62. Several members have spoken for and against the proposition before the assembly. What guides the presiding officer in recognizing members?
    A. The member who is fastest on his feet and rises first.
    B. The member who has not yet spoken on the issue, provided that he represents the opposite side from the speaker who just yielded the floor.
    C. The member who, by calling "Mr. Speaker" most loudly and clearly, indicates that he is anxious to speak.
    D. The seconder of the original motion, if he seeks recognition.
    E. The maker of the motion who now wishes to speak a second time.

63. An appeal from the decision of the chair
    A. is subject to debate on a debatable motion.
    B. does not require a second.
    C. may be made only by the person who raised the original point of order.
    D. requires a two-thirds vote to reverse the decision of the chair.
    E. is not permitted to interrupt the speaker.

64. If the chair of a committee fails to call a meeting, who has the right to call a committee meeting? (Assume that **RONR** is the parliamentary authority.)
    A. The president of the organization.
    B. The secretary of the committee (if it has chosen one).
    C. Any two committee members.
    D. The secretary of the organization.
    E. No one.

65. Which officers are essential in order to conduct business in a deliberative assembly?
    A. presiding officer and secretary.
    B. presiding officer, secretary, and parliamentarian.
    C. presiding officer, secretary, and treasurer.
    D. presiding officer, vice chair, secretary, and treasurer.
    E. nobody is indispensable except the presiding officer.

66. The member seconding a motion
    A. always favors the motion he seconds.
    B. must do so before debate can begin.
    C. must be acceptable to the mover of the original motion.
    D. may not speak or vote against the motion.
    E. must rise and secure recognition from the chair before offering his second.

67. According to **RONR**, when the privileged motion to adjourn is pending, which one of these motions or procedures is still in order?
    A. Motion to lay on the table.
    B. Point of order.
    C. An amendment specifying a future time for adjournment.
    D. Motion to recess.
    E. None of these are possible while the motion is pending.

68. Which of the following procedures is amendable?
    A. Appeal from the decision of the chair.
    B. Close debate (previous question).
    C. Request to withdraw a motion.
    D. Postpone definitely.
    E. Division of the assembly.

69. Which of the following motions is classified as an incidental motion?
    A. Appeal.
    B. Recess.
    C. Extend the limits of debate.
    D. Question of privilege of the assembly.
    E. Rescind.

70. Assume that all of the following motions are before the assembly. Which is the immediately pending question?
    A. Postpone definitely.
    B. Limit debate.
    C. Amend.
    D. Withdraw.
    E. Refer (Commit).

71. Before the motion has been stated by the chair, the request to withdraw requires
    A. only the wish of the maker of the motion.
    B. permission of the chair.
    C. two-thirds agreement by the members of the assembly.
    D. either unanimous (general) consent or a majority vote of the members.
    E. None of these will work; the motion must come to a vote, aye or no.

72. A second implies that the person offering the second
    A. believes that the motion should come before the assembly for debate.
    B. believes that the motion should be entered into the minutes.
    C. believes that the motion should be passed.
    D. will speak for and vote for the motion.
    E. will refrain under all circumstances from speaking against the motion.

73. Which one of the following motions may be made without obtaining recognition from the chair?
    A. Adjourn.
    B. Lay on the table.
    C. Division of a question.
    D. Division of the assembly.
    E. Question of privilege.

74. An appeal from the decision of the chair
    A. can interrupt a speaker because it must be made immediately or not at all.
    B. requires a second.
    C. is sustained by a tie vote.
    D. cannot be amended.
    E. all of these describe the motion to appeal from the decision of the chair.

75. The motion for the previous question (close debate) may be applied
    A. only to main motions and applicable subsidiary motions.
    B. to all pending debatable motions.
    C. only to two main motions and their amendments.
    D. this motion can be applied to any motion or procedure.

76. A question of privilege
    A. may be either personal and individual or relate to the entire assembly.
    B. is given the right to interrupt a speaker if necessary.

C. is usually granted (or refused) by the presiding officer.
D. if stated in the form of a motion, requires a second.
E. all of these describe a question of privilege.

77. If the motion to recess is made when no motion is pending it is classified as
    A. a main motion.
    B. a privileged motion.
    C. a subsidiary motion.
    D. an incidental motion.
    E. none of these accurately describes the motion to recess under these circumstances.

78. Which one of these motions requires a second?
    A. Motions made in a small board or committee.
    B. Nominations made from the floor.
    C. Recommendations for action made by a committee.
    D. Call for a division of the assembly.
    E. Motion to withdraw a subject from a committee to which it has been assigned.

79. Which statement does **not** fit the pattern on the motion to close nominations?
    A. It is not advised by either **RONR** or **AIPSC**.
    B. It is normally made unnecessary by a simple statement by the chair, once there are no further nominations.
    C. It requires a two-thirds vote when permitted (even asked for) by the chair.
    D. A second is required.
    E. It should not be recognized while any member seeks to make nominations.

80. Assume that after a careful count of the vote by the secretary or tellers committee the result is clearly a tie. What happens then?
    A. Debate resumes and another vote is taken some time later.
    B. The chair must vote to break the tie.
    C. The motion is defeated.
    D. Since the chair is a member, nothing can be done.
    E. The motion is automatically held over and comes up under unfinished business at the next meeting.

81. **AIPSC** recognizes the specific main motion Adopt in-lieu-of. Which of the statements does **not** apply to this motion?
    A. The motion is debatable and amendable.
    B. The motion expedites business by considering similar resolutions at one time.
    C. The motion is used when a resolution committee reports its recommendations to the assembly.
    D. All submitted resolutions must be considered before adoption of the motion to Adopt in-lieu-of may be voted on.
    E. If the motion to Adopt in-lieu-of is not adopted, the underlying resolutions may be considered.

82. Which of the following statements does **not** apply to an honorary member or officer?
    A. Such titles are conferred as a compliment to the person recognized.
    B. Honorary members may attend meetings and speak on issues.
    C. If he or she is a member of the organization, honorary officers lose their regular membership rights.
    D. Honorary titles are normally perpetual unless specified in the bylaws.
    E. Honorary members may not make motions or vote unless specified in the bylaws.

83. Assume that several candidates have been nominated for office and that no one receives a majority vote on the first ballot. What does **RONR** say should be done?
    A. A run-off election should be held between the top two vote-getters, as is customary in elections for public office.
    B. When repeated balloting for an office is necessary, the names of all nominees are kept on the ballot.
    C. The nominee who receives the smallest number of votes must withdraw.
    D. The presiding officer should ask the membership for instructions.
    E. After the number of ballots specified in the bylaws, a plurality vote should be sufficient to elect.

84. **RONR** offers a detailed discussion of filling blanks. All but one of the following accurately describes the procedure. Which does **not** fit the set?
    A. The number of alternatives is not limited as it would be in the ordinary process of amendment.
    B. Members have an opportunity to weigh all choices before voting.
    C. Each proposal is debatable and is treated independently.
    D. Voting on proposals always takes place in the order in which they are proposed.
    E. The chair, may, without objection, create a blank in a situation in which that seems appropriate to him.

85. Which of the following motions is both amendable and debatable?
    A. Resume consideration (take from the table).
    B. Postpone to a certain time (postpone definitely).
    C. Suspend the rules.
    D. Appeal from the decision of the chair.
    E. Rescind.

86. Committees whose duties are specified in the constitution or bylaws are known as
    A. constitutional committees.
    B. standing committees.
    C. special committees.
    D. reference committees.
    E. procedural committees.

87. When individuals gather to form a new organization, the first order of business is to
    A. elect a committee to write a set of bylaws.
    B. compile a roster of charter members.

C. elect a temporary presiding officer and temporary secretary (president and secretary pro tem).
D. introduce a keynote speaker.
E. ask someone to explain the purpose of the proposed organization.

88. May a member debating a proposal before the assembly yield his time to another member? If so, to whom is the time charged?
    A. The speaker who did not use all the time permitted.
    B. The speaker to whom the time was yielded.
    C. The time is not charged against anyone.
    D. Except in legislative bodies operating under their own rules, time allocated to one member cannot be transferred to another member.
    E. The speaker may use the remainder of his time at a later period.

89. The duty of a Reference (Resolutions) Committee is to
    A. make a recommendation to the voting body on each proposal assigned to it.
    B. screen proposals and discard those deemed inappropriate.
    C. rewrite submitted proposals before reporting to the assembly.
    D. reach consensus so that no minority recommendations are made.
    E. determine who may submit resolutions to the committee.

90. **RONR** recommends object to consideration to avoid all debate on a subject. **AIPSC** prefers that members use
    A. Point of order.
    B. Postpone indefinitely.
    C. Table.
    D. Call for the orders of the day.
    E. none of these will achieve the desired result.

91. The recording secretary
    A. must keep a verbatim (audiotape) record of proceedings.
    B. may discard committee reports that recommend no action.
    C. sees to it that inquisitive members do not read the minutes.
    D. may not vote when motions come before the assembly.
    E. may participate in debate and vote on motions.

92. The member elected as vice president
    A. may be asked to preside when the president wishes to discuss a pending question.
    B. serves as presiding officer in the absence of the president.
    C. becomes president on the death, resignation, or permanent incapacity of the president (unless the bylaws provide otherwise).
    D. is often assigned responsibilities by the bylaws or by the board.
    E. all of these make the role of the vice president important.

93. When the president asks the vice president to preside so that he can discuss the pending question before the assembly, he returns to preside when
    A. he has completed his statement on the motion.

B. the motion has been amended or modified to his liking.
C. the end of the business section.
D. the main motion under consideration has been disposed of.
E. the vice president asks him to resume the chair.

94. The nominating committee has submitted a list of nominees. The presiding officer then asks for nominations from the floor. There being no further nominations, he or she
   A. asks the committee chair to close nominations.
   B. asks for a motion to close nominations.
   C. declares the nominations closed.
   D. calls for a majority vote to close nominations.
   E. does nothing.

95. Three members at large are to be elected to the Board of Directors. You take advantage of the bylaws provision permitting cumulative voting by
   A. casting all three of your votes for a single candidate.
   B. casting only one vote, but that for your candidate.
   C. voting over and over again, on successive ballots, for your candidate.
   D. cumulative voting has no special advantage for you or your candidate.
   E. cumulative voting is a violation of the principles of parliamentary law.

96. In a small board or executive committee
   A. minutes are kept by the secretary.
   B. members do not need to seek recognition before speaking, but only one member may speak at a time.
   C. informal discussion of a problem or policy proceeds even in the absence of a formal motion.
   D. when motions are made, no second is required.
   E. all of these accurately describe proceedings in small boards or committees.

97. Why is it unwise to require an affirmative vote of a majority of the members present to pass a motion?
   A. Anyone who abstains becomes automatically a negative vote.
   B. Some members may not understand or have any interest in the motion.
   C. No member can be compelled to vote.
   D. Such a requirement would increase divisiveness and generate hostilities.
   E. All of the above are true.

98. When a vacancy occurs on a committee, it is normally filled by
   A. a new election by the entire membership.
   B. the Board of Directors of the society.
   C. the appointing power, whatever authority is so identified in the bylaws.
   D. the remaining members of the committee.
   E. the president.

99. According to **AIPSC,** can the maker of a motion speak against it?
   A. Certainly not, that would confuse everyone.

B. Of course, members have a right to change their minds.
C. Only if it has been amended to reverse its intent.
D. **RONR** and **AIPSC** agree that this is permissible.
E. Only if by a majority vote the assembly permits it.

100. **RONR** believes that the motion to postpone indefinitely
    A. is so confusing that the presiding officer should reject it.
    B. is a useful strategic motion giving the opposition a chance to get a test vote without danger of passage.
    C. should be handled by the chair as a motion to table.
    D. should be used only for its legitimate purpose, to postpone for a time.
    E. should not be debated.

101. When someone offers what he calls a "friendly amendment," how should the chair respond?
    A. The chair may look to the original mover and if he agrees, ask whether there is unanimous (general) agreement to adopt the "friendly amendment."
    B. The chair may ask if there is objection, and in the absence of any objection, declare the motion amended.
    C. If the chair has not yet stated the motion ("put" the motion for debate) the original mover may modify it as he chooses, including this amendment.
    D. If anyone objects, including but not limited to the original mover, the chair is well advised to handle this like any other amendment.
    E. All of these are correct.

102. How many candidates should a nominating committee nominate for each office?
    A. At least two so that there is competition for the offices.
    B. As many as find support from a member of the nominating committee.
    C. Any member who wants to run for an office.
    D. Those who meet the qualifications as laid down in bylaws or other document of authority.
    E. None of these is correct.

103. How should a female presiding officer be addressed?
    A. Chair or Chairperson is used by some organizations.
    B. Chairman is traditional and used in Congress, most state legislatures, and some associations.
    C. An organization is free to use whatever address is appropriate for their organization.
    D. When presiding, Madam President (Speaker, Moderator) is often used.
    E. All of these statements are true.

104. Seconds are not required
    A. for motions of routine business matters.
    B. in small committees.
    C. for recommendations made in committee reports.
    D. for requests to be settled by the presiding officer, such as division of the assembly, question of privilege.
    E. all of the above are correct.

© American Institute of Parliamentarians. All rights reserved.

105. All but one of the following are classified as incidental motions, according to **AIPSC**. Which one is **not**?
    A. Appeal from the decision of the chair.
    B. Point of order.
    C. Parliamentary inquiry.
    D. Division of a question.
    E. Postpone to a certain time.

106. The most commonly used method of voting is
    A. a voice vote.
    B. a rising vote.
    C. a show of hands vote.
    D. a roll call vote.
    E. a written (secret) ballot.

107. All but one of the following accurately describes the motion to refer to committee. Which one does **not** fit the set?
    A. Cannot interrupt the speaker.
    B. Requires a second.
    C. Debate may extend into the merits of the main motion.
    D. Requires a majority vote.
    E. Takes precedence over the motion to amend.

108. The usual method for disposing of a committee's written report is to
    A. receive the report.
    B. file the report.
    C. add the report to the agenda at the next meeting for final action.
    D. adopt the report.
    E. dismiss the committee from further study.

109. According to **RONR**, the motion to postpone indefinitely
    A. opens the main motion to debate and gives those who have exhausted their time for debate under the rules a second chance to speak.
    B. is often made by those opposed to a main motion to get a test vote without danger of passage.
    C. does not postpone, but, if adopted, actually kills the main motion.
    D. is not used by **AIPSC.**
    E. all of these are accurate statements.

110. An amendment to a main motion
    A. must be in accord with the purpose of the original motion.
    B. must be germane to the original motion.
    C. may insert a negative ("not") before the action verb of the motion.
    D. may not offer a substitute for the entire motion.
    E. may add to but not subtract from the original motion.

111. A member in good standing
    A. may be defined in the bylaws.
    B. may not apply to a member under disciplinary action.
    C. may be limited in scope of membership rights.
    D. may vary from organization to organization.
    E. All these statements are true.

112. The "common law" requirement for a quorum in a membership organization is
    A. ten percent of the membership.
    B. a third of the regular members of the organization.
    C. a majority of the regular members of the organization.
    D. two-thirds of the members.
    E. there is no "common law" requirement for a quorum.

113. You are presiding when a member moves the previous question. He or she is seeking to:
    A. kill the motion entirely.
    B. secure a "straw vote" on the motion before the assembly.
    C. close debate on the motion before the assembly.
    D. return to the motion that has just been decided.
    E. delay a vote on the motion before the assembly.

114. You are presiding. The results of a voice vote are indecisive. Someone calls for a division of the assembly. What should you do next?
    A. To save time, ask for another voice vote and listen more carefully.
    B. Ask the secretary to call the roll of members.
    C. Ask those favoring the motion to sit on your right and those opposed on your left and appoint a tellers committee to count the vote.
    D. Ask for a rising vote.
    E. Ask for debate on whether or not a division is really needed.

115. The agenda item of Unfinished Business refers to
    A. any topic discussed at an earlier meeting.
    B. repeal or rescinding a previous action.
    C. any motion left pending by adjournment of the last meeting.
    D. a motion postponed definitely from the last meeting.
    E. both C and D should appear under Unfinished Business.

116. The motion to close nominations
    A. is the best strategic method of preventing competition once your favorite candidate has been nominated.
    B. is a desirable tactic once two candidates have been nominated.
    C. must be made, seconded, and passed before nominations can be closed.
    D. should not be accepted until members have made all desired nominations.
    E. requires only a majority vote.

117. The presiding officer should ask a member to yield the floor and resume his seat if he or she
   A. speaks longer than the time specified in standing or special rules.
   B. attacks another member by name.
   C. discusses the main motion when an amendment is the immediately pending question.
   D. uses language offensive to a sizable part of the membership.
   E. the presiding officer should do so in all cases described.

118. You have volunteered (or been elected) to be secretary for an organization. Your minutes should always include
   A. all motions or resolutions, with the name of the proposer and the disposition of each motion.
   B. a running summary of debate on critical substantive resolutions.
   C. the name of the person seconding a very substantive motion.
   D. approval of members who make extraordinary contributions to the debate.
   E. notes that the debate was "heated" or a report especially "able."

119. Debate may be limited
   A. by the presiding officer when he believes that there has been enough debate for members to make up their minds.
   B. whenever several members "call the question."
   C. whenever debate becomes repetitious, with nothing new offered.
   D. by a motion made, seconded, and carried by a two-thirds vote.
   E. this should not be done until all members have had their say.

120. The member seconding a substantive main motion
   A. must do so before debate begins.
   B. needs to be identified and recorded in the minutes.
   C. always favors the motion he seconds.
   D. should be called on by the presiding officer as soon as the original proposer has made his/her speech.
   E. must rise and secure recognition before offering a second.

121. A meeting is held in continuation of the immediately preceding regular meeting. Work is taken up at the point where it was interrupted. Minutes of the preceding meetings are read. That later meeting is considered what type of meeting?
   A. Annual.
   B. Special.
   C. Session.
   D. Executive.
   E. Adjourned.

122. The provisions of the bylaws of an organization may be suspended
   A. by majority vote, but only with advance notice.
   B. by two-thirds vote, but only with advance note.
   C. by unanimous (general) consent.
   D. by majority vote on authorization by the executive committee.
   E. may not be suspended by any vote unless authorized in the document.

123. All but one of the following statements about the motion to reconsider is accurate. Which one does **not** fit the set?
    A. It can interrupt proceedings if necessary, e.g., even after the assembly has voted to adjourn but before the presiding officer has spoken.
    B. It does not require a second.
    C. It applies to votes on main motions taken at the same meeting.
    D. It requires only a majority vote to reconsider even if vote of the original motion required a two-thirds vote.
    E. It is debatable.

124. Which one of the following statements does **not** accurately describe "point of order?"
    A. It may interrupt a speaker.
    B. It requires a second.
    C. It normally requires a ruling by the chair but no vote of the assembly.
    D. It is undebatable unless the chair is in doubt and refers the matter to the assembly.
    E. It cannot be amended.

125. An ex officio non-member of a committee
    A. may speak (have "voice") but not vote.
    B. may vote but not participate in debate.
    C. is not permitted to make motions.
    D. has the same rights as any other member unless the bylaws say otherwise.
    E. retains the position until the committee has completed its assignment.

# Short Response Questions

These study questions are intended only for general parliamentary study. They are intended to show the type of questions that may be used but are to be taken only as a starting point for further study.

# Short Response Questions

1. The appointed chair of a newly created special committee fails to call a meeting. Does this mean that the committee does not meet? What can be done to call the meeting and what are the responsibilities of the person calling the meeting?

2. Are there important differences between procedures in small committees (for instance 5-7 members) and large committees? If so, what are they?

3. A committee has five members plus the president of the organization, who is made an ex officio member of all committees. What is the quorum for the committee under **RONR**? Under **AIPSC**? Explain.

4. Suppose that a committee member fails to attend meetings or cooperate with other members. What can be done, and by whom?

5. What are some of the restrictions for a committee to hold an electronic meeting? Is the meeting considered to be a deliberative body even though not meeting face-to-face?

6. What is a plurality vote and are there circumstances where this might be a preferred choice?

7. Assume that your motion to hire an executive director for your favorite organization has been defeated. During the next several months you believe that the need for such a position and the ability of the organization to sustain it has been amply demonstrated. What is your procedure?

8. What does **AIPSC** mean by repeal by implication? What term does **RONR** use?

9. Under **RONR**, what is the purpose of the motion to Reconsider and Enter on the Minutes?

10. When you raise a point of order, the chair has three options among which he must choose. What are they?

11. The chair rules that your point of order "is not well taken." What are your options?

12. Under **AIPSC**, someone moves that the main motion (and of course all pending amendments and other adhering motions) be tabled. Assume that you are chairing the meeting. What vote would you require to adopt the motion and why? What is the effect of adoption of the motion?

13. The president is often made an ex officio (or a consultant) member of all committees—except one. What is it and why?

14. A committee report closes with a resolution for adoption by the assembly, but the reporting committee member fails to move its adoption. What then? How do you as presiding officer resolve the situation?

15. You as presiding officer conduct a voice vote, but are in doubt about the outcome. What do you do?

16. The assembly has decided to elect three members to a special committee. Five nominations are received and on the first ballot two receive a majority vote and are declared elected. Since you are conducting the election, what do you do next?

17. In a large assembly you as presiding officer need to appoint tellers to distribute, collect, and count the ballots. How do you decide whom to appoint?

18. A large national organization employs a professional parliamentarian. Assume that you are that parliamentarian. Discuss your duties and your relationship with the presiding officer.

19. You are parliamentarian and there is a challenge to the tellers' report on the officer elections. You are asked by the presiding officer for guidance. How do you advise under **RONR**? Under **AIPSC**?

20. Members sometimes want to suspend the rules because they prove inconvenient at a particular point of the meeting. You as presiding officer need to know what rules cannot be suspended, even by two-thirds vote or unanimous agreement. What are these rules?

21. What is the meaning of the term precedence? What is the difference between precedence and precedent?

22. A member makes a correction to the minutes being approved. How does the secretary record the correction? Why is this process used?

23. What is the role of the president-elect?

24. The convention adjourns *sine die*. What does that mean?

25. Give three legitimate examples of Privilege of the Assembly as distinguished from Personal Privilege.

26. In an election conducted by ballot, what kinds of ballots are illegal?

27. What is the basic Order of Business recognized by **RONR**? What is the basic Order of Business recognized by **AIPSC**?

28. A mass meeting has been called for supporting a candidate for office. What is the quorum for this meeting?

29. What is meant by raise a question of privilege as opposed to questions of privilege?

30. The treasurer reports at each monthly meeting, summarizing receipts and expenditures, and calling attention to any unusual items. How do you as presiding officer handle the report? What action, if any, does the assembly need to take?

31. Many organizations still include on the agenda an item called "Old Business." This is, however, a misleading name. Why? What is the better term for this agenda item?

32. What types of items are included in unfinished business?

33. A president pro tem is presiding. Does this member have all the authority of the elected president? If not, what, if any limitations are placed on this pro tem officer?

34. On certain occasions it may be desirable to offer some background or little-known information as a preamble to a resolution. What term introduces these clauses? Do you see any potential danger in the use of one or more such clauses? Do all resolutions require a preamble?

35. You have been elected a delegate to the national convention of the local organization to which you belong. Should you ask for and be given instructions on how to vote on particular issues to come before the convention?

36. A minority on a committee wishes to present a minority report. Do they have the right to do so?

37. Main motions normally require a second. There are, however, some exceptions. Name some of these exceptions.

38. As presiding officer, you ask the assembly, "Is there any Unfinished Business?" The parliamentarian whispers that this is a mistake. Why?

39. You think that the society should not hear any discussion of a particularly touchy subject and you do not want to have it be discussed at all. If **RONR** is your authority, what do you do? If **AIPSC** is the authority, what then?

Short Response Questions

40. At a convention, what can be done before the first report of the Credentials Committee?

41. What parliamentary authority do legislative bodies (state and national) use?

42. What is the highest internal authority for a voluntary organization? What other documents must be considered and what is their order of rank?

43. What is the difference between the privileged motions to recess and to adjourn?

44. Is it true that in most organizations a member **not** nominated cannot be elected?

45. Who has the authority to fill a vacancy in a committee or office?

46. Sometimes an organization may need to use a non-member presider. What is the most common situation where this may arise? What is the process to place that person into the position of presider?

47. As president of an organization meeting annually, you call for the report of the minutes approval committee. Then what?

48. A member asks you, as presiding officer, if he may divide the question that is before the assembly. You do not think this is a good idea and advise that the motion would be out of order. What then?

49. May a member of a nominating committee become a candidate for office?

50. Explain the meaning of a "disappearing quorum."

51. Discussion of the immediately pending question has been going on for some time. The presiding officer decides that debate has continued long enough and calls for a vote. What do you do?

52. You are presiding. In preparation for an election, nominations are being made. Someone rises and wants to second a nomination. How do you handle it?

53. Can the bylaws (resolution) committee kill any proposed amendment by refusing to report it to the voting body? What procedural limits does the committee have?

54. A majority vote is sometimes defined as 50% plus one. Is this correct? How is a majority

© American Institute of Parliamentarians. All rights reserved.

generally defined?

55. Can a plurality vote ever be sufficient to elect an officer or adopt a motion?

56. **RONR** differentiates among Committee of the Whole, Quasi Committee of the Whole, and Informal Consideration. How does **AIPSC** handle the matter?

57. Ordinarily the bylaws specify the number or percentage of the membership required for a quorum and the legal conduct of business. Suppose the bylaws are silent. What then?

58. Assume that there are a motion, an amendment, and a motion to refer to committee before the assembly. Someone moves to close debate. To what does this form of the motion apply and what other forms of the motion may be applied to the pending motion(s)?

59. What is the purpose of a continued (adjourned) meeting, and how does it differ from simple adjournment?

60. What happens if an organization with no fixed date and time for a monthly or quarterly meeting fails to call a meeting? Does the organization default?

61. The presiding officer tells a member that an amendment may be hostile but must be germane. Explain.

62. What is an ad hoc committee?

63. Identify the differences between **RONR** and **AIPSC** on the privileged motion to adjourn.

64. A member offers a motion with a blank. You are the presiding officer. How would you process the motion under **RONR**? How would you process the motion under **AIPSC**?

65. People change their minds all the time. Decisions made at one point in time may later be rescinded. What are exceptions to this rule?

66. In an assembly, someone wants to make a speech before offering his motion. How do you as presiding officer handle this situation?

67. There is a difference between a general order and a special order. What is the difference, and how are these two orders handled?

68. Differentiate between standing and special committees.

69. Assume that an organization to which you belong takes some action of which you heartily disapprove. Can you resign?

70. You are involved in the creation of a new organization and have been assigned the task of preparing a set of bylaws. What vote and procedure are required for their adoption according to **RONR**? According to **AIPSC**?

71. Your organization already has a set of bylaws. What vote and procedure is required to amend them according to **RONR**? According to **AIPSC**? May notice of a proposed amendment be withdrawn?

72. Suppose that instead of amending the existing bylaws, your organization decides to write a completely new set. How is this different from amending the bylaws? Does this differ under **RONR** and **AIPSC**?

73. You are the author of a motion before the assembly. As you listen to the debate, you become convinced that it is not really a good idea after all. Can you now speak against it?

74. Someone proposes that the organization spend $50 on refreshments for the next meeting. You think the idea is ill-advised and rise to amend by inserting the word "not" before the word "spend." Is this legitimate?

75. Votes may be conducted in many different ways. There is a generally accepted order in which votes are taken within an assembly. What is this order? Is it different in **RONR** and **AIPSC**?

76. You have been asked to take a proxy for a member who will be unable to attend your organization's meeting but would like to vote on business that will be coming up at the meeting. What is a proxy? How are proxies used? Does **RONR** or **AIPSC** recommend the use of proxies?

77. Once you have voted, can you change your mind and your vote?

78. In a regular meeting of an organization can the chair vote?

79. Can a member abstain from voting? When is an abstention considered a negative vote?

80. Should the presiding officer call for abstentions, count them, and make that part of his report?

81. What is meant by the precedence of motions?

# Short Response Questions

82. Do all motions fit into the order of precedence?

83. According to **AIPSC,** what are Specific Main Motions? How are these motions identified in **RONR**?

84. Suppose that the organization adjourns while debating a piece of business. What happens to that motion?

85. Why is the notice of meetings—and of proposals (like amendments to the bylaws) that require advance notice to the members—so critically important?

86. What may an organization do if previous notice was not given and there is an item of business that needs to be taken up?

87. May a member vote for someone who was **not** nominated by a nominating committee or from the floor?

88. What is preferential voting and when is it desirable?

89. What does the term cumulative voting mean? Explain the process.

90. What does the term bullet-voting mean?

91. Following an election, a member rises to move that the secretary cast a unanimous ballot for the winning candidate. Is this permissible?

92. As secretary, you ask for the name of the member seconding a motion so that you can put that name in the minutes, but the president tells you that this is not necessary. Why?

93. How are the members of a special committee chosen?

94. Is there a time limit on a member's right to raise a point of order?

95. Suppose an officer resigns from office. Can he or she have a change of mind and resume the office before another election takes place or appointment is made?

96. If an organization meets only quarterly, semi-annually, or annually, it is difficult for members to

remember what happened in the last meeting, and therefore to correct the minutes with any sense of certainty. How does an organization avoid this problem?

97. **RONR** places a limitation on members eligible to move to reconsider a previous vote. How does this differ under **AIPSC**?

98. If at the appointed time to call the meeting to order a quorum is not present, what can those present do? Does this mean that the meeting was not officially held?

99. **RONR** gives the highest precedence to the motion to fix the time to which to adjourn which allows an organization to set an adjourned meeting. How does **AIPSC** handle setting of a future meeting?

100. A member, while speaking to a motion, concludes by moving the previous question. What is **RONR**'s position in this situation? How does **AIPSC** handle this situation?

# Essay Questions

These study questions are intended only for general parliamentary study. They are intended to show the type of questions that may be used but are to be taken only as a starting point for further study.

# Essay Questions

1. Discuss the basic principles of parliamentary law and why they are important.

2. You have been elected president of an organization. One of your duties is to preside over membership meetings and probably those of the executive committee (or board). Discuss other requirements of your new position.

3. What is the importance of the secretary as a leader in an organization? List some of the essential duties of the secretary.

4. Describe how a board (executive board) is created. What is its purpose and powers?

5. You have been elected secretary of a small organization.
    a. What should the minutes include?
    b. What should the minutes not include?

6. What is previous notice and why is it important? How should previous notice be given?

7. An organization meets only annually. At the first business session the president asks for corrections to and approval of the minutes, which were distributed as members registered for this meeting. Is there a better way than asking members to remember what happened a year ago? Explain any options an organization may have.

8. During an election, no candidate receives a majority on the first ballot. How does **RONR** proceed with subsequent ballots? Does **AIPSC** agree or does **AIPSC** have a different procedure? Explain.

9. You are the presiding officer. There are circumstances that may occur during a meeting where you should step down. What are some of these circumstances and for what period of time do you relinquish the chair?

10. You are the presiding officer and a member requests that a particular item of business be taken up out of order on the adopted agenda. Does the presiding officer have the authority to change the agenda on his or her own? Discuss how this is handled under **RONR** and under **AIPSC**.

11. A complex motion with several different provisions is moved. Discuss the intent of the motion to divide and when a motion to divide would **not** be in order.

12. Is it really necessary for an organization to observe parliamentary procedures during its meetings? Discuss why parliamentary procedures should be used in meeting of all sizes.

Essay Questions

13. You have been asked to serve as parliamentarian for the annual meeting of an organization to which you do not belong. Discuss your role as parliamentarian—noting especially your relationships to the presiding officer and to the members of the organization.

14. The president appointed a committee to review the minutes of a board meeting that lasted two days. After the meeting, copies of the minutes prepared by the secretary were mailed to members of the minutes committee. The committee agreed that certain corrections needed to be made and sent them to the secretary. The secretary disagreed with the changes made by the committee and refused to accept them. Now what happens?

15. Both **RONR** and **AIPSC** deal with committees within an organization—whether standing or special. Discuss why they are important and what part committees have in the decision process of an organization.

16. Who can attend committee meetings? Why is this significant?

17. A motion is referred to a committee with instructions to report with recommendations at the next meeting. However, no committee member is present at that meeting and no report is presented. What can or cannot the assembly do?

18. Suppose that the bylaws and the body's parliamentary authority disagree. Which controls the way the body operates? Is there a rank of authority for other documents that may impact decisions of an organization? If so, what are they and what is their order of precedence?

19. The bylaws of the society state "The president shall preside at all meeting of the organization." The assembly does not want the president to preside at the current meeting due to a major conflict within the organization, but the president has refused. Can they suspend the bylaws to allow some other officer to preside?

20. The Congress of the United States uses the motion to table to kill a pending motion. Is this applicable to an ordinary assembly? Why or why not? How do **RONR** and **AIPSC** use the motion to table?

21. The terms Reference Committee and Resolutions Committee are used interchangeably. In what context is this committee, under either name, appropriate? What are its functions?

22. "Majority vote" can be an ambiguous term. A majority of what? Discuss briefly several different ways in which the term can be defined. Which one "most commonly approves a motion or elects a candidate?"

Essay Questions

23. You are the parliamentarian for an annual meeting. A member has the floor debating a controversial motion before the body. Another member rises and asks if the speaker would yield for a question. How would you advise the chair if your parliamentary authority was **RONR**? Would it be different if the parliamentary authority was **AIPSC**?

24. A motion has been made, seconded, stated by the chair, and is being debated. An amendment has been offered, seconded, and is being debated. Another member of the assembly, rises, secures recognition from the chair, and says, "Mr. Chairman, I wish to offer a substitute motion." How would you advise the presiding officer?

25. A proposal is before the assembly to designate certain persons as honorary members (or even honorary officers). Members seem unsure about what this would mean. The presiding officer turns to you as parliamentarian to explain honorary membership to the body. How do you explain what being an honorary member or officer means?

# Scripts

The study questions are intended only for general parliamentary study. The questions are intended to show the type of questions that may be used on a credentialing exam but are to be taken only as a starting point for further study.

Scripts

Instructions: The following rules must be observed when writing your scripts:

1. The script must indicate the request for recognition to the chair.
2. The script must indicate the proper recognition by the chair whenever recognition is required.
3. The script must indicate seconds for motions that require a second.
4. The chair must ask for discussion on any debatable motion; however actual debate is not required.
5. In announcing the result of a vote, the chair must state both the number of votes in the affirmative and the number in the negative.
6. Use the following format:

    CHAIR:        [Response]

    MEMBER _:     [Response]


1. Instructions: Prepare a script, using **RONR** as your parliamentary authority, for the conclusion of a meeting of the 25 member Board of Directors of the National Parliamentarians Organization (NPO). The organization has a delegate body of 25 members. The script includes the following:

    A. An original main motion is proposed.
    B. An objection to its consideration is proposed and defeated.
    C. An amendment to make an addition to the main motion is entertained.
    D. A ruling by the chair that this amendment is not germane.
    E. This ruling is appealed and overturned.
    F. A motion to fix the time of an adjourned meeting is proposed and carried.
    G. A motion to adjourn is proposed and carried.


2. Instructions: Prepare a script, using **RONR** as your parliamentary authority. Complete the following script:

    A.   A motion to divide the question into three parts is adopted.
    B.   The first "Resolved" clause is amended and then adopted.
    C.   The second "Resolved" clause is defeated.
    D.   The third "Resolved" clause is adopted.
    E.   The following rules must be observed when writing your script:

SCRIPT OPENING:

CHAIR:        The following resolution is pending:

              Resolved, That this society endorses the political platform of Mary Smith; and be it further

              Resolved, That this society authorizes the expenditure of $1,000 to promote the candidacy of Mary Smith; and be it further

              Resolved, That this society urges its members to vote for Mary Smith in the general election.

# Scripts

|  |  |
|---|---|
| | Is there any discussion? |
| MEMBER A: | Madam Chairman. |
| CHAIR: | The chair recognizes Member A. |
| MEMBER A: | I move to divide the question into three parts and to consider each "Resolved" clause separately. |
| MEMBER B: | Second. (CONTINUE SCRIPT) |

# ANSWERS SECTION

# Multiple Choice Answers

> The study questions and answers are intended only for general parliamentary study. The "answers" given are intended to show the type of responses that may be used but are not to be taken as complete answers—only as a starting point for further study.

# Multiple Choice Answers

1. **ANSWER: D. binding.**
The manual is binding except in the cases cited which take precedence over any parliamentary authority. **RONR** p. 16, ll. 20-27. "When a society of an assembly has adopted a particular parliamentary manual—such as this book—as its authority, the rules contained in that manual are binding upon it in all cases where they are not inconsistent with the bylaws...." **AIPSC** p. 5. "A parliamentary authority is a written set of principles and specific procedural rules that can be adopted by motion or stated in bylaws that determine the rules to be followed in all meetings of the organization."

2. **ANSWER: A. persuasive.**
**RONR** pp. 16-17, ll. 29-3. "In matters on which an organization's adopted parliamentary authority is silent, provisions found in other works on parliamentary law may be *persuasive* ... but they are not binding on the body." **AIPSC** p. 277. "When no answer is otherwise clear, provisions found in other respected parliamentary authorities may provide persuasive authority on how to address a situation. ... "

3. **ANSWER: E. include all of the above.**
See **RONR** pp. 601-602, ll. 29-2.

4. **ANSWER: E. It can be applied to any breach of the assembly's rules.**
This applies to any failure to observe the assembly's rules, whether by the chair or by any member. **RONR** p. 248, l. 34. "2. Can be applied to any breach of the assembly's rules."; **AIPSC** p. 90. "A point of order calls the attention of the assembly and of the presiding officer to a violation or potential violation of the rules, an omission, a mistake, or an error in procedure." Do not confuse this with an *Appeal from the Decision of the Chair* which can be used if the member believes that the chair ruled incorrectly.

5. **ANSWER: E. A, B, and C are all cases in which the motion loses its privileged status.**
**RONR** p. 234, ll. 9-21. When the motion to adjourn loses its privileged status, it becomes subject to amendment (and debate) specifying (for instance) the time and place of the next meeting. **AIPSC** p. 79. "If a main motion is not pending, the motion to adjourn is a main motion and is open to full debate and amendment—it is subject to all the rules of a main motion."

6. **ANSWER: D. the motion's urgency.**
**AIPSC** p. 16 states "The precedence of motions is logical and is based on the relative urgency of each motion."

7. **ANSWER: E. all of the above are accurate statements.**
**RONR** pp. 257-258; table II, #18 Permits the chair to open and close the debate. He may also vote to break or create a tie. **AIPSC** p. 84-86. Permits the chair to debate first and uses the term "sustain the decision of the presiding officer."

8. **ANSWER: E. if not elected or appointed, the committee elects its own chair.**
**RONR** p. 175, ll. 24-34. "If the chair appoints or nominates the committee, he has the duty to select its chairman ... and the committee cannot elect another.... but if he neglects to state this fact, the designation nevertheless is automatic unless the first-named member immediately declines the chairmanship...." **AIPSC** p. 189. "If no committee chair is elected or appointed, one may be selected by the committee from its own membership."

9. **ANSWER: B. Domination by the chair is unlikely since he must remain neutral.**
**RONR** p. 500, ll. 17-18 "In committees, the chairman is usually the most active participant in the discussions and work of the committee." **AIPSC** p. 189 "the chair of a committee takes an active part in its discussion and deliberations...."

10. **ANSWER: E. an ex-officio member has the same rights, responsibilities, and duties as any committee member, including the right to vote.**
**RONR** p. 483, p. ll. 26-27. "…, if the ex-officio member of the board is under authority of the society,… there is no distinction between him and the other board members." **AIPSC** p.190. "Unless the organization's governing documents provide otherwise, an ex officio member has all the rights, responsibilities, and duties of other members of the committee, including the right to vote."

11. **ANSWER: D. consider informally.**
**RONR** p. 529 refers to three devices—committee of the whole, quasi committee of the whole, and informal consideration—that may function similar to committees in their deliberations, **AIPSC** p. 89 provides a method for the assembly to consider a proposal in a form close to committee function with rules of debate relaxed.

12. **ANSWER: D. refer to committee.**
**RONR** p. 170, ll. 31-35. "… in the case of a standing committee, as to the committee to which the main question is to be referred; in the case of a special committee, as to the committee's composition and manner of selection; and in the case of any form of committee, as to any instructions the committee is to follow. " **AIPSC** p. 61. "4. Amendments restricted to such details as the committee selected, membership, or duties of the committee, or instructions to it."

13. **ANSWER: A. a majority of votes cast by legal voters.**
Those who elect not to vote (abstain) allow those who do vote to make the decision for the entire body. **RONR** p. 400, ll. 8-11 "… and when the term *majority vote* is used without qualification … it means more than half of the votes cast by persons entitled to vote,…."; **AIPSC** p. 135. "A majority vote,… unless otherwise qualified, is defined as a majority of the legal votes cast by members present and voting."

14. **ANSWER: C. close debate and vote immediately.**
**RONR** pp.197 still prefers the historical term *Previous Question* and brings the assembly to an immediate vote on one or more pending questions. **AIPSC** p. 67. "A motion to close debate and vote immediately prevents or stops discussion on the pending question or questions … and to bring the pending question or questions to an immediate vote."

15. **ANSWER: D. postpone indefinitely.**
**RONR** p. 126, ll. 4-5. "*Postpone Indefinitely* is a motion that the assembly decline to take a position on the main question." **AIPSC** p. 70 uses the motion *Table* which disposes of a main motion without a direct vote on the main motion.

16. **ANSWER: A. Point of Order.**
This procedure insists that something has gone astray and needs to be considered immediately since it often affects the speaker who has been assigned the floor. **RONR** p. 249, ll. 31-33. "It is the right of every member who notices a breach of the rules to insist on their enforcement." **AIPSC** p. 90. "A point of order calls the attention of the assembly and of the presiding officer to a violation or potential violation of the rules, an omission, a mistake, or an error in procedure."

17. **ANSWER: D. prevent unnecessary and undesirable nominations from reaching the floor.**
Appointment or election of a nominating committee does not rule out nominations from the floor.
**RONR** p. 435, ll. 10-12. "After the nominating committee has presented its report and before voting for the different offices takes place, the chair must call for further nominations from the floor." **AIPSC** p. 160. "Unless the bylaws provide otherwise, nominations from the floor are always permitted …"

© American Institute of Parliamentarians. All rights reserved.

p. 162. "... it is essential that ... that both the committee and the membership be protected by permitting nominations from the floor.... It [nominating committee] should choose the candidates on the basis of what is good for all the members and not with the view that office is a reward to be given to a deserving member.

18. **ANSWER: D. call for a Division of the Assembly.**
RONR pp. 52; 280 ll.10-11. "Whenever a member doubts the result of a voice (viva voce) vote or a vote by show of hands ... he can call for the *Division of the Assembly*, thereby requiring the vote to be taken again by rising." **AIPSC** p. 102 "Division of the assembly is called to verify an indecisive voice vote or an indecisive show of hands vote by requiring members to rise and, if necessary, to be counted."

19. **ANSWER: D. rise to a point of order that the negative vote must be called for.**
RONR p. 45, ll. 4-8 "The chair must always call for the negative vote, no matter how nearly unanimous the affirmative vote may appear, except that this rule is commonly relaxed in the case of noncontroversial motions of a complimentary or courtesy nature, but even in such a case, if any member objects, the chair must call for the negative vote.." **AIPSC** p. 32. "Following the completion of the affirmative vote, the presiding officer must always take the negative vote even if it appears that the affirmative vote is unanimous."

20. **ANSWER: B. I move that we suspend our rules to allow our distinguished visitor from national headquarters to address us for ten minutes.**
RONR p. 260, ll.19-22. "When an assembly wishes to do something during a meeting that it cannot do without violating one or more of its regular rules, it can adopt a motion to *Suspend the Rules* interfering with the proposed action...." **AIPSC** p. 88 "The motion to suspend the rules allows an assembly to take a specific action, within the meeting, that would otherwise be improper under its procedural rules."

21. **ANSWER: C. Rescind.**
RONR pp. 305, ll.6-7. "... the assembly can change an action previously taken or ordered."; "*Rescind ...* is the motion by which a previous action or order can be canceled or countermanded.; p. 306, ll. 6-7. "Are debatable; debate can go into the merits of the question which it is proposed to rescind or amend." **AIPSC** pp. 49 "Adoption of a motion to rescind repeals, cancels, nullifies, or voids a motion from the time of the adoption of the motion to rescind."; 3. Is debatable and opens to debate the motion it proposes to rescind.

22. **ANSWER: D. an affirmative vote of a majority of the entire membership.**
RONR p. 310, ll. 11-13. "Adoption of the motion requires an affirmative vote of a majority of the entire membership, and may be inadvisable unless the support is even greater." **AIPSC** includes all corrections to minutes as one process and does not recognize the RONR motion to expunge from the record.

23. **ANSWER: D. the presiding officer, without leaving the chair, may open and close debate.**
The presiding officer does not have to leave the chair to give his/her rationale for the decision. The question should be put thus: "Shall the decision of the chair be sustained?" Only a majority negative vote will overrule the chair's decision. **RONR** p. 258, ll. 1-3. "... no member is allowed to speak more than once except the presiding officer—who need not leave the chair while so speaking...." **AIPSC** p. 84. After the appeal has been stated by the presiding officer, the presiding officer states the reasons for the ruling. In doing so, the presiding officer is not required to leave the chair."

24. **ANSWER: E. all of these statements are accurate.**
A request to withdraw is seldom denied by the assembly, but if anyone objects, a motion, second, and majority vote are required to withdraw. **RONR** pp. 295-297. **AIPSC** pp. 97-98.

25. **ANSWER: E. the motion requires either advance notice or a two-thirds vote.**
**RONR** p. 320, ll. 32-33. "7. Requires only a majority vote, *regardless of the vote necessary to adopt the motion to be reconsidered*." **AIPSC** p. 47. "5. Requires a majority vote."

26. **ANSWER: C. Create a Blank**
**RONR** Chart IV pp. 40-41; p.163, ll. 26-28. "The motion to create a blank requires a second, but it is neither debatable nor amendable; ...." **AIPSC** p. 55. "The motion to create a blank requires a second and is not debatable." None of the other motions listed require a second to come before the assembly for consideration.

27. **ANSWER: E. any of the above may interrupt the speaker.**
All these procedures may interrupt the speaker. **RONR** Table II. pp. 6-29 generally agrees but adds a few qualifications and several additional provisions. **AIPSC** Motions Table.

28. **ANSWER: E. any of the above may be included.**
Any one or a combination of these may be included. **RONR** p. 191, ll. 19-25. "... can limit debate by: (1) reducing the number or length of speeches permitted,... or (2) requiring that, at a certain later hour or after debate for a specified length of the, debate shall be closed.... allowing more and longer speeches...."
**AIPSC** pp. 65-66. "A motion to limit debate on a pending question or to modify limitations already set up usually relates to the number of speakers who may participate, the length of time allotted to each speaker, the total time allotted for discussion of the motion, or some variation or combination of these limitations."

29. **ANSWER: E. none of the above may be suspended by any vote.**
Not even a unanimous vote can suspend any of these. The bylaws may be amended (not suspended) in the way prescribed in its amendment article. **RONR** p. 260, ll. 21-26. "When an assembly wishes to do something ... it cannot do ... provided that the proposal is not in conflict with the organization's bylaws (or constitution), with local state, or national law ... or with a fundamental principle of parliamentary law." **RONR** p. 412, ll. 24-26 "When the bylaws require a vote to be taken by ballot, this requirement cannot be suspended, even by a unanimous vote."; **AIPSC** pp. 86-87. "... an assembly cannot suspend: 1. A rule stated in statute, charter, or the organization's constitution or bylaws unless a specific provision in these documents of authority provides for suspension of the rule 2. Rules governing ... voting methods (such as the requirement for a ballot vote)." Also see **AIPSC** Chapter 2. *Fundamental Principles of Parliamentary Law*.

30. **ANSWER: C. The minority report is voted on before the majority committee report**.
**AIPSC** p. 203. "... if a motion to dispose of the majority report is pending, the minority report is not voted on unless a motion is made to substitute it for the majority report. If such a motion to substitute is adopted and the report as amended by substitution is adopted,... the majority report is filed for reference. If the motion to substitute fails, the minority report is filed for reference."

31. **ANSWER: E. Authorship committee appointed by the American Institute of Parliamentarians.**
**AIPSC** p. vi. "The authorship team, composed of members of AIP, includes Barry Glazer, James N. Jones, James Lochrie, Michael Malamut, Mary Randolph, Ann Rempel, Mary Remson, and Thomas Soliday. All team members are certified parliamentarians, are well-respected professionals in the field, and have a wide range of experience through their clients and the American Institute of Parliamentarians."

32. **ANSWER: A. Official actions require a formal decision of those present and voting.**
**RONR** p. 503, ll. 16-21. "... a report of a board or committee can contain only what has been agreed to by a majority vote at a regular or properly called meeting of which every member has been notified ... where a quorum of the board or committee was present." **AIPSC** p. 194, "Decisions are often made by general consent (without objection), but when this is done, care should be taken that the exact wording of actions is recorded and reflects exactly what everyone agreed to; if this is not the case, amendments and majority vote may be required to adopt an action."

33. **ANSWER: D. the executive committee, or a minutes committee appointed especially for that purpose, should review the minutes as soon as possible and report their approval (with or without corrections) at the next meeting.**
**RONR** pp. 474-475. ll. 35, 2. "... the executive board or a committee appointed for the purpose should be authorized to approve the minutes. **AIPSC** p. 232. If an organization does not meet often, it is important to have a committee on minutes to which all proposed minutes are referred for correction and approval."

34. **ANSWER: B. that will not be controversial.**
**RONR** p. 361, ll. 13-14. Uses the term *Consent Calendar*. "... routine or noncontroversial matters ...."
**AIPSC** p. 120. "This is a part of the printed agenda listing matters that are routine or expected to be noncontroversial and on which there are likely to be no questions or discussion."

35. **ANSWER: D. standing rules permitting only members to speak during debate.**
**RONR** p. 263, footnote. "In contrast, the rules may be suspended to allow a nonmember to speak in debate." **AIPSC** p. 86. "Only rules of procedure can be suspended.... [the assembly] may vote to suspend the rules that interfere with the accomplishment of the specific purpose or the particular action required."

36. **ANSWER: B. names of all guests present.**
Names of guests are not an essential part of the minutes, though under certain circumstances it may be desirable to include them somewhere in the record. **RONR** p. 468, ll. 23-35. "1) the kind of meeting ... 2) the name of the society or assembly; 3) the date and time of the meeting, and the place ... 4) the fact that the regular chairman and secretary were present or ... in their absence, the names of the persons who substitute for them; and ..." **AIPSC** p. 229. "The opening paragraph records the date, hour, and place at which the meeting was called to order, the type of meeting (regular, special, or continued), the name of the presiding officer and a reference to the person recording the meeting (secretary or secretary pro tem)."

37. **ANSWER: B. When a main motion is pending.**
**RONR** p. 234, ll. 9-25. "A motion to adjourn is always a privileged motion *except* in the following cases: 1) When the motion is qualified in any way ... 2) When a time for adjourning is already established ... 3) When the effect ... would be to dissolve the assembly ...." **AIPSC** p. 79. "When a main motion is pending, the motion to adjourn is a privileged motion that takes precedence over all other ranked motions."

38. **ANSWER: C. requires a second.**
This motion is not often used, but is legitimate in any organization with **RONR** as its parliamentary authority. See **RONR** pp. 267-268, ll. 26-15. "1.... The objection can be raised only before there has been any debate or any subsidiary motion .... 2. Can be applied to original main motions .... 4. Does not require a second. 7. A two-thirds vote *against consideration* is required to sustain the objection." **AIPSC** does not use the motion *Object to Consideration*, but instead allows a motion to be "killed" by the motion to *Table*.

## Multiple Choice Answers

39. **ANSWER: B. since it is the right of any member, does not require a second.**
To facilitate accountability and prevent "game playing" both **RONR** and **AIPSC** require that more than one member desire to appeal the chair's decision, hence the requirement of a second. **RONR** pp. 255-256, ll. 29-3: "But any two members have the right to *Appeal* from his [the chair's] decision on such a question. By one member making (or "taking") the appeal and another seconding it, the question is taken from the chair and vested in the assembly for final decision." **AIPSC** p. 85 Basic rules "2. Requires a second."

40. **ANSWER: B. in order to provide continuity, ex officio members continue membership after expiration of their term of office.**
Since "ex officio" means "by reason of office," when the member leaves office, membership on designated committees also changes to the new officer. **RONR** p. 484, ll. 6-8. "When an ex-officio member of a board ceases to hold the office that entitles him to such membership, his membership on the board terminates automatically." **AIPSC** p. 190. "When an ex officio member ceases to hold office, that person's membership on the committee terminates, and the new holder of the office assumes the ex officio membership."

41. **ANSWER: A. a primary amendment.**
Sometimes a member wishes to replace the entire motion before the assembly. It must, of course, be "germane," **RONR** pp. 153-154, ll. 31-4. "A substitute offered for a main motion or resolution, or for a paragraph within a resolution, is a primary amendment …. If a motion proposes to replace one or more paragraphs that are involved in a pending primary amendment, it is a secondary amendment to which the term *substitute* is also applicable." **AIPSC** p. 55. "The substitute motion is a primary amendment and therefore is subject only to a secondary amendment. In other words, an amendment to a substitute motion cannot be amended because amendments of both first rank and second rank are already pending."

42. **ANSWER: C. if the proposal seems useful, the chair may ask if there is any objection, and if not, declare the motion as amended before the assembly.**
This calls for judgment by the presiding officer, but if the original mover and others seem to approve, the chair may save time and energy by asking if there is any objection. **RONR** p. 162, ll. 15-19. "Regardless of whether or not the maker of the main motion 'accepts' the amendment, it must be opened to debate and voted on formally (unless adopted by unanimous consent) …." **AIPSC** p. 274. "A friendly amendment is an amendment made by a member who believes that the change will be acceptable to the maker of the motion or the assembly and that the amendment could be incorporated into the motion by general consent (without a formal vote)," p. 56. "If the original motion has already been stated by the presiding officer, then the presiding officer asks it there is an objection to this acceptance."

43. **ANSWER: B. applied to all debatable motions of any type.**
It may be applied to any debatable motion, whether main, subsidiary, or incidental but the pending motion itself is not debatable. **RONR** p. 191, ll. 13-16. "The subsidiary motion to *Limit or Extend Limits of Debate* is one of the two motions by means of which an assembly can exercise special control over debate on a pending question or on a series of pending questions." **AIPSC** p. 66. "The motion to limit or extend debate may be applied to all pending debatable motions or to only the immediately pending motion."

44. **ANSWER: B. permits partisans of a particular view to plot strategy.**
**RONR** pp. 606, ll. 31-35. "The term caucus is also sometimes applied to a similar meeting of all the known or admitted partisans of a particular position on an important issue … who meet to plan strategy toward a desired result within the assembly." This is not the only purpose of a caucus, but it is one of the most important.

## Multiple Choice Answers

45. **ANSWER: C. election of the nominating committee by the membership is preferred.**
**RONR** p. 433, ll. 10-16. The nominating committee should be elected by the organization wherever possible,... the president should not appoint this committee or be a member of it—ex officio or otherwise." **AIPSC pp.** 161-162. "A nominating committee should be a representative committee.... When possible the committee should represent the demographics of the whole organization.... The president, president-elect, and immediate past president should not appoint any members of the nominating committee, serve on the committee, give the committee instructions, or take any part in its deliberations."

46. **ANSWER: E. All are accurate statements.**
**RONR** p. 433, ll. 22-28. "Although it is not common for the nominating committee to nominate more than one candidate for any office, the committee can do so unless the bylaws prohibit it. It is usually not sound to *require* the committee to nominate more than one candidate for each office, since the committee can easily circumvent such a provision by nominating only one person who has any chance of being elected." **AIPSC** p. 164. "A single slate, meaning one nominee for each office, frequently offers certain advantages provided that nominations may also be made from the floor and that election by write-in votes is not forbidden. For a number of reasons, it is usually not best practice to require the nominating committee to submit more nominations than there are positions to be filled."

47. **ANSWER: A. the immediately pending question only.**
**RONR** pp. 193, ll. 28-32. "If a series of debatable questions is pending and a motion to *Limit or Extend Limits of Debate* does not specify the motions to which it is to apply, then only the immediately pending question is affected." **AIPSC** p. 66. "The motion to limit or extend debate may be applied to all pending debatable motions or to only the immediately pending motion. To illustrate, if a main motion, an amendment, and an amendment to the amendment are pending and the proposer of the motion to limit debate does not specify the motion or motions to which the limit is to apply, only the immediate pending question—in this case, the amendment to the amendment—is affected."

48. **ANSWER: B. any main motion with pending amendments.**
**RONR** p. 169, ll. 5; 22-23. "1. Takes precedence over the main motion ... 2. Can be applied to main motions, with any amendments that may be pending; ...."; **AIPSC** p. 60. "The adoption of a motion to refer transfers the main motion and its amendments (if any) to the committee immediately."

49. **ANSWER: A. any motion that was passed, no matter how long ago.**
**RONR** p. 307, ll. 20-22. "... there is no time limit on making these motions after the adoption of the measure to which they are applied,...." **AIPSC** p. 48. "Any main motion that was adopted, no matter how long before, may be rescinded, but the rescission does not include action taken before adoption of the motion to rescind."

50. **ANSWER: E. Adjourn.**
When any other motion is pending, adjournment is privileged and outranks all others. **AIPSC** p. 79. "When a main motion is pending, the motion to adjourn is a privileged motion that takes precedence over all other ranked motions." **RONR** p. 235, ll. 16-17. "1. Takes precedence over all motions except the *privileged* motion to *Fix the Time to Which to Adjourn* ...." The highest ranking motion according to **AIPSC** is *Adjourn*. **AIPSC** p. 17. "1. When a motion is being considered, any motion of higher rank may be proposed, but no motion of lower rank may be proposed."

51. **ANSWER: B. demands that the predetermined agenda be followed.**
**RONR** p. 219, ll. 4-8. "A *Call for the Orders of the Day* is a privileged motion by which a member can require the assembly to conform to its agenda, program, or order of business, or to take up a general or special order that is due to come up at the time." **AIPSC** p. 90 uses the motion *Point of Order*. "A point of

order calls the attention of the assembly and of the presiding officer to a violation or potential violation of the rules, an omission, a mistake, or an error in procedure."

52. **ANSWER: D. consider seriatim (or by paragraph or section).**
**RONR** p. 277, l. 9. "4. Must be seconded." **AIPSC** p. 101. "2. Requires no second if granted by the presiding officer as a request, but if offered as a motion, requires a second."

53. **ANSWER: D. the seconder must concur in the request to withdraw the motion.**
The seconder, who is usually anonymous and whose name should not appear in the minutes, has no more right to object than any other member. **AIPSC** p. 97. "Only the mover of a motion has the right to request that it be withdrawn; the consent of the seconder in not necessary."

54. **ANSWER: C. Postpone Indefinitely.**
**RONR** p. 127, ll. 12-14. uses *Postpone Indefinitely* to "kill" the pending motion for the current session. "5. Is debatable; and, unlike the case of any other subsidiary motion, debate on the motion to *Postpone Indefinitely* can go fully into the merits of the main question." **AIPSC** p.71. uses the motion to Table to "kill" a motion for the current session without a direct vote. "Adoption of a motion to table stops debate on the main motion and removes it, with amendments and other adhering motions, from the consideration of the assembly during the current meeting or convention."

55. **ANSWER: E. main motion**
**AIPSC** p. 14. " ... However, certain of the subsidiary, privileged, or incidental motions may be proposed when no main motion is pending. In this situation the subsidiary and privileged motions are classified as main motions."

56. **ANSWER: C. withdraw the proposal from committee and bring it back to the floor by two-thirds or majority vote, depending on circumstances.**
This is the most obvious and direct procedure. **RONR** pp. 310-311, ll. 31-2. "By means of the motion to *Discharge a Committee* from further consideration of a question or subject, the assembly can take the matter out of a committee's hands after referring it to the committee and before the committee has made a final report on it, and the assembly itself can consider it." **AIPSC** p. 191. "Any subject or duty that has been assigned to a special committee may be withdrawn at any time and assigned to another committee or considered by the body as a whole. Any proposal or assignment of work to a standing committee may be withdrawn by the governing body unless the subject or motion is assigned exclusively to the committee by the bylaws." It is clear that although C is the best answer both B and D are possible under certain circumstances. E is another possibility before taking the action to remove the committee.

57. **ANSWER: C. may not be amended.**
Philosophically there is no reason for stopping at the second order amendment, but practically anything more would be excessively confusing. **RONR** p. 135, ll. 22-23. "An amendment of the third degree is not permitted." **AIPSC** p. 53. "Amendments of the third rank are not in order."

58. **ANSWER: B. may be applied to any main motion along with any pending amendments.**
**RONR** p. 169, l. 22-23. "2. Can be applied to main motions, with any amendments that may be pending; ..." **AIPSC** p. 61. "6. Takes precedence over the main motion and a motion to amend the main motion."

59. **ANSWER: D. Division of the Assembly.**
This is a demand for a rising vote. Sometimes the presiding officer announces the results of a vote quickly and rushes ahead to the next agenda item. This violates the rights of all members to be sure that any vote is reported correctly. See **RONR** p. 281, ll. 14-15 "3. Is in order when another has the floor and is called for without obtaining the floor; ll. 30-32 "If a member desires the vote on the division to be counted, he

must make a motion to that effect, which requires a majority vote. **AIPSC** p. 103. A call for division of assembly requires that the presiding officer take a standing vote on the motion just voted on and may count the votes if there is any doubts as to which side prevailed." "1. Can interrupt proceedings because it requires an immediate decision."

60. **ANSWER: A. to any decision made earlier in the same session.**
Reconsideration applies to motions, whether adopted or defeated, but only on the same day as the original action (except in conventions). **RONR** pp. 315-335 discusses this motion at length. **RONR** p. 316, ll. 22-26 "In a session of one day—such as an ordinary meeting of a club or a one-day convention—the motion to *Reconsider* can be made only on the same day the vote to be reconsidered was taken." **AIPSC** p. 45 "The vote on a main motion can be reconsidered at the same meeting or convention, except when, as a result of the vote, something has been done that cannot be undone.... The motion to reconsider can be applied only to the vote on the main motion, some specific main motions, and main motions that have been tabled."

61. **ANSWER: C. draw a line around the offending language and write "rescinded and ordered expunged."**
**RONR** p. 310, ll. 15-19 "If such a motion is adopted, the secretary, in the presence of the assembly, draws a single line through or around the offending words in the minutes, and writes across them the words, 'Rescinded and Ordered Expunged.' with the date and his signature.... In any published record of the proceedings, the expunged material is omitted."

62. **ANSWER: B. the member who has not yet spoken on the issue, provided that he represents the opposite side from the speaker who just yielded the floor.**
**RONR** pp. 31, ll. 8-13 "3) In cases where the chair knows that persons seeking the floor have opposite opinions on the question,... the chair should let the floor alternate, as far as possible, between those favoring and those opposing the measure." **AIPSC** p. 128 "3. The presiding officer should alternate between proponents and opponents of a motion whenever possible. ... "

63. **ANSWER: A. is subject to debate on a debatable motion.**
The presiding officer who made the ruling may open and close the debate. It requires a second and may be made by any member. A majority or tie vote (and the chair may vote to create a tie) sustains the decision of the chair. Because the appeal must be made immediately or not at all, it is given the right to interrupt a speaker. **RONR** p. 258, ll. 1-8 allows the chair to make an opening and closing statement, other members may only speak once. **AIPSC** pp. 83-85 permits normal debate rules.

64. **ANSWER: C. any two committee members.**
**RONR** p. 499, ll. 21-25 "If its chairman fails to call a meeting, the committee must meet on the call of any two of its members, unless (for very large committees) the assembly's rules prescribe, or empower the assembly or the committee to require a larger number." **AIPSC** p. 193 "If the chair fails to call a meeting, a majority of the committee members may do so, or the organization's president may call a meeting of the committee."

65. **ANSWER: A. presiding officer and secretary.**
**RONR** p. 22, ll. 1-5. "The minimum essential officers for the conduct of business in a deliberative assembly are a *presiding officer*, who conducts the meeting and sees that the rules are observed, and a *secretary*, or *clerk*, who makes a written record of what is done—usually called 'the minutes'." **AIPSC** p.178. "The president and the secretary are recognized by law as the legal representatives of the organization."

66. **ANSWER: B. must do so before debate can begin.**
The seconder is anonymous and should not be recorded in the minutes. He can speak or vote for or against the motion; the member's second simply indicates that the motion should be discussed, nothing more. Seconds are not required in legislative (representative) bodies, or in small boards or committees.
**RONR** p. 36, ll. 26-28. "The requirement of a second is for the chair's guidance as to whether he should state the question on the motion, thus placing it before the assembly." **AIPSC** p. 29. "It [the second] merely indicates that the member wishes the motion to be considered by the assembly." ... If there is no response [to the inquiry for a second] the presiding officer then proceeds to other business.

67. **ANSWER: B. Point of Order.**
Even so, any member may point out that an important matter needs action before adjournment. **RONR** pp. 238-239, ll. 21-9. lists six motions or procedures that are in order even while the motion to adjourn is pending. **AIPSC** p. 79. allows adjourn to be amended. "The privileged motion to adjourn is subject to restricted debate and may be amended to establish the time when the current meeting will end or will continue."

68. **ANSWER: D. Postpone Definitely (Postpone to a Certain Time).**
Both authorities, however, restrict proposed amendments to those concerning the time of postponement. **RONR** p. 182, ll. 16-18. "6. Is amendable as to the time to which the main question is to be postponed, and as to making the postponed question a *special order*." **AIPSC** p. 65. "4. Amendments restricted to time of postponement, or to making the postponement a special order."

69. **ANSWER: A. Appeal.**
**RONR** p. 69, ll. 21-22. "An incidental motion is said to be *incidental* to the other motion or matter out of which it arises." **AIPSC** p.12. "Incidental motions arise incidentally out of the business before the assembly. They do not relate directly to the main motion or to specific main motions but usually relate to matters incidental to the conduct of the meeting."

70. **ANSWER: D. Withdraw.**
Any motion may be withdrawn, either with no objection or by majority vote of the assembly. If the motion is withdrawn, the other motions become irrelevant. **RONR** p. 61, ll. 12-14. "The rules under which secondary motions take precedence over one another have been gradually evolved through experience. While these rules are proper to each of the specific motions, they follow patterns that are related to the division of secondary motions into the classes of *subsidiary, privileged,* and *incidental* motions." **AIPSC** p.16. "The rank of a motion determines its priority when it is proposed and the sequence in which it must be considered and disposed of.... The precedence of motions is logical and is based on the relative urgency of each motion."

71. **ANSWER: A. only the wish of the maker of the motion.**
**RONR** p. 295, ll. 28-30. "*Permission* for him to do so [withdraw] is required only after the motion to which it pertains has been stated by the chair as pending." **AIPSC** p. 97. "Before a motion has been stated by the presiding officer, its proposer may modify it or withdraw it without the assembly's permission,..." "D" comes into effect once the chair has stated the motion to the assembly for debate.

72. **ANSWER: A. believes that the motion should come before the assembly for debate.**
The seconder, who is anonymous, does not necessarily wait for recognition, does not necessarily support the motion and may, if he wishes, speak and vote against it. The second just says that the motion deserves consideration by the assembly. **RONR** p. 36, ll. 9-11. "A second merely implies that the seconder agrees that the motion should *come before the meeting* and not that he necessarily favors the motion." **AIPSC** p. 29. "Seconding a motion is not necessarily an endorsement of the motion."

73.     **ANSWER: D. Division of the assembly.**
**RONR**; p. 52, ll. 10-12; 20-21. "… any member (without a second) has the right to require that a voice vote (or even a vote by show of hands) be retaken as a rising vote,… To do so, the member, without obtaining the floor, calls out the single word 'Division!' …" **AIPSC** p. 102. "A call for a division is a demand that an indecisive vote, which has been taken by voice or a show of hands, be verified by a standing vote and, if necessary to determine the result, that the vote be counted."

74.     **ANSWER: E. all of these describe the motion to Appeal from the decision of the chair.**
**RONR** pp. 256-258, ll. 11-19. Characteristics of the motion to appeal are listed on pages 256-258. Robert adds that "b. when the chair rules on a question about which there cannot possibly be two reasonable opinions, an appeal would be dilatory and is not allowed." This ignores the probability that the person bringing the appeal probably has an opinion that is "reasonable" in his/her eyes, and possibly in the eyes of others. **AIPSC** pp. 84-85 covers the characteristics of the motion to appeal.

75.     **ANSWER: B. only main motions and applicable subsidiary motions.**
**RONR** pp. 198-199. ll. 18-19. "1. Takes precedence over all debatable or amendable motions to which it is applied, and over the subsidiary motion to *Limit or Extend Limit of Debate,*…." **AIPSC** p. 70. "6. Takes precedence over all subsidiary motions except to table."

76.     **ANSWER: E. all of these describe the Question of Privilege.**
**RONR** p. 226, ll. 13-14. "3. Is in order when another has the floor if warranted by the urgency of the situation." p. 227, ll. 12-15. "Questions of privilege are of two types: (1) those relating to the privileges of the assembly as a whole, and (2) questions of personal privilege. p. 226, ll. 26-27. "4. … the member states it in the form of a motion; such a motion must be seconded.… 7. Is ruled upon by the chair. No vote on the question's admissibility is taken unless the chair's ruling is appealed." p. 228, ll. 13-14. "… the chair rules whether the question is a question of privilege." **AIPSC** pp. 73-76. "Privileged motions deal with basic members rights, actions requiring immediate attention, and actions of the assembly as a whole.… The presiding officer may decide that a particular motion is not a proper question of privilege and rule it not in order.… When a question of privilege is presented as a motion, it is a main motion which is given special privilege. It follows all the rules of a main motion except.… Proposing a question of privilege secures appropriate action by the presiding officer on a request, or by the assembly on a motion, in order to meet an immediate need of emergency."

77.     **ANSWER: A. a main motion.**
**RONR** p. 230, ll. 29-32. "A motion to recess that is made *when no question is pending* … is a *main motion*, and the eight characteristics … apply to it." **AIPSC** p.78. "As with all privileged motions, the motion to recess is privileged only if it is proposed when a main motion is pending. If it is proposed when no main motion is pending, it is a main motion."

78.     **ANSWER: E. motion to withdraw a subject from a committee to which it has been assigned.**
**RONR** p. 311, l. 3. The motion to Discharge a Committee "4. Must be seconded." **AIPSC** p. 191. "Any subject or duty that has been assigned to a special committee may be withdrawn at any time and assigned to another committee or considered by the body as a whole."

79.     **ANSWER: D. is required.**
**RONR** pp. 288-289, ll. 22-2. "In the average society, a motion to close nominations is not a necessary part of the election procedure and it should not generally be moved. When nominations have been made by a committee or from the floor, the chair should inquire whether there are further nominations; and when there is no response, he declares that nominations closed. … it is out of order if a member is rising, addressing the chair, or otherwise attempting to make a nomination, and it always requires a two-thirds vote." **AIPSC** pp. 160-161. "When there appear to be no further nominations for a particular office, the

presiding officer may declare nominations for that office closed. A motion to close nominations is not required but, if made is unamendable and undebatable and requires a two-thirds vote for adoption. The presiding officer should not recognize a motion to close nominations or declare them closed if any member is rising for the purpose of making a nomination."

80.    **ANSWER: C. the motion is defeated.**
Remember that nothing (except an appeal) passes on a tie vote. **RONR** p. 405, ll. 21-22. "... the presiding officer, if a member of the assembly, can (but is not obligated to) vote whenever his vote will affect the result ..." **AIPSC** p. 142-143. "The presiding officer, if a member of the assembly, does have the right to cast a vote. However, in an assembly the presiding officer customarily exercises that right only when the vote is by ballot or when his or her vote will make a difference in the result....The presiding officer cannot be required to cast a vote."

81.    **ANSWER: D.   All submitted resolutions must be considered before adoption of the motion to Adopt in-lieu-of may be voted on.**
**AIPSC** p. 224. "The reference committee recommends that its motion, which is fully stated, be adopted in lieu of the other resolutions, specifically identifying those to be replaced.... When the vote is taken on the motion to adopt in-lieu-of, an affirmative vote adopts, and that is the only vote needed. If adopt in-lieu-of fails, no options have been eliminated."

82.    **ANSWER: E. all of these describe the honorary member or officer.**
**RONR** p. 463, ll. 8-22; "An honorary office is in fact ... a complimentary title that may be bestowed on members or nonmembers.... they must be authorized in the bylaws.... is perpetual—unless rescinded or its duration is limited by the bylaws. Rights carried with the honor include the right to attend meetings and to speak, but not to make motions or vote unless the person is a regular member,..." **AIPSC** p. 181. "Honorary titles are created as a compliment to those on whom they are conferred. Honorary titles generally carry with them the right to attend meetings and to speak. However, they do not confer the right to propose motions, vote, or preside."

83.    **ANSWER: B. when repeated balloting for an office is necessary, the names of all nominees are kept on the ballot.**
**RONR** p. 441, ll. 5-10. When repeated balloting for an office is necessary, individuals are never removed from candidacy on the next ballot unless they voluntarily withdraw—which they are not obligated to do. The candidate in lowest place may turn out to be a 'dark horse' on whom all factions may prefer to agree." In some cases this may prove to be true, but not many organizations have the patience to sit through an interminable number of ballots. (Note footnote page 441.)

84.    **ANSWER: D. voting on proposals always takes place in the order in which they are proposed.**
**RONR** pp. 162-166 offers a choice of methods for arranging and voting on proposals. **AIPSC** p. 55 recommends D. "... the presiding officer opens discussion on the suggestions followed by a vote on each suggestion in the order in which each was proposed."

85.    **ANSWER: B. Postpone to a Certain Time (Postpone Definitely).**
**RONR** and **AIPSC** both agree that debate and amendments are limited, that debate must not go into the merits of the main motion more than absolutely necessary, and that amendment is limited to the time of postponement. **RONR** p. 182, ll. 12-15. "5. Is debatable; but debate is limited in that it must not go into the merits of the main question any more than is necessary to enable the assembly to decide whether the main question should be postponed and to what time." **AIPSC** p. 64. "3. Debate restricted to brief discussion on reasons for, or time of, postponement."

86. **ANSWER: B. standing committees.**
**RONR** p. 491, ll. 6-7. "A standing committee must be constituted by name (a) by a specific provision of the bylaws or (b) by a resolution which is in effect a special rule of order … " **AIPSC** p. 188. "A standing committee is a committee that has a fixed term of office and does the work within its particular field that is assigned to it by the bylaws or referred to it by the organization, or the governing board."

87. **ANSWER: C. elect a temporary presiding officer and temporary secretary (president and secretary pro tem).**
**RONR** p. 547, ll. 1-5. "A chairman and a secretary are in general the only officers required by a mass meeting. Their election takes place immediately after the meeting is called to order…." **AIPSC** p. 254. "At the organizing meeting for an unincorporated association (sometimes referred to as a 'mass meeting'), a member of the organizing group calls the meeting to order and nominates or calls for nominations for a temporary presiding officer."

88. **ANSWER: D. Except in legislative bodies operating under their own rules, "time allocated to one member cannot be transferred to another member."**
**RONR** p. 388, ll. 12-15. "Rights in regard to debate are not transferable. Unless the organization has a special rule on the subject, a member cannot yield any unexpired portion of his time to another member, or reserve any portion of his time for a later time…." **AIPSC** p. 132. "If debate has been limited, time allocated to one member cannot be transferred to another member. In legislative bodies, members may yield portions of debate time to other members, but this is not permitted in ordinary organizations."

89. **ANSWER: A. make a recommendation to the voting body on each proposal assigned to it.**
**RONR** p. 635, ll. 16-26. "In the simplest arrangement, the Resolutions Committee has only the power to put resolutions in proper form, eliminate duplication where similar resolutions are offered, and ensure that all resolutions relating to a specific subject will be offered in a logical sequence. In other cases the committee is given the authority to make substantive alterations in a resolution, but only with the sponsor's consent; …. Except as the rules may provide otherwise, the Resolutions Committee is required to report all resolutions referred to it; …." **AIPSC** pp. 212, 217. "A reference committee system is usually provided for in the bylaws of the organization with the duties defined in the organization's convention rules…. "All items referred to the reference committee must be reported back to the full assembly for action."

90. **ANSWER: C. Table.**
**AIPSC** pp. 70-71. "On occasion an assembly may wish to dispose of a main motion without any debate or without further debate and without a direct vote on the main motion…. It permits the assembly to sidestep an unwelcome issue quickly and decisively. **RONR** p. 267, ll. 16-20. "The purpose of an *Objection to the Consideration of a Question* is to enable the assembly to avoid a particular original main motion altogether …"

91. **ANSWER: E. may participate in debate and vote on motions.**
**RONR** p. 448, ll. 3-5. "An office carries with it only the rights necessary for executing the duties of the office, and it does not deprive a member of the society of his rights as a member." **AIPSC** p. 179. "The elected secretary does not forfeit any rights of membership by reason of holding office and may propose motions and discuss and vote on all measures."

92. **ANSWER: E. all of these make the role of the vice president important.**
Members sometimes look down on the significance of the vice president, but both **RONR** and **AIPSC** stress the importance of this office. **RONR** pp. 457-458, ll. 34-2. "In the absence of the president, the vice-president serves in his stead; thus, it is important to elect a vice-president who is competent to perform the duties of the president." **AIPSC** p. 177. "The vice president has only a few responsibilities

established by parliamentary law, but is often assigned other duties through the bylaws. Vice presidents frequently direct departments of work or study; head important committees ...; serve on the governing board; and perform other assigned tasks."

93. **ANSWER: D. the main motion under consideration has been disposed of.**
**RONR** p. 395, ll. 15-18. "The presiding officer who relinquished the chair then should not return to it until the pending main question has been disposed of, since he has shown himself to be a partisan as far as that particular matter is concerned." **AIPSC** p. 131. "... the presiding officer should not resume the chair until the pending main motion is disposed of."

94. **ANSWER: C. declares the nominations closed.**
The president acts on his own authority. **RONR** p. 288, ll. 25-28. "When nominations have been made by a committee or from the floor, the chair should inquire whether there are any further nominations; and when there is no response, he declares that nominations are closed." **AIPSC** p. 160. "When there appear to be no further nominations for a particular office, the presiding officer may declare nominations for that office closed."

95. **ANSWER: A. casting all three of your votes for single candidate.**
"It is a 'bunching up' of votes for one or more candidates, instead of the casting of single votes for a number of different candidates." **RONR** p. 443, ll. 30-34. "In this form of voting, each member is entitled to cast one vote for each position, so that, if, for example, three directors are to be elected, each member may cast three votes. These votes may all be cast for one, two, or three candidates, as the voter chooses." **AIPSC** p. 275. "Cumulative voting is a method that allows a member to place multiple votes for a single candidate instead of casting of single votes for a number of different candidates. This form of voting must be authorized in the bylaws."

96. **ANSWER: E. all of these accurately describe proceedings in small boards or committees.**
**RONR** p. 487, ll. 26-29. "In a [small] board meeting ... some of the formality that is necessary in a large assembly would hinder business." See list of rules on pages 487-488. **AIPSC** p. 193. "Committees should function under procedures that are appropriate for the applicable circumstances.... Procedure is often relaxed by permitting debate without limits on the number or length of speeches..., permitting members to remain seated while speaking, allowing discussions to occur prior to introduction of formal motions, permitting motions without seconds, and allowing the chair to participate fully in the committee deliberations, including debate and voting."

97. **ANSWER: E. all of the above are true.**
**RONR** p. 403, ll. -13-21. "Voting requirements based on the number of members present—a majority of those present, two thirds of those present, etc.—while possible, are generally undesirable. Since an abstention in such cases has the same effect as a negative vote, these bases deny members the right to maintain a neutral position by abstaining. For the same reason, members present who fail to vote through indifference rather than through deliberate neutrality may affect the result negatively." **AIPSC** p. 139. "In large assemblies a vote based on a majority of members present can cause problems if votes are generally close...."

98. **ANSWER: C. the appointing power, whatever authority is so identified in the bylaws.**
**RONR** p. 177, ll. 19-29. "The power to appoint a committee includes the power to fill any vacancy that may arise in it. The resignation of a member of a committee should be addressed to the appointing power, and it is the responsibility of that power to fill the resulting vacancy ... the appointing authority has the power to remove or replace members of the committee ...." **AIPSC** p. 191. "Unless otherwise provided in the bylaws or in a resolution establishing a committee, all committees are responsible to and work under the direction and control of the authority that created or established them.... The members of a committee

may be replaced by the appointing or electing authority."

99. **ANSWER: B. of course, members have a right to change their minds.**
Parliamentarians differ on this, since opponents may convince the member that he or she was wrong, or the motion may have been amended to make it unacceptable. **AIPSC** p. 126. "Every member may speak for or against a motion; the maker of the motion, while the need is unusual, may speak against the motion he or she moved." p. 274. "The maker of a motion has the right to speak for or against and vote against his or her own motion." **RONR** p. 393, ll. 20-22. "In debate, the maker of a motion, while he can vote against it, is not allowed to speak against his own motion."

100. **ANSWER: B. is a useful strategic motion giving the opposition a chance to get a test vote without danger of passage.**
**RONR** p. 128, ll. 17-19. "The motion to *Postpone Indefinitely* is sometimes employed by strategists to test their strength on a motion they oppose."

101. **ANSWER: E. all of these are correct.**
The chair can often save time and avoid confusion by asking for unanimous consent to approve an amendment that seems genuinely "friendly." A single objection, however, requires the chair to handle it like any other amendment. **RONR** p. 162, ll. 15-19. "Regardless of whether or not the maker of the main motion 'accepts' the amendment, it must be opened to debate and voted on formally (unless adopted by unanimous consent) and is handled under the same rules as amendments generally." **AIPSC** p. 274. "… after the motion has been stated by the presiding officer, any member (including the presiding officer) may object to the proposed friendly amendment. On hearing an objection, the presiding officer should seek a second for the amendment, call for discussion, and take a vote on the amendment."

102. **ANSWER: D. Those who meet the qualifications as laid down in bylaws or other document of authority.**
**RONR** p. 433, ll. 22-25. "Although it is not common for the nominating committee to nominate more than one candidate for any office, the committee can do so unless the bylaws prohibit it." **AIPSC** p.163. "Qualifications for each office should be stated in the bylaws or document of authority as designated in the bylaws, such as a policy established by the board or by the members."

103. **ANSWER: E. all of these statements are true.**
Organizations develop their own language and are free to adopt whatever terms seem comfortable to and understood by its members. **RONR** pp. 22-23, ll. 33-3. "The president or chief officer of an organized society, who normally presides at its meeting, is then addressed as … 'Madam President' (whether a married or unmarried woman),… 'Mr. [or Madam] Moderator,' or whatever may be … her official title. In the lower house of a legislative body, this officer is most commonly 'Mr. [or Madam] Speaker.' A vice-president is addressed as 'Mr. President' or 'Madam President' while actually presiding." **AIPSC** p. 27. "… addresses the presiding officer by his or her official title."

104. **ANSWER: E. all of the above are correct.**
**RONR** pp. 35-36, footnote; ll. 15-33. "A motion made by direction of a board or duly appointed committee of the assembly requires no second from the floor…. In handling routine motions, less attention is paid to the requirement of a second." Tinted p. 40, IV Motions and Parliamentary Steps." **AIPSC** pp. 29-30. "Seconds may be assumed by the presiding officer on routine items of business if that is the custom of the organization…. A second is not required for motions when they are submitted by a committee to the superior body. When a motion is presented in a small committee or small board, it does not require a second."

105. **ANSWER: E. Postpone to a Certain Time.**
**AIPSC** pp. 12-13; 61. "Incidental motions arise incidentally out of the business before the assembly. They do not relate directly to the main motion or to specific main motions but usually relate to matters incidental to the conduct of the meeting...." The purpose of a motion to postpone to a certain time is to put off consideration, or further consideration, of a pending main motion and to fix a definite time for its consideration."

106. **ANSWER: A. voice vote.**
**RONR** pp. 409; 45, ll. 27-29. "A vote by voice is the regular method of voting on any motion that does not require more than a majority vote for its adoption." **AIPSC** p. 148. "Voting by voice is the most commonly used method of voting."

107. **ANSWER: C. Debate may extend into the merits of the main motion. RONR** p. 170, ll. 26-29. "5. Is debatable. The debate can extend only to the desirability of committing the main question and to the appropriate details of the motion to *Commit*,... and not to the merits of the main question." **AIPSC** p. 61. "3. Debate restricted to brief discussion on the advisability of referring, and to the committee selected, membership, or duties of the committee, or instructions to it."

108. **ANSWER: B. file the report.**
**RONR** p. 525, ll. 1-5 "*A Report Containing Only Information*.... Apart from filing such a report, however, no action on it is necessary and usually none should be taken." **AIPSC** p. 201. "1. The report may be filed. This is the usual method for disposing of a committee report. It may be filed automatically or ordered filed by a motion, or the presiding officer may announce, 'The report will be filed,' and proceed to the next item of business. A report that is filed is not binding on the assembly but is available for information and may be considered again at any time."

109. **ANSWER: E. all of these are accurate statements.**
**RONR** p. 126-127, ll. 4-14"*Postpone Indefinitely* is a motion that the assembly decline to take a position on the main question. Its adoption kills the main motion (for the duration of the session) and avoids a direct vote on the question. ... 5. Is debatable; and, unlike the case of any other subsidiary motion, debate on the motion to *Postpone Indefinitely* can go fully into the merits of the main question."

110. **ANSWER: B. must be germane to the subject of the original motion.**
**RONR** p. 136, ll. 6-9. "... an amendment must be *germane* to be in order. To be *germane*, an amendment must *in some way involve* the same question that is raised by the motion to which it is applied." **AIPSC** p. 52. "The most important principle concerning amendments is that they must be germane to the pending motion; that is, they must be relevant to and have direct bearing on the subject of the pending motion that the amendment seeks to change."

111. **ANSWER: E. All these statements are true.**
**RONR** p. 6 footnote. "Members in good standing are those whole rights as members of the assembly are not under suspension as a consequence of disciplinary proceedings or by operation of some specific provision in the bylaws...." **AIPSC** p. 261. "Organizations often use the term 'member in good standing' and variations of it in their documents of authority.... Consequences of loss of good standing might include the loss of some or all of the rights of membership."

112. **ANSWER: C. a majority of the regular members of the organization.**
**RONR** pp. 21; 346. p. 21, ll. 17-22. "In the absence of such a provision [for a quorum] in a society or assembly whose real membership can be accurately determined at any time—that is, in a body having an enrolled membership composed only of persons who maintain their status as members in a prescribed manner—the quorum is a majority of the entire membership, by common parliamentary law." **AIPSC**

p. 122. "In the absence of such a bylaw clause [establishing a quorum] or applicable statutory provision, under parliamentary law ... (1) in the case of membership organizations with a verifiable roll of members, the quorum is fixed at a majority of the voting members ...."

113. **ANSWER: C. close debate on the motion before the assembly.**
**RONR** p. 197, ll. 24-23. "The *Previous Question* is the motion used to bring the assembly to an immediate vote on one or more pending questions.... 1) immediately closes debate on, and stops amendment of, the immediately pending question and such other pending questions as the motion may specify ...." **AIPSC** p. 67. "A motion to close debate and vote immediately prevents or stops discussion on the pending question or questions. Such a motion is made to prevent the proposal of other subsidiary motions except to table the main motion, and to bring the pending question or questions to an immediate vote."

114. **ANSWER: D. ask for a rising vote.**
**RONR** pp. 52, ll. 9-21. *Division of the Assembly*.... "any member (without a second) has the right to require that a voice vote (or even a show of hands) be retaken as a rising vote, so long as he does not use the procedure as a dilatory tactic...." **AIPSC** p. 102-103. "A call for division is a demand that an indecisive vote, which has been taken by voice or show of hands, be verified by a standing vote.... Any member who feels a vote has not been correctly announced or reported has the right to insist on verification, but a member cannot use this privilege to obstruct business by calling for division on an obviously decisive vote."

115. **ANSWER: E. both C and D should appear under unfinished business.**
**RONR** p. 358, ll. 19-30. "a) The question that was pending when the previous meeting adjourned ... b) Any questions that were unfinished business at the previous meeting but not reached before it adjourned ... c) Any questions which, by postponement or otherwise were set as general orders for the previous meeting ... but were not reached before it adjourned." Also includes general orders not reached before adjournment of the previous meeting. **AIPSC** pp. 118. "1. Any motion or report that was being considered and was interrupted when the previous meeting adjourned. 2. Any motion or report that was postponed to the current meeting except those which have been set for a particular hour on the agenda."

116. **ANSWER: D. should not be accepted until members have made all desired nominations.**
**RONR** p. 286, ll. 26-27. "... a formal motion to close the polls should not be recognized until all have presumably voted." **AIPSC** pp. 160-161. "The presiding officer should not recognize a motion to close nominations or declare them closed if any member is rising for the purpose of making a nomination."

117. **ANSWER: E. the presiding officer should do so in all cases described.**
**RONR** p. 450, ll. 9-10. "*Duties of the Presiding Officer of an Assembly.* 6) To enforce the rules relating to debate and those relating to order and decorum within the assembly." **AIPSC** p. 131. "The presiding officer has the responsibility of controlling and expediting debate."

118 **ANSWER: A. all motions or resolutions, with the name of the proposer and the disposition of each motion.**
**RONR** p. 470, ll. 26-27. "The name of the maker of a main motion should be entered in the minutes, but the name of the seconder should not be entered unless ordered by the assembly." **AIPSC** p. 229. "Some organizations do not indicate the original maker of the motion as this is often confusing when the motion has been modified and no longer is the same proposal the member originally presented. If the mover of the motion is indicated in the minutes, it is good practice to state the original motion and the motion as finally adopted."

119. **ANSWER: D. by a motion made, seconded, and carried by a two-thirds vote.**
**RONR** p. 193, ll. 1-8. [The motion to *Limit or Extend Limits of Debate*] "4. Must be seconded.... 7. Requires a two-thirds vote—because it suspends the rules, and because limiting debate takes away the basic rights of all members to full discussion and may restrict a minority's right to present its case." **AIPSC** p. 67. "Rules governing the motion to limit or extend debate include: ... 2. Requires a second ... 5. Requires a two-thirds vote because it limits freedom of debate or modifies already adopted limitations on debate." When A, B, or C occur, the presiding officer may ask for a motion to limit or close debate.

120. **ANSWER: A. must do so before debate begins.**
**RONR** pp. 36, ll. 9-11; 26-28;. "A second merely implies that the seconder agrees that the motion should *come before the meeting* and not that he necessarily favors the motion.... The requirement of a second is for the chair's guidance as to whether he should state the question on the motion, thus placing it before the assembly." p. 37, ll. 2-6. However, until debate has begun ... or, if there is not debate, until the chair begins to take the vote and any member has voted—a point of order can be raised...." **AIPSC** p. 29. "Seconding a motion is not necessarily an endorsement of the motion. It merely indicates that the member wishes the motion to be considered by the assembly.... Seconds may be assumed by the presiding officer on routine items of business if that is the custom of the organization. If any member objects to the lack of a second, the presiding officer must call for one, unless debate by more than one member has already occurred...."

121. **ANSWER: E Adjourned.**
The adjourned meeting, according to **RONR** pp. 93-94, ll. 25-27; 11-15. "An adjourned meeting is a meeting in continuation of the session of the immediately preceding regular or special meeting.... An adjourned meeting takes up its work at the point where it was interrupted in the order of business or in the consideration of the question that was postponed to the adjourned meeting, except that the minutes of the preceding meeting are first read." **AIPSC** p. 107. A continued meeting is sometimes referred to as an *adjourned meeting*, but the term *continued meeting* is recommended because it is less confusing concerning the intent of the action taken. The continued meeting is legally a continuation of the previous meeting." The term adjourned meeting can be used for opposite meanings— a meeting that has ended, or a meeting that has been reconvened.

122. **ANSWER: E. unless authorized in the document, the bylaws may not be suspended by any vote.**
**RONR** p. 263, ll. 1-6. "Rules contained in the *bylaws* (or constitution) cannot be suspended—no matter how large the vote in favor of doing so or how inconvenient the rule in question may be—unless the particular rule specifically provides for its own suspension, or unless the rule properly is in the nature of a rule of order...." **AIPSC** p. 86. Which Rules Cannot be Suspended? "Suspension of the rules cannot deny a member or members any fundamental right whether inherent in parliamentary law or defined by the rules of the organization.... 1) A rule stated in a statute, charter, or the organization's constitution or bylaws unless a specific provision in these documents of authority provides for suspension of the rule." The bylaws may be amended, not suspended.

123. **ANSWER: B. does not require a second.**
**RONR** p. 320, ll. 6-11. "4. Must be seconded at the time it is made.... The *calling up* of the motion to *Reconsider* does not require a second." **AIPSC** p. 47. Basic Rules Governing the Motion to Reconsider "2. Requires a second."

124. **ANSWER: B. requires a second.**
**RONR** p. 249, l. 17. "4. Does not require a second." **AIPSC** p. 92. "2. Requires no second."

125. **ANSWER: D. has the same rights as any other member unless the bylaws say otherwise.**
**RONR** p. 483, ll. 30-33. "If the ex-officio member is not under the authority of the society, he has all the privileges of board membership, including the right to make motions, and to vote, but none of the obligations ...." **AIPSC** p. 190. "Unless the organization's governing documents provide otherwise, an ex officio member has all the rights, responsibilities, and duties of other members of the committee, including the right to vote.... Anyone who is not expected to be a regular working member of the committee should be designated as an advisory or consultant member instead of being given ex officio status."

# Short Response Answers

> The study questions and answers are intended only for general parliamentary study. The "answers" given are intended to show the type of responses that may be used but are not to be taken as complete answers—only as a starting point for further study.

Short Response Answers

1. ANSWER: **RONR** p. 499, ll. 21-27. 1) Two members of the committee may call the meeting, 2) It is the responsibility of the person or persons calling a committee meeting to ensure that reasonable notice of its time and place be sent to every committee member. **AIPSC** p. 193. "If the chair fails to call a meeting, a majority of committee members may do so, or the organization's president may call a meeting of the committee."

2. ANSWER: **RONR** pp. 487-488. ll.33-20; 500-501, ll. 4-8; 2-6.1) In small committees, the chair may act as secretary, members may raise a hand for recognition, motions need not be seconded, there is no limit on speaking, motions to limit or close debate are not allowed, vote may be taken without motion by unanimous consent or by show of hands, chair need not rise to take a vote, chair may fully participate. 2) Large committees may function best in the manner of a full-scale assembly, a secretary may be chosen, specific instructions may be given by the parent body. **AIPSC** pp. 193-194. "Committees should function under procedures that are appropriate for the applicable circumstances. While committees preferably function with relaxed procedures, greater formality may be appropriate as the committee size increases ..." Meeting functions for all committees include: chair as presiding officer, chair should designate a member as secretary, debate without limits, members may remain seated during deliberations, discussions may occur prior to motions, motions do not require seconds, chair may fully participate, decisions may be made by general consent, procedures may be determined by the committee unless otherwise instructed.

3. ANSWER: The quorum is three under **RONR** and four under **AIPSC**. **RONR** p. 497, ll. 25-29. "... the president is an ex-officio member who has the right, but not the obligation, to participate in the proceedings of the committees, and he is not counted in determining the number required for a quorum or whether a quorum is present at a meeting." **AIPSC** p. 190. "Unless the organization's governing documents provide otherwise, an ex officio member has all the rights, responsibilities, and duties of other members of the, including the right to vote. The ex officio member is a full-fledged working member of a committee and is counted in determining the quorum. Anyone who is not expected to be a regular working member of the committee should be designated as an advisory or consultant member instead of being given ex officio status."

4. ANSWER: Generally the appointing power (parent body) has the right to fill vacancies and to remove and replace members. That power may be, and often is, the president. In other cases the entire assembly chooses committee members and the assembly would have to remove and replace. **RONR** p. 501, ll. 14-21. "A standing or special committee may protect itself against breaches of order by its members during committee meetings, and against annoyance by nonmembers, by employing the procedures outlined on pages 645-49 [Disciplinary Procedures], but the committee, instead of itself imposing any penalty on a disorderly member, can only report such behavior to the committee's parent body, which may then take such action as it deems advisable. However, *if there will be no opportunity for this to occur* within the time needed ... the committee may... requiring the disorderly member to leave the meeting room during the remainder of the meeting." **AIPSC** p. 191. "The members of a committee may be replaced by the appointing or electing authority. A member of a committee who is unable or fails to participate in committee activities should be removed and notified of the removal by the president or by the body that appointed the committee, and another member should be chosen to fill the vacancy."

5. ANSWER: **RONR** pp. 97-99, ll. 22-30. Electronic committee meetings must be authorized in the bylaws, expressly by a standing rule, or by motion establishing the particular committee. Other requirements may include: provisions for onsite participation, instructions on how to participate, type of equipment required, how to determine quorum and continuation of quorum, methods to seek recognition, ways to submit motions in writing, methods of taking and verifying votes. **AIPSC** pp. 109, 194. "Such a meeting is as proper as a physical meeting of the members, provided the other requirements for conducting a meeting have been met." Conference calls and electronic meetings must be authorized in the bylaws and applicable law. Meeting rules should include, recognition of members, taking votes, ensuring

© American Institute of Parliamentarians. All rights reserved.

only members attend, a quorum established by roll call, discussion rotation, votes by roll call or general consent. Internet or e-mail discussion may be used for information only and not for action except as specifically authorized.

6.   ANSWER: **RONR** pp. 404-405, ll. 35-14. "A *plurality vote* is the largest number of votes to be given any candidate or proposition when three or more choices are possible; the candidate or proposition receiving the largest number of votes has a plurality." A plurality election may be the best choice in an international or national society where the election is conducted by mail ballot to avoid additional balloting. **AIPSC** pp.140-141. "A plurality vote means more than the number received by any other candidate or alternative Proposition. There is no requirement in plurality voting that a candidate or any proposition receive a majority vote." "While election by plurality is simple and fast, it is usually not advisable."

7.   ANSWER: You renew the motion (a main motion). **RONR** pp. 88, ll. 15-24; 340-341, ll. 33 1. "… a main motion that was introduced but not adopted during one session can,… be renewed at any later session unless it has become absurd." **AIPSC** p. 25. "If a main motion was *rejected* at an earlier meeting or convention, it may be renewed by being introduced as a new main motion at a subsequent meeting or convention."

8.   ANSWER: **AIPSC** pp. 25-26. "A main motion that has been adopted can be affected by a new main motion that has been introduced at a later meeting. *Repeal by Implication* automatically results from the adoption of a motion that conflicts in whole or in part with another motion or motions previously adopted. The first motion is repealed only to the extent that its provisions cannot be reconciled with those of the new motion.…" Repeal by implications is intended to correct *inadvertent* conflicts, not to be a blanket method for disposing of previously adopted main motions without voting directly on their repeal." **RONR** p. 305, ll. 8-10. "… the assembly can change an action previously taken or ordered. *Rescind*—also known as *Repeal or Annul*—is the motion by which a previous action or order can be canceled or countermanded."

9.   ANSWER: **RONR** p. 332, ll. 32-7. "Its purpose is to prevent a temporary majority from taking advantage of an unrepresentative attendance at a meeting to vote an action that is opposed by a majority of … [the] membership.… when it is moved … it cannot be called up until another day, even if another meeting is held on the same day. Thus, with a view to obtaining a more representative attendance.…"

10.   ANSWER: **RONR** pp. 248-250; 253-254, ll. 24-9; **AIPSC** p. 91-92. 1) The chair may rule on the point of order. 2) The chair may ask for advice from the parliamentarian or from other knowledgeable members and then rule. 3) The chair may "refer it to the assembly for decision."

11.   ANSWER: **RONR** p. 250; **AIPSC** p. 91. 1) The chair's explanation may satisfy you and you may accept his ruling. 2) You may appeal from the decision of the chair.

12.   ANSWER: **AIPSC** p. 70-72. "5. Requires a two-thirds vote because it cuts off debate."

13.   ANSWER: **RONR** pp. 456, ll. 28-32; 579, 24-26. "In some organizations, the president is responsible for appointing, and is ex officio a member of, all committees (with the exception of the nominating committee, which should be expressly excluded from such a provision, and…)." **AIPSC** p. 162. "The president, president-elect, and immediate past president should not appoint any members of the nominating committee, serve on the committee, give the committee instructions, or take any part in its deliberations. This requirement protects both the officer and committee from accusations of favoritism or self-perpetuation."

# Short Response Answers

14. ANSWER: **RONR** p. 507, ll. 25-29. The chair may sometimes expedite matters by assuming and stating the motion if the assembly is accustomed to this method. Another option is to ask the member to resume the floor and move adoption of the resolution. **AIPSC** p. 203. "... the presiding officer may state the motion with the concurrence of the committee chair or reporting member."

15. ANSWER: You call for a rising or counted vote. **RONR** p. 410, ll. 15-18; **AIPSC** p. 148. If in doubt on a voice vote the chair should retake the vote by a rising vote and, if necessary, a counted vote.

16. ANSWER: You would proceed to take a ballot on the unfilled positions. **RONR** p. 441, ll. 2-8. When any office remains unfilled after the first ballot, all candidates remain on the ballot unless they voluntarily withdraw. **AIPSC** p. 145. It would be necessary to take another vote to fill the remaining positions unless the assembly adopts a motion to the contrary.

17. ANSWER: **RONR** p. 414, ll. 12-20. You need to appoint tellers whom you trust to be accurate and dependable, and who will be trusted by the assembly. If distinct sides have developed during the debate, you may want to appoint tellers from each of the positions. **AIPSC** p. 165. Members of the tellers committee should be well respected, not openly supportive of any one candidate, detail-oriented, knowledgeable of election rules, selected from different constituencies or geographic regions, not be members of the nominating committee.

18. ANSWER: **RONR** pp. 465, ll. 10-16; 608-609, ll. 30-15. Your basic duty is to be the advisor and consultant to the president, the officers, and the committee chairmen regarding management of the convention as it relates to the actual transaction of business. While the convention is in progress, you should serve as the principal advisor to the president on procedural questions. Some of your "most important work may well be performed before the convention opens." During the convention you should be seated next to the president so that you can answer questions or give advice. If a script is prepared for use by the presiding officer you should review it if at all possible to point out problems or be prepared to assist when needed. **AIPSC** p. 269-270. Be advisor to the president, governing board, committees, and staff. If possible, you should meet with the president prior to the meeting and determine method of communication to be used. During the meeting you should sit next to the presiding officer to advise, but not rule, on procedural matters, be alert to any developing problems, unobtrusively call attention to serious errors.

19. ANSWER: **RONR** pp. 445-446, ll. 1-10; 6-17. The advice will be determined by the timing of the challenge. If the challenge is timely—promptly at the time the breach occurs, the advice to the chair is to request the body to 1) order a recount, 2) approve the report, 3) give the final decision to a committee or the board with full power to act. **AIPSC** pp. 170-171. 1) The challenge must be done before the adjournment of the meeting or convention unless based on fraudulent activity. 2) Election challenges should be resolved at the same meeting or convention, 3) If not possible to resolve the challenge, the assembly should authorize the board or other body to resolve the issue, 4) If the vote was held by an authorized voting system its reported outcome is presumed to be accurate and may not be challenged on the technology.

20. ANSWER: **RONR** pp. 263-264, ll. 1-13; **AIPSC** pp. 86-87. 1) Rules contained in the bylaw or constitution of the organization, unless provided for, 2) A rule stated in a federal, state, or local law, 3) A basic rule of common parliamentary law such as rules governing notice, quorum, vote requirements, and voting methods, 4) Rules protecting absentees or a basic right of the individual member.

21. ANSWER: **RONR** p. 79, ll. 24-28; 252, ll. 2-5. The term precedence is the order in which a motion may be made or yielded to without causing the motion to be out of order. The term precedent is used when a decision of the assembly is established and later used as a persuasive statement for similar incidents. **AIPSC** p. 306. "Precedence. The rank or priority governing a proposal, consideration, and disposal of motions. Precedent. A course of action or decision that may serve as a guide or rule for similar situations in the particular organization."

© American Institute of Parliamentarians. All rights reserved.

# Short Response Answers

22. ANSWER: **RONR** p. 469, ll. 4-8. "Any correction approved by the assembly is made in the text of the minutes being approved; the minutes of the meeting making the correction merely state that the minutes were approved 'as corrected' without specifying what the correction was." **AIPSC** p. 232. "Corrections are incorporated directly into the pending minutes of the meeting for which the corrections were made." Minutes prior to adoption are drafts and considered the same as a main motion. The minutes may be corrected (amended) and adopted in the same manner as a regular motion and the correction is incorporated into the document before adoption.

23. ANSWER: **RONR** p. 457, ll. 8-21; **AIPSC** p. 177. The president-elect is a "president-in-training," elected in advance and automatically assumes the office of president when the current president's term expires. Responsibilities are to prepare for the office of president, become familiar with the workings of the organization, and usually to preside in the absence or incapacitation of the president (if provided for in the bylaws). In addition, the president-elect is often given specific duties as defined in the bylaws.

24. ANSWER: **RONR** p. 83, ll. 7-15; **AIPSC** p. 80. The term adjournment sine die (SIGN-ee-DYE-ee) refers to the final adjournment of a session or several meeting where the closure dissolves the assembly and where the session will not reconvene until a time prescribed in the bylaws.

25. ANSWER: **RONR** p. 227, ll. 16-23; **AIPSC** p. 75. Questions relating to a privilege of the assembly have to do with the rights, safety, integrity, comfort, or convenience of the whole assembly. They frequently are concerned with the heating, lighting, ventilation, seating of members, noise, disturbances, conduct of officers or members, punishment of members, accuracy of reports, and going into executive session.

26. ANSWER: **RONR** p. 416, ll. 1-33; **AIPSC** p. 166. Ballots marked for more candidates than allowed, two or more ballots folded together, ballots for fictional or ineligible persons, unintelligible ballots, and ballots cast for persons not entitled to vote. It is also noted that **RONR** counts blank ballots in the determination of the total votes cast but does not count blanks in the number of total votes cast for election.

27. ANSWER: **RONR** p. 353, ll. 10-15. Under **RONR,** the basic order of business is: 1) reading and approval of minutes, 2) reports of officers, boards, and standing committees, 3) reports of special (select or ad Hoc committees, 4) special orders, 5) unfinished business and general orders, and 6) new business. **AIPSC** p. 115. Under **AIPSC** the basic order of business is: 1) Call to order, 2) Reading and disposal of minutes, 3) reports of officers, 4) reports of boards and standing committees, 5) reports of special committees, 6) unfinished business, 7) new business, 8) announcements, 9) adjournment.

28. ANSWER. **RONR** p. 345, ll. 19-21; **AIPSC** pp. 122; 254. Those present at a mass meeting, no matter what their number, count as a quorum because the members present constitute the entire membership at that time.

29. ANSWER: **RONR** pp. 67-68, ll. 30-33; 25-28; 224, ll. 25-30; **AIPSC** p. 74. *Raising a Question of Privilege* is the device by which a member may put a request before the chair for a ruling on an emergent item of business. The *Questions of Privilege* are motions that do not relate to the pending business but have to do with important actions that may necessitate immediate consideration. These include the motions to: Call for the Orders of the Day, Question of Privilege, Recess, Adjourn, and (in RONR) Fix the Time to Which to Adjourn.

30. ANSWER: **RONR** pp. 479-480, ll. 5-8; 9-10; **AIPSC** pp. 180; 249. As presiding officer you ask if there are any questions for the treasurer on the report. No action is taken on the report unless it is the audited report.

31. **ANSWER: RONR** p. 358, ll. 4-7.; **AIPSC** p. 119. "Old Business" may refer to almost anything discussed at an earlier date. "Unfinished Business" refers to business carried over from a previous meeting as a result of the meeting having adjourned without completing the business before it.

32. **ANSWER: RONR** pp. 358-359, ll. 19-2. Unfinished business includes0: a) The question that was pending when the previous meeting adjourned, b) Any questions that were unfinished business at the previous meeting but were not reached before it adjourned,... c) Any questions which, by postponement or otherwise, were set as general orders for the previous meeting, 4d) Matters that were postponed to, or otherwise made general orders for, the present meeting. **AIPSC** p. 118. Unfinished business includes the following types of meetings: 1) Items of business being considered at the time of adjournment, 2) motions or reports postponed to the current meeting and not set for a specific time.

33. **ANSWER:** *Pro tem* (or *pro tempore*) means "for the time" and may be used if the president steps down to debate or otherwise vacates the chair temporarily. **RONR** p. 495, ll. 18-20. "When the bylaws provide that the *president* shall appoint all committees, this power does not transfer to the *chair* if someone else presides." **AIPSC** pp. 177, 182. "When acting in the place of the president at a meeting, the vice president has all the powers, duties, responsibilities, and privileges that the president may exercise at a meeting." However, the discretionary powers of the office, such as appointment of committees, cannot be delegated to another.

34. **ANSWER:** These are called the "Whereas" clauses or the preamble. **RONR** pp. 106-107, ll. 34-2.; 10-12. Information within the preamble may encumber the adoption of the motion if the members do not agree with the preamble even though they may agree with the resolved section itself. "*It should be emphasized that neither rule nor custom requires a resolution to have a preamble, and one should not be used merely for the sake of form.*" **AIPSC** p. 37. "The statements contained in the "whereas" clauses are of no legal effect and sometimes are the source of disagreement."

35. **ANSWER: RONR** p. 605, ll. 26-29. "A delegate is free to vote as he sees fit on questions at the convention, except as his constituent unit may have instructed him in regard to particular matters scheduled for consideration." **AIPSC** p. 206. A delegate should know the opinions and concerns of the members they represent, however, "... it is usually not wise for delegates to be instructed by their constituents to take specific actions on items of business."

36. **ANSWER:** A minority report is the presentation of members not concurring with the committee report. **RONR** requires a unanimous or majority vote for a minority report to be considered. **AIPSC** considers this a right and no vote is required. **RONR** pp. 527-528, ll. 28-30;35-1. "...is usually allowed by the assembly when such permission is requested,.... the formal presentation of a 'minority report' is a privilege that the assembly may accord, not a matter of right...." **AIPSC** p. 203. "If any members of a committee disagree with the report submitted by a majority of the committee members, they may submit a minority report signed by members who agree with it [minority report].... A minority has the right to present and read a report, even though a motion is pending to dispose of the majority report."

37. **ANSWER:** Seconds are for the guidance of the chair as to whether more than one member of the assembly wishes the motion to be considered, therefore there are some situations where a second is not required. Motions from committees or boards do not require a second as they have been "seconded" when the motion was adopted by the committee. Motions of routine business may be assumed by the chair without a second but a member may make a point of order and require a second. Motions where debate has begun do not require a second because the member entering into debate has essentially made a second. **RONR** pp. 36-38, ll. 15-17; 26-28; 80, ll. 5-10; 103, ll. 14; **AIPSC** pp. 29-30.

# Short Response Answers

38. ANSWER: The chair does not ask for unfinished business. All the actions under this agenda item have been carried over from previous meetings and the chair should be aware of any business under that agenda item to come before the meeting. No new items can be added to the unfinished business agenda item. The chair simply states the first item on the agenda. **RONR** p. 359, ll. 8-15; **AIPSC** pp. 118-119.

39. ANSWER: Under **RONR** pp. 267-269, ll. 16-20; 1-4. Members may Object to Consideration and do so before any debate has taken place. **AIPSC** pp. 70-71. To table (dispose without direct vote) "kills" the motion for the current session.

40. ANSWER: No *business* can be transacted. A quorum has not yet been established and nothing could be done that requires the presence of a quorum. A convention is under the same rules as any other meeting pertaining to lack of quorum. **RONR** pp. 347-348, ll. 30-32. The convention may, 1) adjourn, 2) recess, 3) take measures to obtain a quorum, or 4) fix the time to which to adjourn. **AIPSC** p. 122. The convention may conduct items that do not require official action such as 1) opening ceremonies, 2) hearing reports (without action), 3) listen to a speaker, 4) program, 5) recess, or 6) adjourn.

41. ANSWER: Both House and Senate, and all state legislatures, have developed their own sets of rules. **RONR** p. 8, ll. 14-17. "Each state or national legislative assembly generally has its own well-developed body of rules, interpretations, and precedents, so that the exact procedure for a particular legislative house can be found only in its own Manual." **AIPSC** p. 4. "Government at its highest level (such as the U.S. House of Representatives and Senate), state legislatures, national parliaments (such as UK Parliament), and most nations around the world that have such governmental structures use parliamentary procedure suited specifically to their needs."

42. ANSWER: Its Corporate Charter (if incorporated), its Constitution, or its Bylaws. Some organizations develop both a Constitution and a set of Bylaws. The latter was generally more specific and easier to amend than the Constitution, which was regarded as the most important and basic document. Some organizations still have both, but one document is much more common today. External documents include laws (by whatever name) from national, state, and local public authorities. These documents take precedence over any internal document. **AIPSC** pp. 238; **RONR** pp. 11-12, ll. 30-32; 8-16.

43. ANSWER: Recess is a short intermission in an assembly's proceedings which does not close the meeting and after which business will immediately be resumed at the point where it was interrupted. Adjourn means to close a meeting and when the meeting is called to order again it is a new meeting. **RONR** p. 85, ll. 4-25; **AIPSC** p. 77.

44. ANSWER: No. Unless the bylaws specifically forbid it, write-in candidates may be (and occasionally are) elected. **RONR** p. 430, ll. 18-20. "… each member is free to vote for any eligible person, whether he has been nominated or not." **AIPSC** p. 161. "Any member receiving the necessary number of votes is elected, whether nominated or not."

45. ANSWER: Who has the authority to fill a vacancy in a committee or office? The general concept is that the power to appoint or elect carries with it the power to replace unless the bylaws provide otherwise. **RONR** pp. 177, ll. 19-21; 467-468, ll. 25-8. The power to appoint or elect carries the power to accept resignations and fill any vacancy. If the executive board has full power and authority between meetings of the society without reserving that right to the society, the board may accept resignations and fill vacancies between society meetings. Filling a vacancy in an office must always be given to the body that elected that member unless otherwise the bylaws provide otherwise. **AIPSC** p. 184. "A vacancy is filled by the same authority that selected the officer, director, or committee member unless the bylaws provide otherwise." The bylaws may provide authority to the board of directors to fill elected vacancies. If the position is filled by any authority other than the appointing body, the position is filled only until the next meeting of the appointing body.

46. **ANSWER: RONR** pp. 453-454, ll. 26-1; 652, ll. 3-7. The most common circumstance is to deal with a problem that has intensely divided the organization. Other circumstances include 1) to preside over specific business items (amending or revision of bylaws being most common), or 2) preside on request of the president because of politics within the organization. Even if the president and vice presidents do not object, the assembly must vote (majority or unanimous consent) to allow the new presider. If the president and/or vice presidents object, the assembly may suspend the rules and authorize the new presider. **AIPSC** pp. 270-271. "The parliamentarian then presides only with the assembly's permission, which is usually granted by general consent."

47. ANSWER: Assuming that the minutes have been distributed beforehand or are available at that annual meeting, the minutes committee (or the executive committee acting as one) reports that the minutes have been approved. No further action is required unless there are corrections to the minutes. No vote is taken by the assembly as the committee has been given approval authority when created or appointed. **RONR** pp. 95, ll. 2-3; 474-475, ll. 35-7. *"When the next regular meeting will not be held within a quarterly time interval ... the executive board or a committee appointed for the purpose should be authorized to approve the minutes."* In conventions, the convention may authorize the board or a committee to approve the minutes. This does not preclude corrections to the minutes at a later meeting or convention. **AIPSC** pp. 232-233. When an organization does not meet frequently, the governing documents should give authority to a minutes approval committee to approve minutes between meetings and report to the organization. The members of the committee have final authority over the content of the minutes and no further action is required by the assembly. This does not preclude corrections to the minutes even at a later meeting or convention.

48. ANSWER: The member may accept the chair's explanation or may put the motion before the assembly indicating exact wording for the division. If the chair then rules the motion not in order, that may then be appealed. **RONR** p. 259, ll. 1-9. No appeal may be made from the chair's response to a ... inquiry since this is only an opinion of the chair. If the member moves the motion and the chair then rules the motion not in order, the member may then appeal from the decision of the chair. **AIPSC** pp. 83-84. Answering a question or providing information cannot be appealed. If a motion is made and the presiding officer rules it out of order, that decision may be appealed.

49. ANSWER: **RONR** p. 433, ll. 29-30 "Members of the nominating committee are not barred from becoming nominees for office themselves. To make such a requirement would mean, first, that service on the nominating committee carried a penalty by depriving its members of one of their privileges; and second, that appointment or election to the nominating committee could be used to prevent a member from becoming a nominee." **AIPSC** p. 163. "Members who are likely to become candidates should not serve on a nominating committee, but members of the committee can become candidates. A member of a nominating committee who becomes a candidate should resign from the committee immediately."

50. ANSWER: Once established, a quorum is presumed to be present until challenged. Even if members leave, business continues until either the presiding officer decides that a quorum is no longer present, or some member challenges the existence of a quorum and a count shows that one is no longer present. Despite its common usage in parliamentary circles, neither **RONR** nor **AIPSC** use the term. The term appears in neither index, nor in the sections devoted to quorum. **RONR** p. 349, ll. 8-21. states: "When the chair has called a meeting to order after finding that a quorum is present, the continued presence of a quorum is presumed unless the chair or a member notices that a quorum is no longer present. If the chair notices the absence of a quorum, it is his duty to declare the fact, at least before taking any vote or stating the question on any new motion—which he can no longer do except in connection with the permissible proceedings related to the absence of a quorum... *Debate* on a question already pending can be allowed to continue at length after a quorum is no longer present, however, until a member raises the point." Decisions made before the challenge to the existence of a quorum are held as valid actions of the assembly. **AIPSC** p. 125. "The question as to the presence of a quorum at the time of a vote on a particular motion must be raised at the time the vote is taken, if it is to be raised at all. It cannot be raised later. Unless the minutes document that a quorum was not present at the time of voting

on a motion, it is presumed that since the minutes show that a quorum was present when the meeting began, a quorum continued to be present until recess or adjournment. It is not permissible at some later time to question the validity of an action on the grounds that there was not a quorum present at the time the vote was taken."

51.     ANSWER: **RONR** p. 387, ll. 3-8. "The right of members to debate or introduce secondary motions cannot be cut off by the chair's attempting to put a question to vote so quickly that no member can get to the floor—either when the chair first states the question or when he believes debate is ended. Debate is not closed by the presiding officer's rising to put the question." A point of Order may be raised only at the time of the chair's action. **AIPSC** p. 132. "The presiding officer should never end discussion arbitrarily. It should be ended only the by the assembly, whether by general consent …, by a vote on the motion to close debate, or by a previously adopted limitation on debate.… The presiding officer does, however, have a responsibility to assist the assembly in disposing of its business efficiently. If all debate has been on one side of an issue and the presiding officer has called for debate on the other side with no response, it may be appropriate to ask the assembly, "Are you ready to vote?"

52.     ANSWER: **RONR** p. 435, ll. 12-15. "This is another stage of nomination and election procedure for which a number of details should be established by rule or custom of the particular organization." **AIPSC** p. 160. "It is customary in some organizations to permit a nominator to give reasons for supporting the nominee. Nominations do not require seconds, but some organizations permit other members to give endorsing statements, which are called "seconding speeches."

53.     ANSWER: **RONR** p. 635, ll. 28-31; p. 636, ll. 5-9. "Except as the rules may provide otherwise, the Resolutions Committee is required to report all resolutions referred to it; but the committee can, if it wishes, report a resolution with 'no recommendation'." "In this connection, it should be noted that voting 'not to report' a resolution, reporting it with 'no recommendation,' and reporting it with the recommendation that it be rejected by the convention are each quite different." **AIPSC** p. 211. "The bylaws or governance committee may be empowered to: (1) approve the text of the amendment as written for submission to the assembly, (2) reword the amendment to accomplish the intent of the maker in proper form used by the organization, (3) combine several similar resolutions, with the permission of their proposers, and (4) comment on and make recommendations regarding the proposed amendments.… The committee should not be empowered to prevent the adoption of any proposed amendment by failing to report it to the voting body."

54.     ANSWER: No. The definition works perfectly for even numbers such as 20. But if the membership of the board or organization were 21, then 50% plus one would be 12, since it is impossible to divide an individual in half. A majority is properly defined as more than half. **RONR** p. 400, ll. 7-12. " The word *majority* means 'more than half"; and when the term *majority vote* is used without qualification—as in the case of the basic requirement—it means more than half of the votes cast by persons entitled to vote, excluding blanks or abstentions, at a regular or properly called meeting." **AIPSC** p. 135. "A *majority vote* in this book, unless otherwise qualified, is defined as a majority of the legal votes cast by members present and voting."

55.     ANSWER: **RONR** p. 405, ll. 2-6; 8-12. "A plurality that is not a majority never chooses a proposition or elects anyone to office except by virtue of a special rule previously adopted.… In an international or national society where the election is conducted by mail ballot, a plurality is sometimes allowed to elect officers, with a view of avoiding the delay and extra expense that would result from additional balloting under these conditions." **AIPSC** p. 140. "A plurality vote does not elect a candidate or adopt a motion except when the bylaws provide for a decision by plurality vote."

56.     ANSWER: **RONR** p. 529, ll. 30-35. "The *committee of the whole* and its two alternate forms, the *quasi committee of the whole (or consideration as if committee of the whole)* and *informal consideration*, are devices that enable the full assembly to give detailed consideration to a matter under conditions of freedom approximating those of a committee." **AIPSC** p. 133. "There are times when it is wise to set

© American Institute of Parliamentarians. All rights reserved.

aside the formal rules governing discussion and have relaxed rules of debate.... Informal consideration permits freedom in the length and number of speeches, allows possible amendments and motions to be discussed together, and gives broader latitude in debate."

57.     ANSWER: "In the absence of such a provision, parliamentary law fixes the quorum at a majority of the members. **RONR** pp. 345-346, ll. 14-13. "...voluntary societies should provide for a quorum in their bylaws, but where there is no such provision, the quorum, in accordance with the common parliamentary law, is as follows: 1) In a mass meeting ... the number of persons present.... 2) In organizations ... in which there is not ... a list of the bona-fide members,... the quorum consists of those who attend. 3) In a body of delegates ... the quorum is a majority of the number who have been registered as attending .... 4) In any other assembly with enrolled membership ... the quorum is a majority of all members." **AIPSC** p. 122. "In the absence of such a bylaws clause [setting a quorum] or applicable statutory provision, under parliamentary law: (1) ... membership organizations ... a majority of the voting members; (2) ... indefinite number of members ... the voting members who attend a meeting."

58.     ANSWER: **RONR** p. 199, ll. 7-11. "...When stated as 'I move the previous question' then it applies only to the immediately pending question. In its qualified form, however, it can be applied to include consecutively any series beginning with the immediately pending question." **AIPSC** p. 68. "If the motion to close debate and vote immediately is unqualified—'I move that we close debate,' for example—it applies to the immediately pending motion only. If more than one motion is pending, the motion to close debate should specify the pending motions to which it applies."

59.     ANSWER: A continued (adjourned) meeting is legally a continuation of the original meeting. The interval between the two meetings, no matter how long, is technically a recess, and when the organization reconvenes, business begins at the point where it was interrupted by the motion to hold a continued meeting at a definite later time. **RONR** pp. 93-94, ll. 25-1. "An *adjourned meeting* is a meeting in continuation of the session of the immediately preceding regular or special meeting.... If a regular meeting or a special meeting is unable to complete its work, an adjourned meeting can be scheduled for later the same day or some other convenient time before the next regular meeting, by the adoption (as applicable)of a main or a privileged motion to fix the time to which to adjourn, or a main motion to adjourn until the specified time." **AIPSC** p. 80. When an assembly cannot consider all its important business in the time available for a meeting, it may be desirable to continue the meeting at a later time. No exact form is required in stating such a motion to adjourn, but it must be clear that the meeting is to continue at a later date, and the time and place of the continued meeting must be specified." p. 107. "A continued meeting is sometimes referred to as an *adjourned meeting*, but the term *continued meeting* is recommended because it is less confusing concerning the intent of the action taken. The continued meeting is legally a continuation of the previous meeting."

60.     ANSWER: No, the members may call a meeting under the organization bylaws or applicable statute. **RONR** p. 576, ll. 7-10. [The bylaws should include] "A section authorizing the calling of special meetings should state by whom such meetings can be called—such as the president, the board, or a specified number of members nearly equal to a quorum— and the number of days' notice required." **AIPSC** p. 110. "If officers or directors fail to call a meeting in accordance with the organization's governing documents, members may demand that a meeting be scheduled and that the membership be notified.... If the leadership fails to perform its duty to issue the call, statutes may provide that a group of members or a single member may call the meeting and designate the time and location. In such cases, the requirements of any applicable statute should be strictly complied with."

61.     ANSWER: **RONR** p. 136, ll. 6-9; 16-19. "... an amendment must be *germane* to be in order. To be *germane*, an amendment must *in some way involve* the same question that is raised by the motion to which it is applied.... An amendment cannot introduce an independent question; but an amendment can be hostile to, or even defeat, the spirit of the original motion and still be germane." An amendment must always be germane—that is, closely related to or having bearing on the subject of the motion to be

amended." **AIPSC** pp. 52-53. "The most important principle concerning amendments is that they must be germane to the pending motion; that is, they must be relevant to and have direct bearing on the subject of the pending motion that the amendment seeks to change.... An amendment may be hostile. This means that it may be directly opposed to the actual intent of the original motion.... An amendment that merely changes an affirmative statement of a motion to a negative statement of the same motion is not in order."

62.  ANSWER: An *ad hoc* or special committee is created for a particular purpose and is discharged once that purpose has been achieved. **RONR** p. 492, ll. 3-9. *A special (select, or ad hoc) committee* is a committee appointed, as the need arises, to carry out a specified task, at the completion of which—that is, on presentation of its final report to the assembly—it automatically ceases to exist. A special committee may not be appointed to perform a task that falls within the assigned function of an existing standing committee." **AIPSC** p. 188. A special committee performs a specific task assigned by the organization. Even if it is called by another name, such as an ad hoc committee, a task force, a commission, or anything else, and unless otherwise designated by the organization, groups of members that are performing a specific task assigned by the organization are, in practice, special committees and are subject to the same rules as special committees. A special committee ceases to exist when its final report is issued."

63.  ANSWER: **RONR** p. 233, ll. 17-21 "The *privileged* motion to *Adjourn* (which is always moved in an unqualified form with no mention of a time either for adjourning or for meeting again) is a motion to close the meeting immediately, made under conditions where some other provision for another meeting exists".... p. 234, ll. 9-13."A motion to adjourn is always a privileged motion *except* in the following cases: 1) When the motion is qualified in any way, as in the case of a motion to adjourn at, or to, a future time." **AIPSC** p. 79. "When a main motion is pending, the motion to adjourn is a privileged motion that takes precedence over all other ranked motions.... The privileged motion to adjourn is subject to restricted debate and may be amended to establish the time when the current meeting will end or will continue. If a main motion is not pending, the motion to adjourn is a main motion and is open to full debate and amendment—it is subject to all the rules of a main motion.

64.  ANSWER: Following a second, the chair states the motion and then members may make, without seconds, suggestions to fill the blank. Following the close of suggestions, the proposals are debated and then voted on separately. **RONR** and **AIPSC** differ on the order that the suggestions are sequenced and how the vote to fill the blank is taken. **RONR** p. 164, ll. 25-26. "Each proposal is treated as an independent original to be voted on separately until one is approved by a majority." **RONR** differentiates the order in which the suggestions are submitted to a vote by the type of proposal; names, money, or places, dates or numbers. **AIPSC** pp. 55-56. "... the presiding officer opens discussion on the suggestions followed by a vote on each suggestion in the order in which each was proposed. Each member can vote for or against each suggestion, casting as many votes a there are suggestions.... The suggestion receiving the highest vote, provided that it is a majority, is inserted in the blank.

65.  ANSWER: **RONR** p. 308, ll. 12-30. The motion to *Rescind* ... is not in order when: a) the question can be reached by the motion to *Reconsider*, b) something has been done, as a result of the original vote , that is impossible to undo, c) when a resignation, election to (or resignation from) office and the person has been notified. **AIPSC** p. 48. "Any main motion that was adopted, no matter how long before, may be rescinded, but the rescission does not include action taken before adoption of the motion to rescind."

66.  ANSWER: **RONR** p. 34, ll. 7-13; 19-23. "Under parliamentary procedure, strictly speaking, discussion of any subject is permitted only with reference to a pending motion. When necessary, a motion can be prefaced by a few words of explanation, which must not become a speech; or a member can first request information, or he can indicate briefly what he wishes to propose and can ask the chair to assist him in wording an appropriate motion,... For a member to begin to discuss a matter while no question is pending, without promptly leading to a motion, implies an unusual circumstance and requires permission of the assembly ... in addition to obtaining the floor." **AIPSC** pp. 28-29. "... the presiding officer may inquire whether the member wishes to put the statement in the form of a motion. The presiding officer

may assist members in clarifying the wording of motions. Aside from an occasional brief explanatory remark, no discussion is permissible until the presiding officer states the motion to the assembly."

67. ANSWER: Both general and special orders postpone a main motion (or subject) until a future time. **RONR** p. 358, ll. 9-12. "A *general order* ... is any question which, usually by postponement, has been made an order of the day without being made a special order." pp. 364-365, ll. 32-6. "Orders of the day are divided into the classes of *general orders* and *special orders*. A special order is an order of the day that is made with the stipulation that any rules interfering with its consideration at the specific time shall be suspended except those relating: (a) to adjournment or recess; (b) to questions of privilege; (c) to special orders that were made before this special order was made; or (d) to a question that has been assigned priority over all other business at a meeting by being made *the* special order for the meeting ..."
A general order (postponement) requires a majority vote; a special order requires a two-thirds vote to postpone to a specific time. **AIPSC** pp. 62-63. "Any main motion that is postponed to a certain time becomes a general order for that time.... To postpone a main motion and designate it as a general order for a particular time requires a majority vote.... Instead of designating a postponed motion as a general order, the assembly may vote to make it a special order. This means that when the specific time arrives, the matter must be taken up immediately, regardless of whether something else is pending at that time.... Because a special order interrupts pending business, a two-thirds vote is required to postpone a main motion and make it a special order."

68. ANSWER: The general answer is that standing committees are those named in the bylaws and special committees are not. *Standing committees* are assumed to be permanent; special (or *ad hoc*) committees are created for a particular purpose and "discharged" when that task is accomplished. **RONR** pp. 490-491, ll. 4-6; 32-34; 6-10. "Ordinary committees are of two types—*standing committees* (which have a continuing existence) and *special committees* (which go out of existence as soon as they have completed a specific task).... Standing committees are constituted to perform a continuing function, and remain in existence permanently or for the life of the assembly that establishes them.... A standing committee must be constituted by name (a) by a specific provision of the bylaws or (b) by a resolution which is in effect a special rule of order and therefore requires for its adoption either previous notice and a two-thirds vote or a vote of a majority of the entire membership." **AIPSC** pp. 188-189. "A standing committee is a committee that has a fixed term of office and does the work within its particular field that is assigned to it by the bylaws or referred to it by the organization, or the governing board. The term of service for members of standing committees is usually the same as the terms of the officers.... A special committee performs a specific task assigned by the organization.... A special committee ceases to exist when its final report is issued.... Special committees are created and appointed as directed by the assembly or the organization's bylaws. Special committees report to the authority that established and appointed them."

69. ANSWER: While it is possible for a member to resign from the organization, it may or may not be the action of choice. **RONR** p. 2, ll. 9-10. "Failure to concur in a decision of the body does not constitute withdrawal from the body." p. 291, ll. "A member in good standing with his dues paid cannot be compelled to continue his membership to that additional obligations are incurred." **AIPSC** p. 265. "A member has the absolute right to resign from an organization at any time."

70. ANSWER: A majority vote will be sufficient to adopt by both authorities. **RONR** p. 569, ll. 28-32. "After the proposed bylaws are approved by the committee, the report of the committee is presented to the assembly and is considered seriatim—article by article and, whenever an article consists of more than one section, section by section." p. 558, ll. 25-31. "Each article or section is read separately, each provision being carefully explained by the chairman of the bylaws committee, as described above; and after the last one has been completed, the chair gives opportunity to insert additional paragraphs or sections and to correct any inconsistency or oversight that may have arisen during the process of amendment,..." p. 559, ll. 21-24. "Unlike the case of amending or revising the bylaws of an organization already established, the adoption of the bylaws through which a society is brought into being requires only a majority vote. The bylaws take effect immediately upon their adoption." **AIPSC** p. 240. "When the

presiding officer calls for the report of the committee appointed to draft the bylaws, the committee chair first moves the adoption of the proposed bylaws in order to bring them before the assembly for consideration and discussion.... The committee chair reads the first section of the first article, and the presiding officer calls for discussion, questions, or amendments to it.... The presiding officer then calls for the reading of the next section and follows the same procedure. ...When all proposed amendments have been voted on and no one rises to discuss the bylaws further, the presiding officer takes the vote on the motion to adopt the bylaws. A majority vote is required for adoption of the original bylaws."

71.     ANSWER: **RONR** pp. 592-593, ll. 3-25. "A motion to amend the bylaws is a particular case of the motion to *Amend Something Previously Adopted*; it is therefore a main motion, and it is subject to the same rules as other main motions with the following exceptions: 1) Special requirements for this motion's adoption should be specified in the bylaws, and they should always include at least notice *and* a two-thirds vote,... (with a vote of a majority of the entire membership as an allowable alternative), 2) Permissible primary and secondary amendment ... is usually limited by the extent of change for which notice was given ... 3) An affirmative vote on the motion to amend the bylaws cannot be reconsidered ... 4) the rule that, when a main motion is adopted, no other conflicting main motion is thereafter in order is not applicable ... since several notices of proposals representing different approaches to the same problem may have been given ..." p. 596, ll. 25-27. "When notice has been given of a bylaw amendment, it becomes a general order for the meeting at which it is to be considered." **AIPSC** p. 241-244. "The bylaws of most organizations require previous notice for amendments, review by a bylaws or reference committee, and at least a two-thirds vote for adoption.... A notice of motion may be withdrawn up to and including the last date of the notice period. Beyond the notice period, a notice of a motion may not be withdrawn.... "Since a proposed amendment to the bylaws is a specific main motion to *amend a previous action*, it may be amended, and an amendment to that amendment is also in order.... When the required notice concerning a proposed amendment to bylaws, the law ... gives the assembly wide discretion in amending the proposed amendment. Parliamentary law, however, provides that: 1.The proposed amendment must be germane to the section to which it applies. 2) No amendments can be proposed that cannot reasonably be implied by the notice given ... "The vote required to amend the bylaws should be stated in the bylaws.... If ... the bylaws are silent on the vote required to amend or revise the bylaws, it requires a majority of the legal votes cast. If the bylaws are silent on the notice required ... advance notice is required at the previous meeting or with the notice of the meeting."

72.     ANSWER: **RONR** pp. 593-594, ll. 16-22; 33-35. "Changes of the bylaws that are so extensive and general that they are scattered throughout the bylaws should be effected through the substitution of an entirely new set of bylaws, called a *revision*. Notice of such a revision is notice that a new document will be substituted that will be open to amendment as fully as if the society were adopting bylaws for the first time.... [A]s in case of any other bylaw amendment, the old document is not pending; and therefore, while the revision can be rejected altogether, leaving the old bylaws intact, the old document cannot be altered with a view to retaining it in a changed form." p. 570, ll. 3-6. "b) a revision of bylaws is adopted by the vote required to amend the existing ones ... rather than by a majority vote as in the case of bylaws that bring a society into being." **AIPSC** p. 244-245. "A revision proposes, in effect, a new set of bylaws, and the revision is presented and considered in the same manner as an amendment of the bylaws. A revision requires the same vote and advance notice that is required to amend the bylaws. The original bylaws, which are still in effect, are not before the assembly for consideration."

73.     ANSWER: **RONR** p. 393, ll. 19-25. "In debate, the maker of a motion, while he can vote against it, is not allowed to speak against his own motion. He need not speak at all, but if he does he is obliged to take a favorable position. If he changes his mind while the motion he made is pending, he can, in effect, advise the assembly of this by asking permission to withdraw the motion." **AIPSC** p. 126. "The right of every member to participate in the discussion of any matter of business that comes before the assembly is one of the fundamental principles of parliamentary law. Every member may speak for or against a motion; the maker of the motion, while the need is unusual, may speak against the motion he or she moved."

© American Institute of Parliamentarians. All rights reserved.

# Short Response Answers

74. ANSWER: **RONR** p. 138, ll. 9-23. "The following types of amendment are out of order: ... 2) One that merely makes the adoption of the amended question equivalent to a rejection of the original motion. Thus, in the motion that 'our delegates be instructed to vote in favor of the increase in Federation dues,' an amendment to insert 'not' before 'be' is out of order because an affirmative vote on not giving a certain instruction is identical with a negative vote on giving the same instruction. But it would be in order to move to insert 'not' before 'to' ('instructed not to vote in favor'), since this would change the main motion into one to give different instructions." **AIPSC** p. 53. "An amendment may be hostile. This means that it may be directly opposed to the actual intent of the original motion. An amendment that merely changes an affirmative statement of a motion to a negative statement of the same motion is not in order.... such a motion is not in order because the same result can be attained by voting against the main motion.... The negative wording of the motion can also confuse members who are casting votes."

75. ANSWER: **RONR** pp. 409-410, ll. 23-36. Regular Methods of Voting on Motions ... 1) by *voice* (*viva voce*)—the normal method of voting on a motion; 2) by *rising*—used in verifying an inconclusive voice vote, and in voting on motions requiring a two-thirds vote for adoption; and 3) by *show of hands*—an alternative methods that can be used in place of a rising vote in very small assemblies if no member objects. In some small groups, a vote by show of hands is also used in place of a voice vote as a normal method of voting." **AIPSC** p.147. " The usual methods of voting are: 1. General consent, 2. Voice vote, 3. Standing vote or show of hands, 4. Roll call, 5. Ballot."

76. ANSWER: **RONR** pp. 428-429, ll. 28-2. "A *proxy* is a power of attorney given by one person to another to vote in his stead; the term also designates the person who holds the power of attorney. Proxy voting is not permitted in ordinary deliberative assemblies unless the laws of the state in which the society is incorporated require it, or the charter or bylaws of the organization provide for it. Ordinarily it should neither be allowed nor required because proxy voting is incompatible with the essential characteristics of a deliberative assembly in which membership is individual, personal, and nontransferable." **AIPSC** pp. 153-154. "A *proxy* is a written authorization empowering another person to act, in a meeting, for the member who signs the proxy.... The term *proxy* may mean either the statement authorizing another to act in place of the member signing it, or it may refer to the person who attends the meeting in place of the absent member.... In addition to voting, unless otherwise restricted by the proxy, the proxy holder may act in all ways for the absent member, including speaking in debates and making motions.... In nonprofit organizations, voting by proxy is authorized in most jurisdictions. In some jurisdictions, the applicable corporate statute allows proxies unless prohibited in the charter or bylaws, while in other, the charter or bylaws of the organization must specifically authorize the use of proxies.... If the organization uses this book as its parliamentary authority, the proxy holder is given discretion to vote on ... motions unless the proxy statement or the bylaws say otherwise."

77. ANSWER: **RONR** pp. 408-409, ll. 21-4. "A member has a right to change his vote up to the time the result is announced; after that, he can make the change only by the unanimous consent of the assembly requested and granted, without debate, immediately following the chair's announcement of the result of the vote.... After the result of a vote has been announced, members can ... request unanimous consent to change his vote.... if any of these actions is to apply to a vote after the result has been announced, it must be taken immediately after the chair's announcement, before any debate or business has intervened." p. 48, ll. 30-35; 18-24. "... whenever it is stated in this book that a certain procedural motion relating to a vote that has been taken is in order immediately after the result of a vote has been announced, that interval begins as soon as the chair has pronounced the first two points.... Report of the voting itself, stating which side 'has it' and ... declaration that the motion is adopted or lost." **AIPSC** p. 157. "When a vote is taken by voice, a show of hands, standing, or roll call, members may change their votes up to the time that the result of the vote is announced.... When voting is by ballot, a member may not change the ballot after it has been placed in the ballot box. "

78. ANSWER: Philosophically, if the chair (presiding officer) is a member, "he has the same voting *right* as any other member. **RONR** pp. 405-406, ll. 19-26; 14-15. If the presiding officer is a member of the assembly, he can vote as any other member when the vote is by ballot. In all other cases the presiding

officer, if a member of the assembly, can (but is not obligated to) vote whenever his vote will affect the result—that is, he can vote either to break or to cause a tie; or, in a case where a two-thirds vote is required, he can vote either to cause or to block the attainment of the necessary two thirds.... The chair

cannot vote twice, once as a member, then again in his capacity as presiding officer." **AIPSC** pp. 142-143. "The presiding officer, if a member of the assembly, does have the right to cast a vote. However, in an assembly the presiding officer customarily exercises that right only when the vote is by ballot or when his or her vote will make a difference in the result. This preserves the presiding officer's duty of impartiality and objectivity. The presiding officer cannot be required to cast a vote."

79. ANSWER: The rules of representative bodies, like a state legislature, usually require that members vote in all cases except where self-interest is involved. **RONR** p. 407, ll. 12-19; 22-25. "Although it is the duty of every member who has an opinion on a question to express it by his vote, he can abstain, since he cannot be compelled to vote.... No member should vote on a question in which he has a direct personal or pecuniary interest not common to other members of the organization." p. 403, ll. 13-18. "Voting requirements based on the number of members present—a majority of those present, two thirds of those present, etc.—while possible, are generally undesirable. Since an abstention in such cases has the same effect as a negative vote, these basis deny members the right to maintain a neutral position by abstaining." **AIPSC** p. 140. "An abstention is not considered a vote and is therefore not counted in determining the result. A member who abstains has in fact relinquished his or her vote.... A member has the right to abstain from voting on any motion, and *must* abstain from voting if the member has a financial interest or conflict of interest in the outcome of the vote."

80. ANSWER: **RONR** p. 45, ll. 14-19. "The chair should not call for abstentions in taking a vote, since the number of members who respond to such a call is meaningless. To 'abstain' means not to vote at all, and a member who makes no response if 'abstentions' are called for abstains just as much as one who responds to that effect." **AIPSC** p. 140. "An abstention is not considered a vote and is therefore not counted in determining the result. A member who abstains has in fact relinquished his or her vote."

81. ANSWER: **RONR** p. 61, ll. 12-17; 21-23. "The rules under which secondary motions take precedence over one another have been gradually evolved through experience. While these rules are proper to each of the specific motions, they follow patterns that are related to the division of secondary motions into classes of *subsidiary*, *privileged*, and *incidental* motions.... The five privileged motions fall into a definite *order of precedence*, which gives a particular *rank* to each of these thirteen motions." **AIPSC** p. 306. "Precedence. The rank or priority governing a proposal, consideration, and disposal of motions. p. 16. The rank of a motion determines its priority when it is proposed and the sequence in which it must be considered and disposed of.... The precedence of motions is logical and is based on the relative urgency of each motion."

82. ANSWER: **RONR** p. 62, ll. 4-6. "Incidental motions have no rank among themselves, and none of them can be assigned a *position* in the order of precedence of motions. p. 70, ll. 2-7. "The order in which the incidental motions are listed ... has no relation to what other motions they may take precedence over or yield to. **AIPSC** p. 17. "*Incidental motions* have no order of ranking. They can arise incidentally out of the immediately pending business at any time."

83. ANSWER: **AIPSC** p. 11. "There are six main motions that ... are referred to as specific main motions because they perform unique and specific functions. They do not present a new proposal, but they concern actions that were previously taken." **RONR** p. 75. ll. 20-24. "The motions that bring a question again before the assembly enable the assembly,... to reopen a completed question during the same session, or to take up one that has been temporarily disposed of, or to change something previously adopted and still in force."

84. ANSWER: **RONR** p. 358, ll. 13-20. "The heading of *Unfinished Business and General Orders* includes items of business ... [which include] ... a) The question that was pending when the previous

# Short Response Answers

meeting adjourned, if that meeting adjourned while a question other than a special order was pending." **AIPSC** p. 118. "Unfinished business includes ... 1. Any motion or report that was being considered and was interrupted when the previous meeting was adjourned."

85.    ANSWER: **AIPSC** p. 111. "Common parliamentary law provides for full protection of every member by rigid enforcement of notice requirements before a meeting. It does not protect absentees who have received notice but who fail to attend, or members who come late or leave early.... When proper notice has been given and a quorum is present, it cannot be contended that those members present are 'not representative' or that the meeting is 'not representative,' since legally all members are equal."

86.    ANSWER: **RONR** p. 404. "The vote of a majority of the entire membership is frequently an alternative to a requirement of previous notice, and is required in order to rescind and expunge from the minutes. Otherwise, prescribing such a requirement is generally unsatisfactory in an assembly of an ordinary society, since it is likely to be impossible to get a majority of the entire membership even to attend a given meeting, although in certain instances it may be appropriate in conventions or in permanent boards where the members are obligated to attend the meetings." **AIPSC** p. 114 "If there was a mistake in a notice or a failure to send notice to every member and yet every member is present at the meeting and no one protests a lack of notice, the members waive notice simply their attendance and their participation in the meeting. Members may also waive notice by signing a written waiver of notice before, during, or after a meeting."

87.    ANSWER: **RONR** p. 430, ll. 17-20. "Strictly speaking, nominations are not necessary when an election is by ballot or roll call, since each member is free to vote for any eligible person, whether he has been nominated or not." **AIPSC** p. 161. "A member need not be nominated for an office, either from the floor or by a committee, when the vote for election is taken by ballot or by roll call. Unless the bylaws require a nomination, members may vote for anyone who is eligible, regardless of whether the person has been nominated, by writing in the name of their choice on the ballot or voting for that person during roll call."

88.    ANSWER: **RONR** pp. 425-426. "The term *preferential voting* refers to any of a number of voting methods by which, on a single ballot when there are more than two possible choices, the second or less-preferred choices of voters can be taken into account if no candidate or proposition attains a majority. While it is more complicated than other methods of voting ... preferential voting is especially useful and fair in an election by mail if it is impractical to take more than one ballot." **AIPSC** p. 156. "There are many preferential voting systems.... This is a single-ballot method of conducting the election as it would occur if repeated ballots were taken,... It is useful when a mail ballot is necessary, or when a meeting will end before counting is completed and the members cannot be reconvened for additional balloting."

89.    ANSWER: **RONR** pp. 443-444, ll. 30-34. "In this form of voting, each member is entitled to cast one vote for each position, so that, if, for example, three directors are to be elected, each member may cast three votes. These votes may all be cast for one, two, or three candidates, as the voter chooses.... this method of voting, which permits a member to cast multiple votes for a single candidate, must be viewed with reservation since it violates the fundamental principle of parliamentary law that each member is entitled to one and only one vote on a question." **AIPSC** p. 275. "Cumulative voting is a method that allows a member to place multiple votes for a single candidate instead of the casting of single votes for a number of different candidates. This form of voting must be authorized in the bylaws."

90.    ANSWER: **RONR** does not recognize the process of bullet voting. **AIPSC** p. 275. "Bullet voting is a method of focusing your voting power on a single candidate by choosing to place a single vote for a single candidate and to abstain from using any additional votes for anyone else. Bullet voting is permitted unless it is prohibited by the bylaws because a member has a right to abstain."

© American Institute of Parliamentarians. All rights reserved.

# Short Response Answers

91. ANSWER: **RONR** p. 413, ll. 1-9. "When a vote is to be taken, or has been taken, by ballot, whether or not the bylaws require that form of voting, no motion is in order that would force the disclosure of a member's vote or views on the matter. A motion to make unanimous a ballot vote that was not unanimous is thus out of order, unless that motion is also voted on by ballot—since any member who openly votes against declaring the first vote unanimous will thereby reveal that he did not vote for the prevailing choice." **AIPSC** p. 169. "One common error is to suppose that a vote that is not unanimous can be made unanimous by adopting a motion to that effect by majority vote. Sometimes the candidate receiving the second highest number of votes, or one of that candidate's supporters, proposes a motion to make the vote unanimous for the elected candidate. This is only a complimentary gesture, and no vote should be taken to make the vote unanimous. This gesture does not change the legal vote."

92. ANSWER: **RONR** p. 36, ll. 9-11; 26-28. "A second merely implies that the seconder agrees that a motion should *come before the meeting* and not that he necessarily favors the motion.... The requirement of a second is for the chair's guidance as to whether he should state the question on the motion thus placing it before the assembly." p. 470, ll. 26-28. "The name of the maker of a main motion should be entered in the minutes, but the name of the seconder should not be entered unless ordered by the assembly." **AIPSC** p. 29. Seconding a motion is not necessarily an endorsement of the motion. It merely indicates that the member wishes the motion to be considered by the assembly.... Seconds may be assumed by the presiding officer on routine items of business if that is the custom of the organization."

93. ANSWER: **RONR** p. 171, ll. 30-35. "If the main question is to go to a special (select, or ad hoc) committee, the motion should specify the number of committee members, and the method of their selection unless the method is prescribed by the bylaws; or, if preferred, the motion can name the members of the special committee." **AIPSC** p. 59. "A member may propose the motion [to refer] in the simple form, 'I move to refer this motion to a committee,' or the member may include provisions such as the type of committee, the number of members and how they are to be selected, the committee chair, or instructions to the committee. If the committee is to have power to act on behalf of the organization, the wording of the motion must provide for this power.... If these provisions are not specified in the motion, the presiding officer may put the motion to refer to a vote and, if adopted, may use his or her judgment in deciding on the membership of the committee, assigning its work, and giving instructions to it. If the presiding officer does not wish to take this responsibility, he or she may ask the assembly to determine the detailed provisions either before or after the motion to refer to committee is voted on."

94. ANSWER: **RONR** p. 250, ll. 18-19;23-25. "If a question [of a point of order] is to be raised, it must be raised promptly at the time the breach occurs. For example, if the chair is stating the question on a motion that has not been seconded, or on a motion that is out of order in the existing parliamentary situation, the time to raise these points of order is when the chair states the motion. After debate on such a motion has begun—no matter how clearly out of order the motion may be—a point of order is too late. **AIPSC** p. 91. "A point of order must be raised immediately after the mistake, error, or omission occurs. It cannot be brought up later in the meeting, or in another meeting, unless the error involves a violation of law or a serious violation of the principles of parliamentary procedure or of the bylaws."

95. ANSWER: **RONR** p. 308, ll. 24-29. Actions That Cannot be Rescinded or Amended. "c) When a resignation has been acted upon, or a person has been elected to or expelled from membership or office, and the person was present or has been officially notified of the action. (The only way to reverse an expulsion is to follow whatever procedure is prescribed by the bylaws for admission or reinstatement....)" **AIPSC** p. 266. "A resignation effective at some future date may be withdrawn until it has been accepted, or until the effective date of the resignation. If, however, the resignation is intended to become effective immediately, it cannot be withdrawn. After the effective date has passed, an officer or director who has resigned either orally or in writing cannot simply resume office because of a change of mind. A person who has resigned from office can be restored to that office only pursuant to the applicable vacancy-filling provision."

© American Institute of Parliamentarians. All rights reserved.

# Short Response Answers

96. **ANSWER: RONR** pp. 474-475, ll. 31-1. "When the next regular business session will not be held within a quarterly time interval, and the session does not last longer than one day, *or in an organization in which there will be a change or replacement of a portion of the membership*, the executive board or committee appointed for the purpose should be authorized to approve the minutes. **AIPSC** p. 232. "If an organization does not meet often, it is important to have a committee on minutes to which all proposed minutes are referred for correction and approval.... Because the approval of minutes is a power normally reserved for the assembly, the authority for a minutes approval committee should be included in the organization's governing documents or granted by adoption of a motion. The members of the minutes committee have the final authority over the content of the document.

97. **ANSWER: RONR** p. 315, ll. 24-33. "To provide both usefulness and protection against abuse, the motion to *Reconsider* has the following *unique characteristics*: a) It can be made only by a member who voted on the prevailing side. In other words, a reconsideration can be moved only by one who voted *aye* if the motion involved was adopted, or *no* if the motion was lost. (In standing and special committees, the motion to *Reconsider* can be made by any member who did not vote on the losing side—including one who did not vote at all.) **AIPSC** p. 47. "This book permits any member to propose the motion to reconsider when it appears justified."

98. **ANSWER: RONR** p. 347, ll. 22-33. "In the absence of a quorum, any business transacted (except for the procedural actions noted in the next paragraph) is null and void.... the inability to transact business does not detract from the fact that the society's rules requiring the meeting to be held were complied with and the meeting was convened—even though it had to adjourn immediately. Even in the absence of a quorum, the assembly may fix the time to which to adjourn, adjourn, recess, or take measures to obtain a quorum." p. 348, ll. 14-16. "The prohibition against transacting business in the absence of a quorum cannot be waived even by unanimous consent, and a notice cannot be validly given." **AIPSC** p. 122. "If a quorum is not present, the presiding officer may call the meeting to order to establish that a meeting was held, but the organization may not transact business. However, agenda items that do not require official action may be dealt with, such as hearing reports, hearing speeches by guests, having a program, or other non-business activities."

99. **ANSWER: RONR** p. 244, ll. 17-21. "Whether introduced as a privileged or a main motion, the effect of this motion is to establish an *adjourned meeting*—that is, another meeting that will be a continuation of the session at which the motion is adopted. **AIPSC** p. 78. "The purpose of a motion to adjourn is twofold: 1. To end a meeting or convention. 2. To end a meeting or convention and set a time to continue the meeting or convention." p. 82. "The rules governing the motion to adjourn include the following: 4. Can be amended to establish a continued meeting or change the time or place of a proposed continued meeting."

100. **ANSWER: RONR** p. 386, ll. 25-29. "A member may both speak in debate and conclude by offering a secondary motion, which is a particular application of the principle that a member having been recognized for *any* legitimate purpose has the floor for *all* legitimate purposes." **AIPSC** p. 68. "The motion to close debate is a powerful tool for expediting business. It may be proposed at any time after the motion to which it applies has been stated to the assembly. It cannot be combined with the motion to which it applies.... If the motion to close debate is proposed as soon as a main motion has been stated to the assembly, its adoption prevents any discussion of the question and the vote is taken immediately."

# Essay Answers

> The study questions and answers are intended only for general parliamentary study. The "answers" given are intended to show the type of responses that may be used but are not to be taken as complete answers—only as a starting point for further study.

1. ANSWER: **RONR** pp. li-lii, "The rules of parliamentary law found in this book will, on analysis, be seen to be constructed upon a careful balance of the rights of persons or subgroups within an organization's or an assembly's total membership. That is, these rules are based on a regard for the rights:
   - of the majority,
   - of the minority, especially a strong minority—greater than one third,
   - of individual members,
   - of absentees, and
   - of all of these together."

**AIPSC** pp. 6-10. "Knowledge of the fundamental principles of parliamentary law enables you to reason out the answers to most questions about parliamentary procedure.... The principles are simple and so familiar that we sometimes fail to recognize their importance. They are the same principles on which democracies are based.... These basic principles serve as a foundation for the framework of democratic group procedures.... *The purpose of parliamentary procedure is to facilitate the orderly transaction of business and to promote cooperation and harmony*.... Right of Association. *Individual persons have the right to associate with other persons to promote and pursue their common interests and aspirations*.... Right of Assembly. *Individual persons or groups have a right to assemble to promote their common interest*.... Equality of Rights. *All members have equal rights, privileges, and obligations*.... Majority Decision. *The majority vote decides*.... Minority Rights. *The rights of the minority must be protected*.... The Right of Discussion. *Full and free discussion of every proposition presented for decision is an established right of members*.... The Right to Information. *Every member has the right to know the meaning of the question before the assembly and what its effect will be*.... Fairness and Good Faith. *All meetings must be characterized by fairness and by good faith*."

2. ANSWER: You must be a leader and administrator as well as presiding officer. Those responsibilities are at least as important as your work at formal meetings. **RONR** p. 456, ll. 22-33. "*Administrative Duties of the President of a Society*.... in many organized societies, the president has duties as an administrative or executive officer; but these are outside the scope of parliamentary law, and the president has such authority only insofar as the bylaws provide it. In some organizations, the president is responsible for appointing, and is ex officio a member of, all committees ...." **AIPSC** pp. 173-174. "The *president*, the head of an organization regardless of the title, usually has three roles—leader, administrator, and presiding officer. Each roll call for different abilities.... The following are important duties performed by the president as an administrator.: 1. Acts as chief administrative officer and legal head of the organization, 2. Exercises supervision over the organization and all its activities and senior employees, 3. Represents and speaks for the organization, 4. Presides at business meetings, 5. Appoints committees as directed by the bylaws or the assembly, 6. Signs letters or documents necessary to carry out the will of the organization, and 7. Presides at meetings of the governing board."

3. ANSWER: The secretary is in the record keeper and custodian of the organization's official documents. The secretary's record (minutes) is, when properly corrected and approved, the official history of the organization. Should there be any legal challenge to its actions, the minutes are the first and best guide consulted. **RONR** p. 447, ll. 3-5. "... the minimum essential officers for the conduct of business in any deliberative assembly are a presiding officer and a secretary or clerk." pp. 458-459, ll. 24-30. A summary of the duties of the secretary vary with the organization. Some of the usual duties are: "1) To keep a record of all proceedings of the organization—usually called the *minutes*. 2) To keep on file all committee reports. 3) To keep the organization's official membership roll ... and to call the roll where it is required. 4) To make the minutes and records available to members upon request. 7) To sign all certified copies of acts of the society. 8) To maintain record book(s) .... 9) To send out to the membership a notice of each meeting,... and to conduct the general correspondence of the organization .... 10) To prepare, prior to each meeting, an order of business for the use of the presiding officer .... 11) In the absence of the president and vice-president, to call the meeting to order and preside until the immediate election of a

chairman pro-tem." **AIPSC** pp. 178-179. "The president and the secretary are recognized by law as the legal representatives of the organization. The secretary has extensive duties, serving as the chief recording and corresponding officer and the custodian of the records of the organization.... responsible for ensuring that the secretarial duties are performed properly, either by performing them personally or by directing the appropriate staff in those duties....The chief duties of a secretary are to: 1. Take careful and accurate notes of the proceedings .... 2. Prepare and certify the correctness of the minutes.... 3. Read or submit the proposed minutes to the organization.... 5. Record the approved minutes as the official minutes of the organization.... 7. Prepare a list of members and call roll when directed.... 11. Assist the presiding officer before each meeting in preparing a detailed agenda. 12. Preserve all records, reports, and official documents of the organization .... 13. Prepare and send required notices.... 16. Sign official documents to attest to their authenticity. 17. Carry on the official correspondence of the organization.... 18. Perform any additional duties required by applicable statutes."

4.  ANSWER: **RONR** pp. 148, ll. 16-20. "Except in the simplest and smallest local societies,... it is generally found advisable to provide in the bylaws for a board to be empowered to act for the society when necessary between its regular meetings, and in some cases to have complete control over certain phases of the society's business." p. 482, ll. 25-29. "A society has no executive board, nor can its officers act as a board, except as the bylaws may provide; and when so established, the board has only such power as is delegated to it be the bylaws or by vote of the society's assembly referring individual matters to it." p. 483, ll. 6-9. "... [N]o action of the board can alter or conflict with any decision made by the assembly of the society, and any such action of the board is null and void." **AIPSC** p. 195. "... provide in the bylaws that a smaller elected group, acting as the representatives of all the members, shall carry on the work of the organization during the intervals between meetings of the membership.... The duties, responsibilities, and powers of the board of directors should be clearly defined in the bylaws. Such a board is usually delegated the duty and power of acting for the membership in the intervals between meetings, except that certain powers are vested exclusively in the members.... [F]inal authority of any organization remains in its members assembled, except as that assembly may direct otherwise by adopting provisions in the bylaws. "

5.  ANSWER: **RONR** pp. 469-471, ll. 13-24. The body of the minutes should contain: "[a] all main motions or motions to bring a main question again before the assembly; ... [b] the wording in which each motion was adopted or otherwise disposed of; ... [c] the disposition of the motion; [d] ... secondary motions that were not lost or withdrawn, in cases where it is necessary to record them for completeness or clarity; [e] ... the complete substance of oral committee reports; [f]... all points of order and appeals ... together with the reasons; [g] ... the name of the maker of a main motion; [h] ... committee report of great importance; [i] ... declaration by the chair in 'naming' and offending member ...." The minutes should not contain: "[a] ... the name of the seconder ... unless ordered by the assembly; ... [b] If the chair voted [on a roll-call vote]; ... [c] The proceedings of a committee or the whole; [d] ... summarize his [speaker's] remarks." **AIPSC** pp. 229-230. "Minutes are generally a record of all actions and proceedings but *not* a record of discussion" The body of the minutes should contain: "[a] ... all main motion or resolutions stated by the chair and the way in which the assembly disposed (temporarily or permanently) of each motion.... [b] The exact wording of the main motion ... in its final form as adopted (or as adopted after amendment).... [c] When a vote is counted or taken by ballot, the number of members voting on each side is recorded.... [d] A motion withdrawn after being stated by the presiding officer. [e] ... any notice of a bylaw amendment; ... [f] Each report ... with the name of the member presenting the report, a brief summary of the report, and the action taken." Minutes should not contain: "[a] ... procedural motions ... except when they affect future action; [b] ... seconds ... unless required by governing documents; [c] ... personal opinions, personal interpretations, or comments.... [d] Criticism ... except when action of a motion to censure or reprimand a member has been stated."

6.  ANSWER: Previous notice is the requirement that certain motions that will be brought up at a meeting have been given to all members. This is a protection for the members and prevents motions of

major impact to come before the assembly without his or her knowledge. **RONR** p.121, ll. 21-30. "The term *previous notice* (or *notice*), as applied to necessary conditions for the adoption of certain motions, has a particular meaning in parliamentary law. A requirement of previous notice means that announcement that the motion will be introduced—indicating its exact content …—must be included in the call of the meeting at which the motion will be brought up, or, as a permissible alternative, if no more than a quarterly time interval … will have elapsed since the preceding meeting, the announcement must be made at the preceding meeting." **AIPSC** p. 113. "A proposal that according to the law, charter, or provision of the bylaws (…) requires advance notice cannot be considered at any meeting unless proper notice of the proposed action has been sent. Even with unanimous approval of the members present at a meeting, if members did not receive advance notice of a proposal, the proposal will be invalid. Amendments to the bylaws or charter, sale of property, large and unusual expenditures, election of officers, and other items of similar importance require whatever notice is specified by the bylaws or rules of the organization. The proposals to be voted on must be stated specifically."

7. ANSWER: **RONR** pp. 474-475, ll. 31-1. *"When the next regular business session will not be held within a quarterly time interval, and the session does not last longer than one day, or in an organization in which there will be a change or replacement of a portion of the membership, the executive board or a committee appointed for the purpose should be authorized to approve the minutes."* **AIPSC** p. 232. An organization that does not meet at least every three months should have a committee to approve the minutes of the meeting. Because the approval of minutes is a power normally reserved for the assembly, the authority for a minutes approval committee should be included in the organization's governing documents or granted by adoption of a motion." p. 117. "If a minutes approval committee has approved the minutes, the approval is announced and no further action is required."

8. ANSWER: **RONR** p. 441, ll. 1-10. "… if any office remains unfilled after the first ballot,… the balloting is repeated for that office as many ties as necessary to obtain a majority vote for a single candidate. When repeated balloting for an office is necessary, individuals are never removed from candidacy on the next ballot unless they voluntarily withdraw—which they are not obligated to do." RONR gives an alternate in the footnote which notes—"An organization could suspend the rules, or adopt a special rule of order, so that the nominee with the fewest votes is dropped from the list of nominees for succeeding ballots in the expectation that voters will then confine their choice to the remaining nominees. Only a bylaws provision, however, could make the dropped nominee ineligible for election so as to render illegal any subsequent votes cast for that nominee." **AIPSC** p. 168. "3. When election to an office requires a majority vote but no candidate receives a majority vote, the requirement for a majority vote cannot be waived, but the assembly can adopt motions to enable it to complete the election within a reasonable time."

9. ANSWER: **RONR** pp. 394-395, ll. 26-17. "If the presiding officer is a member of the society, he has—as an individual—the same *rights* in debate as any other member; but the impartiality required of the chair in an assembly precludes his exercising these rights while he is presiding.… On certain occasions—which should be extremely rare—the presiding officer may believe that a critical factor relating to such a question has been overlooked and that his obligation as a member to call attention to the point outweighs his duty to preside at that time. To participate in debate, he must relinquish the chair; … The presiding officer who relinquished the chair then should not return to it until the pending main motion has been disposed of,…" p. 451, ll. 29-35. "Whenever a motion is made that refers only to the presiding officer in a capacity not shared in common with other members, or that commends or censures him with others, he should turn the chair over to the vice-president or appropriate temporary occupant (…) during the assembly's consideration of that motion, just as he would in a case where he wishes to take part in debate." **AIPSC** p. 176. "The presiding officer does not leave the chair merely to present important fact that need to be presented. However, if a motion is directed at the president personally, the president–elect, if there is one, or the vice president, is asked to take the chair until action on the motions

as been completed. This is true whether the motion affects the president favorably—such as, to award a life membership—or adversely—a vote of censure."

10.    ANSWER: **RONR** p. 363, ll. 9-12. "Any particular item of business can be taken up out of its proper order by adopting a motion to suspend the rules by a two-thirds vote, although this is usually arranged by unanimous consent." p. 364, ll. 1-5. "The chair himself cannot depart from the prescribed order of business, which only the assembly can do by at least a two-thirds vote. This is an important protection in cases where some of the members principally involved in a particular question may be unable to be present through an entire meeting." **AIPSC** p. 120. "Unless the organization has a rule to the contrary, the use of an adopted agenda does not preclude other items of business from being added, deleted, or moved around on the agenda during the meeting. An agenda is flexible, and may be changed by general consent or by a majority vote."

11.    ANSWER: **RONR** pp. 270-273, ll. 30-35. "When a motion relating to a single subject contains several parts, each of which is capable of standing as a complete proposition if the other are removed, the parts can be separated to be considered and voted on as if they were distinct questions—by adoption of the motion for *Division of a Question* (or 'to divide the question').... a motion to divide the main question cannot be made while an amendment to the main question is pending.... A motion cannot be divided unless each part presents a proper questions for the assembly to act upon if none of the other parts is adopted, and unless the effect of adopting all of the parts will be exactly the same—no more, no less—as adoption of the compound main question. ... Another type of motion that cannot be divided is one whose parts are not easily separated.... if separating the elements of action in a proposed resolution would require recasting the parts ... the resolution cannot be divided." **AIPSC** pp. 99-100. "When a motion contains two or more distinct proposals, any member has the right to request that it be divided into separate motions.... each part must be suitable for adoption, even if one or more other parts are defeated.... A motion may contain several proposals that are worded in such a way that they cannot be divided easily or without extensive rewriting."

12.    ANSWER: **RONR** p. lii. "The application of parliamentary law is the best method yet devised to enable assemblies of any size, with due regard for every member's opinion, to arrive at the general will on the maximum number of questions of varying complexity in a minimum amount of time and under all kinds of internal climate ranging from total harmony to hardened or impassioned division of opinion."
p. 456, ll. 13-18. "The president should never be technical or more strict than is necessary for the good of the meeting. Good judgment is essential; the assembly may be of such a nature, through its unfamiliarity with parliamentary usage and its peaceable disposition, that strict enforcement of the rules, instead of assisting, would greatly hinder business." **AIPSC** p. 2. "The purpose of meeting [parliamentary] procedures is to allow members to reach informed business decisions in an effective, efficient, orderly, courteous, and fair manner.... Meeting procedures facilitate group decisions and help members attain the organization's objectives."

13.    ANSWER: **RONR** p. 465. ll. 10-16. "The parliamentarian is a consultant, commonly a professional, who advises the president and other officers, committees, and members on matters of parliamentary procedure. The parliamentarian's role during a meeting is purely an advisory and consultative one—since parliamentary law gives to the chair alone the power to rule on questions of order or to answer parliamentary inquiries." pp. 466-447, ll. 12-34. "During a meeting the work of the parliamentarian should be limited to giving advice to the chair and, when requested, to any other member. It is also the duty of the parliamentarian—as inconspicuously as possible—to call the attention of the chair to any error in the proceedings that may affect the substantive rights of any member or may otherwise do harm. There should be an understanding between the parliamentarian and the presiding officer that there will probably be occasions when it may be essential for the chair to listen to suggestions being made by the parliamentarian, even if it means momentarily not giving full attention to others or asking the assembly to *stand at ease* during the consultation.... In advising the chair, the parliamentarian

should not wait until asked for advice—that may be too late.... The parliamentarian should be assigned a seat next to the chair, so as to be convenient for consultation in a low voice ...." **AIPSC** pp. 269-270. "The parliamentarian is usually chosen by, and works under, the direction of the presiding officer. The parliamentarian may also aid and advise the governing board, committee ... and staff members.... Best practices are for a parliamentarian to meet with the presiding officer to determine the method of communication between them before and during meetings, to review the meeting script, and to discuss any 'what ifs' that may come up during the meeting. At a meeting or convention, the parliamentarian should sit next to the presiding officer. The parliamentarian does not make rulings but advises the presiding officer on procedures. The presiding officer may or may not follow the advice and is responsible for the final ruling,.... The parliamentarian is responsible for seeing that no procedural details are overlooked, for anticipating procedural strategy, and for being certain that all parliamentary requirements are observed. The parliamentarian is not an advocate of causes or a representative of any group or individual within the organization, but is retained to help the members accomplish the legitimate purposes of the organization."

14. ANSWER: **RONR** does not directly address the use of a minutes committee for a multiple day board meeting but does address the ability to present a minority report. Since the secretary is a member of the committee, he or she would have the opportunity to submit a minority report (pp. 528-529, ll. 27-10). However, there is no indication that the secretary does not have to abide by the majority opinion of the minutes approval committee. **AIPSC** p. 233. "The members of the minutes committee have the final authority over the content of the document. The secretary's record of the meeting is considered to be only notes until approved by the committee or assembly. The secretary, if in disagreement with the approval committee, may file a minority report to the assembly after the report of the committee, and the assembly will determine the final copy for the official record."

15. ANSWER: **RONR** p. 168, ll. 3-7. "The subsidiary motion to *Commit* or *Refer* is generally used to send a pending question to a relatively small group of selected persons—a committee—so that the question may be carefully investigated and put into better condition for the assembly to consider." p. 490, ll. 8-17; 26-31. "Generally the term *committee* implies that, within the area of its assigned responsibilities, the committee has less authority to act independently for the society (or other constituting power) than a board is usually understood to have. Thus, if the committee is to do more than report its finding or recommendations to the assembly, it may be empowered to act for the society only on specific instructions; or, if it is given standing powers, its actions may be more closely subject to review than a board's, or it may be required to report more fully.... In large assemblies or those doing a great volume of business, much of the preliminary work in the preparation of subjects for consideration is usually done by committees. In many such bodies, in fact, it is advisable to have every main question go to a committee before final action on it is taken by the assembly." pp. 500-501, ll. 25-1. "A committee may not adopt its own rules except as authorized in the rules of the society or in instructions given to the committee by its parent assembly in a particular case." **AIPSC** pp. 187-189. "Committees and boards are subdivisions of the membership charged with the day-to-day working of the organization.... Committees are important because they perform the bulk of the work of organizations. No committee should be established unless it is needed.... A standing committee is a committee that has a fixed term of office and does the work within its particular field that is assigned to it by the bylaws or referred to it by the organization, or the governing board.... A special committee performs a specific task assigned by the organization.... A special committee ceases to exist when its final report is issued." p. 191. "The powers, rights, and duties of each standing committee and of important special committees that are appointed periodically should be provided for in the bylaws. The powers, rights, and duties of other special committees should be provided for in the motions that create them or in the instructions given to them. Since no committee has inherent powers, rights, or duties, these must be delegated to it by the authority that established the committee."

16. ANSWER: **RONR** p. 501, ll. 7-13. "When a committee is to make substantive recommendations or decision on an important matter, it should give members of the society an opportunity to appear before

it and present their views on the subject at a time scheduled by the committee. Such a meeting is usually called a *hearing*. During actual deliberations of the committee, only committee member have the right to be present." **AIPSC** pp. 192-193. "Since committees often consider business of a confidential nature, which should not be discussed at a meeting of the membership, the confidentiality of committee deliberations must be protected. No officer, member, employee, or outside person has the right to attend any meeting of a committee except by invitation of the committee or by direction of the appointing body.... To further protect the privacy of the proceedings of a committee, its minutes are open to no one except members of the committee, unless its minutes are ordered to be produced by the entity that established the committee."

17. ANSWER: **RONR** p. 311, ll. 3-5. "So long as a question is in the hands of a committee, the assembly cannot consider another motion involving practically the same question." pp. 312-313, ll. 22-27; 1-2; 18-30. "Action to discharge a committee from further consideration of a question or subject is generally advisable only when the committee has failed to report with appropriate promptness or when, for some urgent reason, the assembly desires to proceed on the matter without further aid from the committee, or wishes to drop the matter.... Instead of discharging the committee, the assembly can instruct it to report at a reasonable specified time.... When a committee is discharged from considering a matter, either by adoption of a motion to discharge it or by the submission of its final report, the committee continues in existence if it is a standing committee, but ceases to exist if it is a special committee that was appointed to take up the matter....When a committee is discharged from further consideration of a question which was pending at the time of its referral and which was referred by means of the subsidiary motion to *Commit*, the question comes before the assembly automatically at that time ..." **AIPSC** p.191. "Any subject or duty that has been assigned to a special committee may be withdrawn at any time and assigned to another committee or considered by the board as a whole. Any proposal or assignment of work to a standing committee may be withdrawn by the governing body unless the subject or motion is assigned exclusively to the committee by the bylaws. Any special committee may be dissolved by the authority that created it."

18. ANSWER: **RONR** p. 16, ll. 21-27. "When a society or an assembly has adopted a particular parliamentary manual ... as its authority, the rules contained in that manual are binding upon it in all cases where they are not inconsistent with the bylaws (or constitution) of the body, any of its special rules of order, or any provisions of local, state, or national law applying to the particular type of organization. pp. 3-4, ll. 32-2. "Aside from rules of parliamentary procedure and the particular rules of an assembly, the actions of any deliberative body are also subject to applicable procedural rules prescribed by local, state, or national law and would be null and void if in violation of such law." **AIPSC** p. 245. "Every deliberative organization is presumed by law to be governed by the rules of parliamentary law. The charter, constitution, bylaws, and standing rules of the organization are its highest authority; but in all matters not covered by these rules, the organization is governed by parliamentary law." p. 237. An organization may be governed by statutes, a charter, a constitution, bylaws, or standing rules or by two or more of these. If the organization is incorporated, the primary rules under which it operates are the corporate laws of the state in which it is incorporated. Next in rank are the bylaws and standing rules. The parliamentary authority adopted by the organization controls all matters not covered by these governing documents."

19. ANSWER: **RONR** p. 17, ll. 22-27. "Rules clearly identified as in the nature of rules of order that are placed within the bylaws can (with the same exceptions) also be suspended by a two-thirds vote; but, except for such rules and for clauses that provide for their own suspension, as stated above, rules in the bylaws cannot be suspended. p. 263, ll. 1-6. "Rules contained in the *bylaws* (or constitution) cannot be suspended—no matter how large the vote in favor of doing so or how inconvenient the rule in question may be—unless the particular rule specifically provides for its own suspension, or unless the rule properly is in the nature of a rule of order ..." **AIPSC** pp. 86-87, "Suspension of the rules cannot deny a member or members any fundamental right whether inherent in parliamentary law or defined by the rules of the

organization. For example, an assembly cannot suspend: 1. A rule stated in statute, charter, or the organizations constitution or bylaws unless a specific provision in these documents of authority provides for suspension of the rule."

20.     ANSWER: **RONR** p. 215 footnote. "Some misuses of the motion to *Lay on the Table* probably arise from a misunderstanding of the practice of the United State House of Representatives, where this motion has gradually become converted to a special purpose that is not applicable in ordinary assemblies. The press of legislation in the House is so great ... the majority must be given power to suppress a measure without debate, and the agenda must be tightly regulated .... Consequently, when a matter is laid on the table in the House it is virtually killed." p.209, ll. 26-30. "The motion to *Lay on the Table* enables the assembly to lay the pending question aside temporarily when something else of immediate urgency has arisen or when something else needs to be addressed before consideration is resumed,.... p. 215, ll. 13-15. "It is out of order to lay the pending question on the table if there is evidently no other matter requiring immediate attention." **AIPSC** pp. 70-71. "When adopted a motion to table disposes of a main motion without a direct vote on the main motion. It suppresses or kills a main motion, without further debate, with the intention of avoiding any further action on the main motion in the meeting.... The practice of killing a motion by tabling it is used frequently by the U.S. Congress and by most voluntary organizations ... the motion is so convenient a means of ending discussion and setting a motion aside that it continues to be widely used for that purpose, despite efforts to discourage its use.... the motion to table requires a two-thirds vote to adopt."

21.     ANSWER: **RONR** p. 633, ll. 3-8; 15-23. "The Resolutions Committee—also sometimes called the *Reference Committee* or, in certain cases ... the *Platform Committee*—has as its basic purpose the screening of all original main motions that have not been screened by another committee and that come—or are to come before the convention.... The establishment of a Resolutions Committee in a convention represents a limitation on the ordinary right of members to propose any number of motions from the floor without notice—such limitation arising from the need for keeping within a schedule and disposing of a large amount of business within a short time. The degree of limitation imposed and the manner in which the committee functions vary considerably, depending on the organization,...." **AIPSC** p. 212. When an organization has a very extensive or complex agenda, it may establish reference (or resolutions) committees to assist in the timely conduct of its business and to optimize the decision-making process within the time constraints that exist. Such a system provides for the referral of all motions and reports to one or more reference committees. These committees consider the items referred to them and provide recommendations for action by the full assembly."

22.     ANSWER: **RONR** pp. 400, ll. 5-12; 20-4. "the basic requirement for approval of an action or choice by a deliberative assembly, except where a rule provides otherwise, is a *majority vote*. The word *majority* means 'more than half'; and when the term *majority vote* is used without qualification—as in the case of the basic requirement—it means more than half of the votes cast by persons entitled to vote, excluding blanks or abstentions, at a regular or properly called meeting.... Other bases for determining a voting result,... are required under parliamentary law for certain procedures, or may be prescribed by the rules of the particular body—for decisions in general or for questions of a specified nature .... Regardless of the basis required, a decision can be validly made only when a quorum is present ...." p. 402, ll. 22-31. "By modifying the concepts of a majority vote ... other basis for determining a voting result can be defined and are sometimes prescribed by rule. Two elements enter into the definition of such bases for decision: (1) the proportion that must concur—as a majority, two-thirds ...; and (2) the set of members to which the proportion applies—which (a) when not stated is always the number of members *present and voting*, but (b) can be specified by rule as the number of members present, the total membership, or some other grouping." pp. 403-404, ll. 13-18; 25-27; 8-10; 20-24. Voting requirement based on the *number of members present* [italics inserted for emphasis] ... while possible, are generally undesirable. Since an abstention in such cases has the same effect as a negative vote, these bases deny members the right to maintain a neutral position by abstaining.... A *majority of the entire membership* is a majority of the total

number of those who are members of the voting body at the time of the vote.... The vote of a majority of the entire membership is frequently an alternative to a requirement of previous notice.... Whenever it is desired that the basis for decision be other than a majority vote ... the desired basis should be precisely defined in the bylaws or in a special rule of order." **AIPSC** p. 135 "One of the fundamental concepts in a democracy is that the ultimate authority lies in a majority of the citizens of the democracy.... A majority vote is required to take an action. A *majority vote* in this book, unless otherwise qualified, is defined as a majority of the legal votes cast by members present and voting." pp. 138-139. "Every organization should state in its bylaws the vote required for election of candidates and also the vote required for important decisions. Whenever the basis on which a vote must be computed is not defined in statute, charter, or bylaws, it is a majority of the legal votes cast by members present and voting.... A *majority of all the membership positions* is often required to take an action in organizations having a fixed number of members.... A *majority vote of all the members in good standing* means a vote of more than half of all the members both present and absent.... A *majority vote of the members present* is sometimes required to take an action.... A *majority vote of the quorum*, or a majority of the number or member who are authorized to act for the organization, is the minimum number that some organizations require to make a decision for all the members. It means a majority of those present and voting, assuming a quorum is present, with the further stipulation that the affirmative vote must include a majority of the number required for a quorum.... A *majority of the legal votes cast* is the requirement that most commonly approves a motion and elects a candidate."

23. ANSWER: **RONR** p. 388, ll. 12-20. "Rights in regard to debate are not transferable. Unless the organization has a special rule on the subject, a member cannot yield any unexpired portion of this time to another member, or reserve any portion of his time for a later time—that is, if a member yields the floor before speaking his full ten minutes, he is presumed to have waived his right to the remaining time. If a speaker yields to another member for a question, the time consumed by the question is charged to the speaker." **AIPSC** p. 132. "If debate has been limited, time allocated to one member cannot be transferred to another member. In legislative bodies, members may yield portions of debate to other members, but this is not permitted in ordinary organizations."

24. ANSWER: **RONR** pp. 153-154, ll. 31-34. "A substitute offered for a main motion or resolution, or for a paragraph within a resolution, is a primary amendment and can therefore be moved only when no other amendment is pending." p. 135, ll. 22-26. "An amendment of the third degree is not permitted. To accomplish the same purpose, a member can say, while a secondary amendment is pending, that if it is voted down, he will offer another secondary amendment—which he can then indicate briefly—in its place." **AIPSC** p. 55. The substitute motion is a primary amendment ...." The presiding officer would be well advised to say that the motion is not in order at this time and he will recognize the speaker to offer his substitute as quickly as the amendment(s) on the floor has been disposed of.

25. ANSWER: **RONR** pp. 463-464, ll. 8-1. "An honorary office is in fact not an office but—like honorary membership—a complimentary title that may be bestowed on members or nonmembers. When it is desired to honor a nonmember, it is more usual to elect such a person to honorary membership.... If there are to be honorary officers or honorary members, they must be authorized by the bylaws. Like an honorary degree conferred by a college or university, an honorary office or membership is perpetual—unless rescinded or unless its duration is limited by the bylaws. Rights carried with the honor include the right to attend meetings and to speak but not to make motions or vote unless the person is also a regular member, or unless the bylaws provide full membership rights.... An honorary office entails no duties and in no way conflicts with a member's holding a regular office or being assigned any duty whatever." **AIPSC** p. 181. "Honorary titles are created as a compliment to those on whom they are conferred. Honorary titles generally carry with them the right to attend meetings and speak. However, they do not confer the right to propose motions, vote, or preside. The bylaws of the organization should set forth specific authority for honorary officer or members. Holding an honorary office does not prevent a person who is a member from exercising any rights or from holding a regular office."

# Sample Script Answers

The study questions and answers are intended only for general parliamentary study. The manual is intended to give examples of the types of questions that may be included in a written exam. The "answers" given are intended to show the type of responses that may be used but are not to be taken as complete answers—only as a starting point for further study.

Scripts Answers

SCRIPT 1. ANSWER: Items to look for in the script:

1. Member: "I move that …."

2. (Member may object before it is seconded or after, but only before there has been any debate or any subsidiary motion except *Lay on the Table* has been stated by the chair.)

3. Member: "I object to consideration of the question."

4. No second required.

5. Chair: (NOTE CORRECT WORDING) The consideration of the question is objected to. Shall the question be considered? Those in favor of considering it, rise. Be seated. Those opposed to considering the question, rise. Be seated. There are less than two-thirds opposed and the objection is not sustained. The motion will be considered. Is there a second to the motion?

6. Main motion is seconded, stated by the chair, and opened for discussion.

7. Mr. Chairman.

8. The chair recognizes …

9. Member: "I move to amend the motion by adding the words …."

10. Amendment must be seconded.

11. Chair: It is the ruling of the chair that the amendment is not germane to the main motion.

12. Member: "I appeal from the decision of the chair."

13. Member seconds the appeal.

14. Chair states his reasons for the ruling.

15. Member appealing the decision states his reason for the appeal.

16. Chair: The question is, "Shall the decision of the chair stand as the judgment of the assembly?" (This is a debatable appeal.) "Is there further discussion on the appeal concerning whether or not the amendment is germane?" (Discussion)

-- OR --

17. Chair: "The question is, "Shall the decision of the chair be sustained? Those in favor of sustaining the chair's decision, say aye. Those opposed to sustaining this decision, say no. There being a majority in the negative, the ruling of the chair is overruled."

18. Chair: "It is moved and seconded to amend the main motion by … Is there any discussion?"

19. Member: Mr. Chairman.

20. Chair: The chair recognizes ….

21. Member: "I move that when this meeting adjourns, it adjourn to meet at 8 a.m. on Saturday, March 4."

© American Institute of Parliamentarians. All rights reserved.

Scripts Answers

22. Member: "I second the motion."

23. Chair: It is moved and seconded that when this meeting adjourns, it adjourn to meet again at 8 a.m. on Saturday, March 4. Those in favor of the motion, say aye … Those opposed, say no. The ayes have it and the motion is carried. Is there any further discussion on the amendment to add the words ….

24. Member: Mr. Chairman.

25. Chair: The chair recognizes ….

26. Member: "I move that this meeting be adjourned."

27. Motion is seconded.

28. Chair: "It is moved and seconded that the meeting be adjourned. (NO DEBATE) Those in favor of the motion to adjourn, say aye. Those opposed, say no. The motion is carried. The meeting is adjourned to meet at the adjourned meeting at 8 a.m. on Saturday, March 4."

SCRIPT 2 ANSWER: Penalty for these errors:

1. If the chair calls for discussion on the motion to divide.

2. If the chair asks for or allows a motion and/or second for any of the three parts of the resolution to become pending.

3. If the chair fails to take separate votes on "amend" and "adopt" for the first resolved.

4. If the chair fails to ask for discussion on any of the three resolves. For any of the following minor infractions:

    a. A speaker fails to gain proper recognition by the chair.

    b. A motion that requires a second is not seconded.

    c. The chair fails to announce the final wording of the adopted resolution.

    d. Any other minor infraction.

# Appendix A

Appendix A

## *Parliamentary Law* Opinion Comparisons

Henry M. Robert's 1923 classic *Parliamentary Law* was designed to be a more readable treatise on parliamentary law than the *Rules of Order* which was designed for quick reference. (Henry M. Robert, *Parliamentary Law*, New York: Appleton-Century-Crofts, Inc., 1923, p. v.) Included in *Parliamentary Law* are 390 questions and answers selected from the correspondence of the author. The answers, or opinions, are based on, and cross-referenced to the 1915 edition of the Rules of Order. The opinions remain a valuable resource on interstitial issues of parliamentary law and are still recommended reading for the American Institute of Parliamentarians (AIP) certified professional parliamentarian examination (CPP exam).

This appendix consists of a matrix of selected topics with cross references to the leading authorities on parliamentary law allowing the reader to compare and contrast the treatment of each issue in each authority.

This volume provides a similar comparison for the 390 opinions in *Parliamentary Law*, arranged as follows:

| Column 1 | Number assigned by Robert to each opinion. |
|---|---|
| Column 2 | Summary of the question presented. |
| Column 3 | Summary of answer in *Parliamentary Law*. |
| Column 4 | Proposed answer under Robert, Henry M., *Robert's Rules of Order Newly Revised*, 11th Edition, Eds. Sarah Corbin Robert, Henry M. Robert, III, William J. Evans, Daniel H. Honemann, Thomas J. Balch, Philadelphia: Da Capo Press, 2011 ("RONR"), including page references. |
| Column 5 | Section Number in RONR. |
| Column 6 | Proposed answer under *American Institute of Parliamentarians Standard Code of Parliamentary Procedure*, Eds. Barry Glazer, James N. Jones, James Lochrie, Michael Malamut, Mary Randolph, Ann Rempel, Mary Remson, and Thomas Soliday. New York: McGraw Hill, 2012 ("AIPSC"), including page references. |
| Column 7 | Proposed answer under Cannon, Hugh, *Cannon's Concise Guide to Rules of Order*, Lincoln: Authors Choice Press, 2001 ("Cannon"), including page references. |
| Column 8 | Proposed answer under Demeter, George, *Demeter's Manual of Parliamentary Law and Procedure* Revised Edition, Boston: Little, Brown and Company, 1969 ("Demeter"), including page references. |
| Column 9 | Proposed answer under Riddick, Floyd M., Riddick's *Rules of Procedure*. Ed. Miriam H. Butcher. New York: Scribner, 1985 ("Riddick"), including page references. |

The brief entries in the matrix are not definitive opinions. They are merely proposed analyses with supporting page citations. Readers may differ in their analysis of these issues; the point of *Parliamentary Law* Opinion Comparisons is to provide a convenient reference and starting point for further study and analysis.

Appendix A

| | |
|---|---|
| MM | Main motion |
| PA | Primary amendment |
| SA | Secondary amendment |
| M | Majority |
| MN | Majority with notice |
| MN23 | Majority with notice, 2/3 vote without notice |
| MN23MEM | Majority with notice, 2/3 vote or majority of entire membership. |
| VP | Vice President |
| EB | Executive Board |
| EC | Executive Committee |
| COTW | Committee of the Whole |
| NC | Nominating Committee |
| ROR | Robert's Rules of Order Revised (1915 edition) |
| POO | Point of Order |

Appendix A

| No | Issue | Answer | RONR 11th. Ed | § | AIPSC | Cannon | Demeter | Riddick |
|---|---|---|---|---|---|---|---|---|
| 1 | What is an amendment to something already adopted? | Main motion, not ordinary amendment, p. 407. | Incidental main motion, MN23MEM, p. 305. | 35 | MM to amend action previously taken, same vote, p. 40, but see also repeal by implication, p. 25. | Motion not recognized, instead reconsider -- M or 2/3 if beyond next day, p. 126. | Amend bylaw or previous adoption, p. 171; 2/3 vote, pp. 72, 174. | Amend, rescind, reconsider or de novo replacement by M, pp. 41-2. |
| 2 | Can a member offer two amendments at the same time to different parts of bylaws? | Yes, if no-one objects, p. 407. | Yes, if isolated changes offered as substitute, p. 593. | 57 | Yes, and related changes may be implied, p. 243. | Yes, no express limit on form of amendments, p. 71. | Yes, p. 182. | Yes, amendment must generally be contiguous except by consent, p. 1 |
| 3 | MM -- Boat ride on Severn River; (a) Strike Severn River, insert Placid Lake; (b) Strike boat ride on Severn River, insert dinner. Are the amendments germane? | (a) germane; (b) germane if boat ride and dinner are mutually exclusive, p. 407. | Yes, in some way involves the same question, would preclude consideration of second, can put to Ass'y, pp. 131, 136-37. | 12 | Yes, relevant, direct bearing, p. 52. | Yes, relevant, p.56. | Yes, related, pertinent, pp. 70-71. | Yes, relevant, p. 97. |
| 4 | MM - build clubhouse; PA - cost not to exceed $X; SA strike $X, insert $Y. Is SA in order? | Yes -- germane and PA adoption would preclude SA, p. 408. | Yes, in some way involves the same question, would preclude consideration of second, can put to Ass'y, pp. 131, 136-37. | 12 | Yes, relevant, direct bearing, p. 52. | Yes, relevant, p.56. | Yes, related, pertinent, p. 70-71. | Yes, relevant, p. 97. |
| 5 | MM - swan boats; PA - with roller skates; SA - ice skates. Is SA in order? | Yes, only if SA is not germane to PA must it wait, pp. 408-9. | Yes, in some way involves the same question, would preclude consideration of second, can put to Ass'y, pp. 131, 136-37. | 12 | Yes, relevant, direct bearing, p. 52. | Yes, relevant, p.56. | Yes, related, pertinent, pp. 70-71. | Yes, relevant, p. 97. |

© American Institute of Parliamentarians. All rights reserved.

Appendix A

| No | Issue | Answer | RONR 11th. Ed | § | AIPSC | Cannon | Demeter | Riddick |
|----|-------|--------|---------------|---|-------|--------|---------|---------|
| 6 | Is MM open for further discussion when PA has been voted down? | Yes, p. 409. | Yes, any number can be considered in succession if not questions already decided, p. 135. | 12 | Yes, after PA or SA is adopted or defeated another of same rank is in order, p. 54, 57. | Yes, chair must continue debate and put MM to vote, pp. 103-4. | Yes, no limit to successive amendments, p. 73. | Yes, amendment process indefinite if proper new question, pp. 17-18. |
| 7 | Is discussion on amended MM confined to amendment? | No, discuss MM as it then stands, p. 409. | No, question is then on MM as amended, p. 143. | 12 | No, question is on MM as amended, p. 57. | No, question is on MM as amended, p. 103-4. | No, question is on MM as amended, p. 69. | No, question is on MM as amended, p. 16. |
| 8 | Can chair reput question on own initiative at next meeting: (a) on original MM when friendly amendment was incorporated without a vote and the amended MM lost? (b) if chair failed to put MM to vote after amendment? | No, (a) final by consent to friendly amendment, (b) drops and must be renewed as new business, pp. 409-10. | No, (a) final by consent to amendment, p. 162; (b) main motion must be voted on in amended form, p. 131, but could be brought back for confirmation by unanimous consent, p. 74. | 12 | No, (a) final by general consent, p. 148; (b) final vote on MM is required, pp. 37, 57 -- either failed or approved by general consent. | No, (a) final by consent, pp. 124-5, 104; (b) can use general consent to go back and correct errors, p. 26. | No, (a) final by consent, pp. 309-10; (b) bad practice, but failure to put MM will stand as final if that is understanding and no point of order, p. 69. | No, (a) final by consent, pp. 194-5; (b) chair can back up and reopen debate if something has been overlooked, p. 157. |
| 9 | An amendment is offered but not accepted by maker; chair incorporates over maker's objection. Is this proper? | No, chair has no authority w/o maker or assembly consent, p. 410. | No, except by assembly consent, p. 162, or maker withdraws or modifies, pp. 295, 40. | 12 | No, except by consent of assembly, p. 274, or by maker before motion presented to assembly, p. 56. | No, can work with maker before statement and after with consent of assembly, pp. 102, 104. | No, maker and assembly may informally amend but not chair, p. 70 | No, only the assembly has that power, pp. 12-13, 194-5. |
| 10 | After a substitute motion is passed, should the chair put the original motion or consider that the substitute has passed? | The original motion has been replaced and disposed of; the substitute must now be disposed of p. 410. | Put substitute to vote, p., 161. | 12 | Final vote on substitute MM is required, pp. 57. | Always put MM after amendment; amendment may make it easier to defeat, pp. 103-04. | Bad practice but failure to put MM will stand as final if that is understanding and no point of order, p. 69. | After amendment, question recurs on the MM as amended by the substitute and that must be put to a vote, p. 15. |

© American Institute of Parliamentarians. All rights reserved.

Appendix A

| No | Issue | Answer | RONR 11th. Ed | § | AIPSC | Cannon | Demeter | Riddick |
|---|---|---|---|---|---|---|---|---|
| 11 | When a primary substitute is pending is a secondary substitute in order? | Yes, after a chance to amend the text to be struck, p. 411. | Yes, p. 154n. | 12 | No, amendment by "substitution of a new motion" discusses only primary amendments, pp. 54-5. | Yes, but substitute used in looser sense of delete and add, p. 103. | No, "substitute motion" defined as primary amendment, pp. 79, 81. | No, substitute should be perfected before adoption, p. 15, but no express authority for secondary substitute. |
| 12 | After a MM is amended by substitution, can the substitute be amended by substitution? | No, while pending can have substitute for substitute, but after adoption, can only add or reconsider, pp. 411-2. | No, while pending can have substitute for substitute, but after adoption, can only add or reconsider, pp. 154n, 155. | 12 | Yes, successive amendments may be proposed one at a time, p. 54 | Yes, but substitute used in looser sense of delete and add, p. 103. | No, can only add new matter or reconsider, p. 81. | No, substitute should be perfected before adoption, p. 15. |
| 13 | Speaker engaged for three lectures. At next meeting, moved to amend by striking "three" and inserting "five." Is this out of order? | Out of order if speaker already engaged. Should move to engage for addition two. If not engaged, requires MN23MEM, p. 412. | Out of order if already engaged -- contract entered into, can't be undone, p. 308. Otherwise, amend previous adoption. | 35 | Out of order if engaged, can't unilaterally change terms of contract but motion to attempt to renegotiate terms would be in order, p. 41. | Out of order if engaged; otherwise reconsider -- M or 2/3 if beyond next day, p. 126. | Out of order if engaged but previous adoptions can be amended if not yet carried out, p. 72. | Out of order if a contract has been entered into, but can move to change the part that has not been implemented or put into contractual effect p. 42. |
| 14 | Can assembly amend something already adopted before the time for reconsideration expires? | Yes, but requires 2/3 vote or prior notice, p. 412. | Yes, no time limit, MN23MEM, p. 307, but not after reconsideration has been moved, p. 308. | 35 | No, amend previous action applies to action at previous meeting, p. 40; reconsideration, action at same meeting, p. 45. | Yes, called reconsideration whenever it occurs -- M or 2/3 if beyond next day, p. 126. | Yes, no time limit stated, p. 72. | No, only reconsider is in order on the same or next day p. 42. |

© American Institute of Parliamentarians. All rights reserved.

Appendix A

| No | Issue | Answer | RONR 11th. Ed | § | AIPSC | Cannon | Demeter | Riddick |
|---|---|---|---|---|---|---|---|---|
| 15 | How does assembly change an item in an adopted budget? | Move to amend by striking amount and inserting new amount, MN23MEM p. 412. | Amend something previously adopted, MN23MEM, p. 305, see also budget, pp. 577, 587 (bylaws allow amendment by M). | 35 | Amend action previously taken, same vote, p. 40, see also budget, p. 251. | Called reconsideration -- M or 2/3 if beyond next day, p. 126. | Amend previous adoption, p. 72, 171, 174. | Amend that portion of the budget by substitution to keep entire section intact, p. 42. |
| 16 | Can motion to reconsider be made or seconded by someone who is entitled to debate and make motions but not to vote? | No, reconsider can be moved only by someone who voted on prevailing side (or did not vote on losing side in committee), p. 413. | No, must have voted with prevailing side, or not on losing side in committee, p. 315. | 37 | Yes, reconsider can be moved by any member, p. 46-7. | Yes, reconsider can be moved by any member, p. 127. | No, reconsider can be moved only by voter on prevailing side, p. 156, or not on losing side in committee, p. 159. Any member can second. | Yes, any member can move for reconsideration, p. 166. |
| 17 | Can a motion to reconsider be made at the next regular meeting in organizations meeting weekly or twice a month? | No, must be next calendar day, except for legal holidays. Can be regular, adjourned or special meeting, p. 413. | No, one day session - same day; longer session - same and next day, p. 316. No time limits in committee, pp. 329-30. | 37 | No, must be during same meeting or conventions, p. 45. | Yes, no time limit but M if moved or notice given same or next day, 2/3 thereafter, p. 127. | No, right to move expires on adjournment of meeting or session unless: bylaws extend; notice given; move to reconsider and enter, p. 158. | No, same or next day, p. 166. |
| 18 | Can question that carried be reconsidered at next meeting, regular or special? | Yes, as long as motion was made on the same or next day, p. 413. | Yes, can **make** motion same or next day, p. 316; **call up** by end of next session if within the quarter, same session if not, pp. 321-3. | 37 | No, only within same meeting or convention, pp. 44-5. | Yes, M same or next day, 2/3 later; once motion is made, debate follows, as for any MM, p. 127. | Yes, if moved or noticed same day, or in call of meeting, p. 158. | Yes, if same or next day; once entered, can be called up at same or next meeting but chair should bring it up after pending matter, p. 166. |

Appendix A

| No | Issue | Answer | RONR 11th. Ed | § | AIPSC | Cannon | Demeter | Riddick |
|----|-------|--------|---------------|---|-------|--------|---------|---------|
| 19 | Can a motion decided by a secret ballot be reconsidered? | Yes, maker must state that he voted on the prevailing side and vote on reconsideration must be by ballot, p. 414. | Yes, maker must waive secrecy, p. 316, motion to reconsider must be by ballot, pp. 286, 413. | 37 | Yes, any main motion can be reconsidered, no need for waiver of secrecy because anyone can move, p. 45. | Yes, any question can be reconsidered, no need for waiver of secrecy because anyone can move, p. 127. | Yes, member must state he voted on prevailing side and vote on motion to reconsider must be by ballot, pp. 38, 140. | Yes, any member can move for reconsideration, p. 166. |
| 20 | Instead of reconsidering a ballot vote in an election, can the club order another vote? | No, not unless there is misunderstanding or fraud, p. 414. | No, a vote is never retaken by the same form of voting, p. 410, recount or point of order if prompt, pp. 410, 445. | 45 | No, challenge must be prompt, based on fraud or impropriety **and** violations could have changed results, pp. 170-171. | No, not without misunderstanding or fraud, p. 134. | No, not without prompt raising of fraud or illegality and then only the offices affected, p. 248. | No, challenge to vote must be prompt and base on irregularities, p. 205. |
| 21 | Can a vote taken by secret ballot be rescinded? | Yes, with some exceptions, but vote on rescinding must be by ballot, p. 414. | Yes, can be applied to anything with continuing force, p. 305, any further vote must be by ballot, pp. 286, 413. | 35 | Yes, any adoption can be rescinded, p. 48, privacy of ballots must be protected, p. 166. | Yes, can reconsider any vote at any time and don't need to breach secrecy, pp. 127-8. | Yes, can rescind any adoption, p. 165, should take rescind vote by ballot, pp. 140, 38. | Yes, can rescind any adoption, p. 173. |
| 22 | Bylaws provide name can't be proposed twice in a year for membership. Can one move rescission of a rejection? | No, motion to rescind brings matter again in violation of the bylaws, p. 414 | No, rescind applies to adoptions, p. 305, and bylaws trump rules, p. 14. | 35 | No, rescind applies to adoptions, p. 48, and bylaws trump rules, p. 237. | No, reconsider any vote at any time, p. 128, but bylaws govern, p. 69. | No, rescind applies to adoptions, p. 165, and bylaws govern, p. 308. | No, rescind applies to adoptions, p. 173, and bylaws govern, p. 89. |
| 23 | Ordinance adoption reconsidered, then ordinance amended. Should a vote now be taken on adoption? | Yes, no motion necessary -- reconsideration opens question of adoption of ordinance, pp. 414-5. | Yes, adoption of reconsider immediately places question before assembly, p. 324. | 37 | Yes, motion before assembly as if not voted on before, p. 47. | Yes, resume consideration at point just before vote, p. 128; debate follows as for any MM, p. 127. | Yes, question automatically reopened and must be voted on again, pp. 154-5. | Yes, upon adoption, open to debate, amendment and re-adoption, p. 166. |

Appendix A

| No | Issue | Answer | RONR 11th. Ed | § | AIPSC | Cannon | Demeter | Riddick |
|---|---|---|---|---|---|---|---|---|
| 24 | Ordinance passed; a week later motion to reconsider made, never called up. What is its status? | Motion wasn't in order without special rule; even so, terminated at close of next regular meeting, p. 415. | Not in order. Weekly meeting is a session. Only in order to make motion same day in one-day meeting, p. 316. Ability to call up terminates with adjournment of next regular session, p. 321. | 37 | Not in order - must be same meeting, p. 45. Reconsider terminated, must be taken up immediately if no business pending or as soon as pending business has been handled, p. 46. | In order at any time, and taken up that day, p. 127. No time limit, p. 128, raise by POO. | Not in order, p. 158; and expired, ordinance effective, p. 155. | Not in order, p. 166. Terminated because once entered, can only be called up at same or next meeting, p. 166. |
| 25 | Regular meeting at 2-3 month intervals; Directors meeting in between. Must reconsideration be at next Directors meeting or next regular meeting? | Action at either type can only be reconsidered at that type, p. 415. Can be called at next if made at original meeting. | Only in order to make motion the same day in one day meeting, p. 316. Ability to call up terminates upon adjournment of next regular session, p. 321. | 37 | Must be made at same meeting, p. 45, and is taken up immediately, p. 46. | Same body can reconsider at any time, p. 128. | Must be made at same meeting, p. 158, automatically opens underlying question, unless tabled or postponed, pp. 154-5. | Must be made at same meeting, can be called up at the next meeting (of same body implied), p. 166. |
| 26 | Constitution requires state society 2/3 vote for amendment. An amendment did not get necessary support. Is motion at national convention to reconsider rejection vote in order? | No, must be moved by one on prevailing side on day of vote or next day, pp. 415-6. Votes at issue here were at state society level. | No, maker must be on prevailing side in the same assembly, p. 315, same or next day in same session, p. 316. | 37 | No, must be during same meeting or convention of the same assembly, p. 45. | No, no time limit, p. 127, but state societies would have to act, not convention. | No, can be moved only by prevailing side of same body, p. 156, and expires on adjournment of meeting or session, p. 158. | No, any member may move, but must be member of same body, p. 166. |

Appendix A

| No | Issue | Answer | RONR 11th. Ed | § | AIPSC | Cannon | Demeter | Riddick |
|---|---|---|---|---|---|---|---|---|
| 27 | Can a delegate move reconsideration of a vote where his delegation voted as instructed as a unit on prevailing side? | No, delegates voted as units. Delegate can move reconsideration of instructions at unit level but not at convention, pp. 416-7. | No, delegate must vote as instructed by unit, p. 605. | 58 | No, "not wise" to instruct delegates but implied that instruction is binding, p. 206. | No, not explicit but delegates represent units, p. 3. | No, when instructed, reconsideration must be moved in accord with express wishes of majority of unit, p. 160. | No, delegates must follow instructions, although giving instructions not recommended, p. 80. |
| 28 | Is a motion to rescind in order when a motion to reconsider has been defeated? | No, not at that meeting. Rescind is in order at a future meeting, p. 417. | No, rescind not in order if question can be reached by reconsider, p. 308. After defeat of reconsider, rescind is arguably dilatory on same day, pp. 342-3. | 35 | No, rescind is to repeal approval at previous meeting, can be moved at a future meeting but not same meeting, pp. 45, 48. | No, reconsider and rescind are the same motion. Could move at a future meeting but requires 2/3 vote, p. 127. | No, not in order at same sitting if reconsideration has been moved and lost, p. 165. | No, rescind applied to action at previous meeting, p. 173. Can be moved at future meeting. |
| 29 | A bill rejected, reconsidered and rejected again by one house. Can that house consider identical bill approved by another house? | Yes, new question from coordinate branch. Reconsideration applies only to acts of same assembly, p. 417. | Yes, but other house approval would have to be considered a substantial difference in circumstances, p. 336, or application of special rule, p. 8. | 38 | No, can't be renewed at that meeting, p. 25, but doesn't deal with specific rules of legislatures. | No, p. 127, but doesn't deal with specific rules of legislatures. | No, p. 172, but doesn't deal with specific rules of legislatures. | No, p. 169, but doesn't deal with specific rules of legislatures. |
| 30 | Motion to reconsider and enter. Can the chair refuse the request to enter because it would defeat the purpose of the motion? | Yes, request is out of order if a delay to next day (adjourned or other meeting) would defeat the purpose, p. 417. | Yes, cannot be applied to votes on motions defeated by delay of one day, p. 334. | 37 | Yes, no motion to reconsider and enter recognized, p. 26. | Yes, no motion to reconsider and enter recognized, p. 126-9. | Yes, out of order as "dilatory" if defeats purpose of motion, p. 161. | Yes, no motion to reconsider and enter recognized p. 166. Chair directs secretary to make note only until pending business disposed. |

Appendix A

| No | Issue | Answer | RONR 11th. Ed | § | AIPSC | Cannon | Demeter | Riddick |
|----|-------|--------|---------------|---|-------|--------|---------|---------|
| 31 | Can one rescind a vote and leave the motion in the form it was before the vote? | No, reconsider has that effect but not rescind. Rescind repeals, strikes out, p. 418. | No, rescind strikes out entire MM, p. 305. Reconsideration immediately opens question on which vote was reconsidered, p. 324. | 35 | No, rescind nullifies MM, p. 48. Reconsider cancels vote and reopens motion, p. 47. | Yes, Cannon merges and modifies rescind and reconsider, p. 128. | Yes, rescind abolishes vote and automatically reopens MM to debate, pp. 165-6. | Yes, rescind strikes out, abolishes action, and restores original status, p. 173. |
| 32 | When a member gives notice of intention at next meeting to rescind, does president raise under unfinished business, does noticer raise, or can any member call? | Any of these methods can be used for any motion requiring notice, p. 418. Otherwise member could use notice to block action. | When previous notice has been given, it is usual to wait for the member who gave notice to move, but if he does not, any member can move, p. 307. | 35 | Not explicit about who can move after notice but logically must be any member to prevent noticer blocking other members. | Not explicit about who can move but must be any member to prevent blocking, p. 127. Recommends advance notice of all substantive motions, p. 100. | Any member can move to rescind even after notice, pp. 165-6. | If member who gave notice fails to move, any member may do so, p. 173. |
| 33 | How does one rescind a resolution adopted by a delegated convention last year? | Any member can make motion and rescind by M if notice given at prior meeting even the same day, p. 418. | Any member can move and M can rescind if notice given at prior meeting on at least the previous day, p. 620, 306. | 58 | Delegates should be free to vote as they think best for the organization unless instructed, p. 206. Move to rescind with same vote and notice as original motion, p. 49. | Delegates represent units but, absent instructions, any delegate could move and vote would be MN23, pp. 3, 127. | When instructed, rescind must be moved in accord with express wishes of majority of unit (by analogy to reconsider), p. 160, but otherwise any delegate could move. | Delegates must vote as instructed but giving instructions not recommended, p. 80. Absent instruction, any delegate could move to rescind. |

© American Institute of Parliamentarians. All rights reserved.

Appendix A

| No | Issue | Answer | RONR 11th. Ed | § | AIPSC | Cannon | Demeter | Riddick |
|----|-------|--------|---------------|---|-------|--------|---------|---------|
| 34 | Club voted to send delegate and pay all expenses. Discovered it could not afford more than $50 when too late to reconsider. What is the solution? | Could rescind and adopt a new MM. Or could amend previous adoption by MN23MEM, pp. 418-9. | Rescind or amend something previously adopted, MN23MEM, p. 305. | 35 | Rescind or amend a previous action, same vote as underlying action, pp. 41, 49. | Reconsideration of a vote previously taken (rescind variation), by 2/3 vote, p. 127. | Rescind or incidental main motion to amend previous adoption, by M with notice or 2/3 vote, pp. 165, 171, 237. | Changing previous decisions can be done by amending previous adoptions, rescinding, or adopting de novo resolution, p. 42 same vote as underlying, p. 173. |
| 35 | Can vote rejecting application for membership be reconsidered or rescinded when vote is secret? | Yes, can be reconsidered and can be rescinded unless bylaws prohibit renewals for a certain period, p. 419. | Yes, reconsidered -- maker must waive secrecy, p. 316, and motion to reconsider must be by ballot, p. 286, 413. Rescind applies only to adoptions, p. 305. | 37 | Yes, any MM can be reconsidered and no need to waive secrecy because anyone can move, p. 45. Rescind applies only to adoptions, p. 48. | Yes, any question can be reconsidered and no need to waive secrecy because anyone can move, p. 127. | Yes, member must state he voted on prevailing side and vote must be by ballot, p. 38, 140. Rescind applies only to adoptions, p. 165. | Yes, any member can move for reconsideration, p. 166. Rescind applies only to adoptions, p. 173. |
| 36 | Can a properly approved expulsion be rescinded? | No, p. 419. | No, if the expelled members have been officially notified, can't rescind or amend, must follow bylaw procedure for admission or reinstatement, p. 308. | 35 | No, rescission can't affect action taken (such as notification), p. 48, and suggested mechanism is application for readmission, p. 265. | Yes, any question can be reconsidered or rescinded at any, p. 127. No discussion of discipline or bar on rescinding expulsion. | No, if expelled member has been duly informed, the vote can't be rescinded, p. 167. | No, rescission applies only to what has not already been implemented (giving example of officers already notified of election), p. 173. |

© American Institute of Parliamentarians. All rights reserved.

Appendix A

| No | Issue | Answer | RONR 11th. Ed | § | AIPSC | Cannon | Demeter | Riddick |
|---|---|---|---|---|---|---|---|---|
| 37 | A member resigned and was present when the resignation was accepted. Can the resignation be reconsidered? | No, p. 419. | No, if the member is present when resignation is accepted, can't reconsider, pp. T46, 318-9, must follow bylaw procedure for admission or reinstatement, p. 308. | 37 | No, resignation is effective, p. 265, and reconsider can't be used for something that can't be undone, p. 45. | Yes, any question can be reconsidered or rescinded at any, p. 127. No discussion of resignation or bar on reconsidering resignation. | Yes, accepted resignation can be reconsidered by unanimous consent, p. 208. | No, reconsideration applies only to what has not already been implemented, p. 166, and resignation is effective upon acceptance, p. 174. |
| 38 | Motion passed that all present except for challenged delegates are members. At next meeting motion to rescind and consider everyone present members ruled out of order for combining rescind with rider. Was chair correct? | No, new motion conflicted with old and required repeal of everything in conflict, p. 420. | No, amending something previously adopted allows a change to only part of the previous action, p. 305. | 35 | No, amending a previous action by same vote as underlying action permitted, pp. 41. | No, reconsideration of a vote previously taken (rescind variation), p. 127. | No, incidental main motion to amend previous adoption, by M with notice or 2/3 vote, p. 171, 237. | No, changing previous decisions can be done by amending previous adoptions, rescinding, or adopting de novo resolution, p. 42, same vote as underlying, p. 173. |
| 39 | Single vote approved multiple board recommendations, including bills and signed blank check procedure. Some bills have been paid. How can check procedure be reversed? | Rescind the blank check procedure prospectively, p. 420. | Rescind the blank check procedure prospectively, p. 305. | 35 | Rescind just the blank check procedure prospectively, p. 48. | Reconsider (rescind) the blank check procedure prospectively, p. 127. | Incidental main motion to amend previous adoption, by M with notice or 2/3 vote, p. 171, 237. | Amend to delete the blank check procedure prospectively, pp. 42, 173. |

© American Institute of Parliamentarians. All rights reserved.

Appendix A

| No | Issue | Answer | RONR 11th. Ed | § | AIPSC | Cannon | Demeter | Riddick |
|---|---|---|---|---|---|---|---|---|
| 40 | (a) Is rescind in order when reconsider could be moved? (b) Should chair prompt reconsider if rescind moved? (c) Rule rescind out of order if someone willing to move reconsider? | (a) Yes, but requires MN23MEM vote; (b) Not necessarily; (c) No, p. 421. | (a) Yes, in order any time except when reconsider has been moved, pp. 307-8; (b) No, not among duties, pp. 449-50; (c) No, pp. 307-8. | 35 | (a) No, rescind applies to action at previous meeting, p. 48, reconsider action at same meeting, p. 45; (b) Yes, help members, p. 175: (c) Yes, p. 48, 45. | (a) Yes, same motion, M or 2/3 beyond next day, p. 126; (b) No need, just apply appropriate vote; (c) No, p. 126. | (a) Yes, except when reconsideration has been moved and is pending, p. 167; (b) Yes, duty to enlighten and guide, p. 251; (c) No, p. 167. | (a) No, only reconsider in order on the same or next day p. 42; (b) No, not among duties, pp 146-7; (c) Yes, out of order regardless of willingness to move to reconsider, p. 42. |
| 41 | Can you rescind the unexecuted part of a motion? | Yes, p. 421. | Yes, rescind prospectively, pp. 305, 308. | 35 | Yes, rescind prospectively, p. 48. | Yes, reconsider (rescind) prospectively, p. 127. | Yes, rescind prospectively, p. 165. | Yes, rescind prospectively, pp. 42, 173. |
| 42 | (a) Was attempted rescission at special meeting called for another purpose properly ruled out of order? (b) Was motion to rescind resolution specifying officer qualities in order at the time of election? | (a) Yes, no apparent emergency; (b) Yes, incidental to the election, pp. 421-2. | (a) Yes, only business specified in the call can be transacted at special meeting, p. 93; (b) Yes, rescind can be moved when nothing pending, p. 305, and incidental to election, p. 101. | 35 | (a) Yes, only business in the call can be transacted, p. 106; (b) Yes, can rescind motion from previous meeting, p. 49. | (a) Yes, only business in the notice can be considered, p. 88; (b) Yes, can reconsider (rescind) vote previously taken, p. 127. | (a) No, any business can be considered unless bylaws require notice of special meeting business, p. 13; (b) Yes, can rescind motion previously adopted, p. 165. | (a) Yes, only business in the call can be transacted, p. 183; (b) Yes, can rescind motion from previous meeting, p. 173, procedural motion relating to election, pp. 119-20. |
| 43 | Is it desirable to have both a constitution and bylaws? | Entirely optional. Simpler and easier to classify if not separated. Nothing to be gained if they require same vote to change, p. 423. | Recommended practice is single document, bylaws. Fewer problems of duplication and inconsistency and easier to understand, pp. 12-14. | 2 | One document is desirable because it is simpler and avoids confusion, p. 237. Constitution should be harder to amend if organization has both, p. 238. | Recommended practice is single document, bylaws, for simplicity, p. 70. | Most today have only bylaws, but describes advantages of both approaches, p. 178. | Parliamentary authorities today generally agree that one document is better, p. 58. |

Appendix A

| No | Issue | Answer | RONR 11th Ed | § | AIPSC | Cannon | Demeter | Riddick |
|---|---|---|---|---|---|---|---|---|
| 44 | If an article in the constitution conflicts with an article in the bylaws, which governs? | The article in the constitution and the other is null and void, pp. 423-4. | Constitution supersedes bylaws, p. 14. | 2 | Constitution is fundamental and bylaws supplement, p. 238. | Constitution is the superior authority and bylaws can't conflict, p. 70. | In case of conflict, constitution supersedes bylaws, p. 178. | Constitution is fundamental, p. 58. |
| 45 | Can bylaws be divided into articles? | Yes, generally divided into articles and sections, p. 424. | Generally divided into articles and sections, pp. 570-91. | 56 | Generally divided into articles and sections, p. 239 and Appendix I, p. 299. | Divided into articles and sections, Appendix B, pp. 149-54. | Generally divided into articles and sections, p. 179. | Simple bylaws shown include only articles, p. 34. |
| 46 | Is it true that the law requires that corporations have only bylaws? | Robert knew of no such law, but charter often takes the place of a constitution in incorporated societies, p. 424. | Incorporated society should generally not have constitution and bylaws because constitution would duplicate much in the charter, p. 14. | 2 | Not addressed but advocates minimizing duplication, p. 237. | Not addressed but advocates minimizing duplication, p. 70. | Not addressed but recognizes trend to reduce overlap of governance documents, p. 178. | Not addressed but advocates minimizing duplication, p. 58. |
| 47 | (a) When resolution conflicts with a law or rule, must law or rule be changed first? (b) Can resolution include repeal of all conflicting provisions? (c) Does adoption of resolution automatically repeal conflicting laws or rules? | (a) Yes, resolution conflicting with law or rule is out of order; (b) No, out of order and would require extraordinary vote; (c) No law or rule must first be amended, pp. 424-5. | (a) Yes, out of order if conflicts with rules required by law or previous actions, p. 111. (b) No, but may be able to combine resolution and motion to **suspend** certain rules, p. 260; (c) No, out of order, p. 111. | 10 | (a) Yes, conflicts should be reconsidered or rescinded first, p. 26; (b) No, but can combine suspension of certain procedural rules, p. 86; (c) Yes, inadvertent conflicts can be repealed by implication, p. 26. | (a) Yes, or suspend by 2/3, p. 75; (b) Yes, can combine suspension of certain rules, p. 75; (c) No, should be ruled out of order, p. 102. | (a) Yes, resolution conflicting is out of order, p. 308; (b) No, language attempting repeal is insufficient, p. 308; (c) No, adoption is null and void, p. 308. | (a) Yes, motions conflicting with laws or rules are out of order, p. 116; (b) No, out of order and suspension of rule requires extraordinary vote, pp. 116, 188; (c) No, out of order, p. 116. |
| 48 | Is it necessary to designate the fiscal year in the bylaws in any way other than setting the time of payment of dues? | No, unless fiscal year will close at some other time than the end of the annual meeting, p. 425. | No, fiscal year defaults to calendar year unless different fiscal year is stated in the bylaws, p. 477. | 48 | No, not specified in Finances section of bylaws template, p. 300. | No, not necessary but recommended in Model Bylaws, p. 150. | No, not specified in Model Bylaws, p. 193. | No, not specified in guidelines for bylaws, p. 34. |

© American Institute of Parliamentarians. All rights reserved.

Appendix A

| No | Issue | Answer | RONR 11th. Ed | § | AIPSC | Cannon | Demeter | Riddick |
|---|---|---|---|---|---|---|---|---|
| 49 | How long do officers serve who are elected when first organized? | Until first annual meeting unless bylaws specify a longer term, p. 425. | The term specified in the bylaws, pp. 560, 573. | 54 | The term specified in the bylaws, p. 183. | The term specified in the bylaws, p. 151. | As specified in the bylaws, in the Model Bylaws, until the annual meeting, p. 194. | As specified in the bylaws, usually until the close of the annual meeting, p. 192. |
| 50 | Should the auditor be a member of the executive board and finance committee? | No, auditor should not authorize and audit expenses, ideally a non-member CPA, p. 425. | No, independent CPAs preferred but not specific as to member auditor roles, p. 479. Separation of function generally better. | 48 | No, independent CPAs preferred and officers involved with finances should not even select auditor, p. 250. | No, Model Bylaws suggest independent CPA audit, p. 152. | No, audit by separate committee or CPA preferred to treasurer's report, p. 253 | No, audit by CPA preferred, p. 25. |
| 51 | State constitution has "minimum" dues set for top three levels, no dues set for level 4. (a) Can districts increase their dues? (b) For partial year, are dues applied to this year or next? | (a) No, dues set for districts, level 3; excess if any goes to association; (b) This year unless otherwise stated in bylaws, pp. 425-6. | (a) No, dues set for districts, level 3; additional assessments must be in bylaws, p. 572. Associations, level 4, can set own dues. (b) This year, no general rule of apportionment, pp. 571-2, 584. | 56 | (a) No, dues set for districts, level 3; assessments must be in bylaws; (b) This year, no general rule of apportionment, pp. 259, 300. | (a) No, dues set for districts, level 3; assessments must be in bylaws; (b) This year, no general rule of apportionment, p. 150. | (a) No, dues set for districts, level 3; assessments must be in bylaws; (b) This year, no general rule of apportionment, p. 194. | (a) No, dues set for districts, level 3; assessments must be in bylaws; (b) This year, no general rule of apportionment, p. 34. |
| 52 | Under bylaws, President appoints committees, board ratifies. (a) Is it proper to amend constitution to make committee chairs board members? (b) Would president still appoint? | (a) Yes, (b) Yes, unless bylaws are also amended, p. 426. | (a) Yes, p. 592, but not typical, p. 482; (b) Yes, but not recommended that President control typically elected positions, p. 433. | 57 | (a) Yes, p. 241, but not typical, p. 195; (b) Yes, but not recommended that President control typically elected positions, pp. 162, 195. | (a) Yes, p. 71, but not typical, p. 3; (b) Yes, but not recommended that President control typically elected positions, p. 130. | (a) Yes, p. 171, and committee chairs commonly included, p. 270; (b) Yes, pp. 240, 270. | (a) Yes, p. 36, and standing committee chairs commonly included, p. 28; (b) Yes, but not recommended that President control typically elected positions, p. 122. |

© American Institute of Parliamentarians. All rights reserved.

Appendix A

| No | Issue | Answer | RONR 11th. Ed | § | AIPSC | Cannon | Demeter | Riddick |
|---|---|---|---|---|---|---|---|---|
| 53 | Bylaws provide that board includes elected officers and president-appointed standing committee chairs. Member claims appointee presence in board meeting is illegal. Is claim correct? | No, as long as bylaws do not conflict with laws, rights of members or justice, they trump rules of order, pp. 426-7. | No, but not recommended, p. 482. | 49 | No, but not recommended, p. 162. | No, but not recommended, p. 130. | No, but not recommended, p. 240. | No, but not recommended, p. 122. |
| 54 | Can a constitution require payment of dues in advance? | Yes, p. 427. | Yes, Sample Bylaws require dues in advance, p. 584. | 57 | Yes, bylaws should specify when dues delinquent, p. 300. | Yes, pp. 70, 150. | Yes, Model Bylaws require dues in advance, p. 194. | Yes, bylaws should specify when dues payable, p. 34. |
| 55 | Bylaw provides for executive committee management of all affairs, subject to approval of members, and authorizes payment of funds. Does this authorize payment of bills without approval of members? | No, but approval may be in the form of management plan, and committee must report in sufficient detail for members to provide direction, pp. 427-8. | No, members decide degree of oversight; any ambiguity is determined by M vote of the membership, in harmony with other bylaw provisions and the intention at the time of adoption, p. 588. | 56 | No, members decide degree of oversight; interpretation of bylaws can be delegated but final decision rests with the membership, p. 245. | No, no specific guidance on interpretation but assembly is ultimate authority, p. 2. | No, typically organization itself authorizes payment unless bylaws clearly delegate, p. 253. | No, committee can't authorize payment without clear bylaw authority, p. 96; chair interprets bylaw subject to appeal or submission to assembly, p. 38. |
| 56 | Proposed amendment to constitution -- give board power to reduce dues by 2/3 of entire membership by mail vote. (a) Is it proper to give the board so much power? (b) Is mail vote legal or advisable? | (a) Yes, proper; (b) Yes, legal and advisable for important matters and widely scattered membership, p. 428. | (a) Yes, up to "complete control" between meetings, if circumstances warrant, p. 481; (b) Yes, legal and proper for important issues and widespread membership, p. 424. | 49 | (a) Yes, as long as powers clearly defined in bylaws, p. 195; (b) Yes, legal if in bylaws for important issues but may not be advisable because no opportunity for debate, p. 152. | (a) Yes, can give broad power to govern between meetings, pp. 3, 152; (b) Yes, no express prohibition, pp. 120-5. | (a) Yes, boards may be given unlimited power in bylaws, including fixing dues, p. 270; (b) Yes, can be useful for important decisions, scattered membership, p. 33. | (a) Yes, board authority depends on circumstances, set by bylaws, p. 27; (b) Yes, for important issues and widespread membership, pp. 103, 200-1. |

© American Institute of Parliamentarians. All rights reserved.

Appendix A

| No | Issue | Answer | RONR 11th. Ed | § | AIPSC | Cannon | Demeter | Riddick |
|---|---|---|---|---|---|---|---|---|
| 57 | Board filled vacancy in presidency, an elected office. Bylaws state that board has power to fill all board vacancies. Is claim of illegality correct? | No, organization has the right in the bylaws to authorize its board to fill vacancies, p. 429. | No, an executive board with full power to act between meetings has the power to fill vacancies, p. 467. | 47 | No, bylaws may provide that the board fills vacancies, p. 184. | No, no express prohibition but must be in bylaws, p. 3, 152. | No, bylaws may provide that the board fills vacancies, p. 256. | No, bylaws may provide that the board fills vacancies, and should be filled promptly, pp. 196-7. |
| 58 | Term limits adopted: same office 2 years except registrar; any office 4 years except regent. (a) Are board managers limited along with officers? (b) Does 4 year limit apply to any member or only registrar? (c) Is bylaw retroactive? | (a) Yes, managers "hold office"; (b) Any member; (c) No but prior service counts, pp. 429-30. | (a) Yes, directors (managers) classed as officers, p. 572; (b) Any member -- terms may be limited, pp. 574-5, members interpret only when ambiguous, p. 588; (c) No, immediate effect, but proviso can except incumbents, p. 597. | 56 | (a) No, directors not classed as officers, p. 195; (b) Any member -- terms may be limited in various ways, p. 183; (c) No, immediate effect, except by proviso, p. 240. | (a) Yes, "officer" includes elected and appointed leaders; directors elected, pp 164, 152; (b) Any member -- office broadly defined, p. 164; (c) No, effective immediately, except by proviso, p. 72. | (a) No, directors not classed as officers, pp. 250-4, 270; (b) Any member -- terms may be limited, p. 194; (c) No, effective immediately, pp. 178, 180, 187. | (a) No, officials and directors distinguished, p. 28; (b) Any member -- terms may be limited, p. 125; (c) No, immediate effect unless otherwise specified, p. 37. |
| 59 | If bylaws are amended shortening terms of officers, does it apply to incumbents? | Yes, unless proviso excepts incumbents, p. 431. | Yes, unless proviso excepts incumbents, p. 597. | 57 | Yes, unless proviso excepts incumbents, p. 240. | Yes, unless proviso excepts incumbents, p. 72. | Yes, unless proviso excepts incumbents, p. 180. | Yes, unless proviso specifies otherwise, p. 37. |
| 60 | State bylaw provides that members of clubs may participate in deliberations but only delegates can vote. Can non-delegate members make motions? | Yes, deliberations is used in broad sense and only voting is excluded, p. 431. | Yes, deliberation is a broad term, pp. 1-2. Here only voting is excluded. | 1 | Yes, deliberation is a broad term, p. 4. Here only voting is excluded. | No; deliberate, debate, consideration are interchangeable, p. 6, refer to speeches only. | Yes, no definitions of deliberation changes broad interpretation of the text itself, pp. 25-32. | Yes, deliberate used broadly -- discuss, debate, expose facts, sift evidence, ask questions, persuade and convince, pp. 81-2. |

Appendix A

| No | Issue | Answer | RONR 11th Ed | § | AIPSC | Cannon | Demeter | Riddick |
|---|---|---|---|---|---|---|---|---|
| 61 | State president and VP elected. President dies before national confirmation at annual meeting. How is vacancy filled? | VP becomes president absent bylaw provision to the contrary, pp. 431-2. | VP becomes president absent bylaw provision to the contrary, pp. 578, 457; president took office on election, p. 444. | 56 | VP becomes president absent bylaw provision to the contrary, p. 177. | VP presides absent bylaw provision to the contrary, p. 4. | VP becomes president absent bylaw provision to the contrary, p. 255. | VP becomes president absent bylaw provision to the contrary, p. 127. |
| 62 | Constitution gives corresponding secretary charge of general correspondence. Can board employ someone else to handle mail? | No, not unless the employee is undersecretary's orders or constitution is amended, p. 432. | No, not unless the employee is undersecretary's orders or constitution is amended, pp. 460, 111. | 47 | No, not unless the employee is undersecretary's orders or constitution is amended, pp. 179, 237-8. | No, not unless the employee is undersecretary's orders or constitution is amended, p. 70. | No, not unless the employee is undersecretary's orders or constitution is amended, pp. 252-3, 58. | No, not even by unanimous consent, unless the employee is under secretary's orders or constitution is amended, pp. 181, 31. |
| 63 | Does "duly elected and installed" in constitution require installation exercises? | No, unless there is a rule or custom, elected officers can just assume their duties, p. 432 | No, even if ceremony is prescribed, failure to hold does not affect the time of assuming office, which is when election final, p. 444. | 46 | No, unless bylaws provide otherwise, officer assumes office when declared elected and no formal installation is necessary, p. 170. | No, election is over when election committee report adopted -- no installation required, p. 134. | No, not unless required by law or bylaw; one in possession of office is presumed duly qualified, p. 255. | No, unless bylaws provide otherwise, officer assumes office when declared elected and no formal installation is necessary, p. 101. |
| 64 | National bylaws provide that state branches must have constitutions in harmony with national constitution. What is status of state constitution not in harmony? | Null and void, because state constitution is subordinate and cannot conflict, p. 432. | Null and void -- rules of parent body govern, pp. 10, 12n, conflicting motions out of order, p. 343. | 2 | Null and void -- unit is subject to parent charter, p. 238. | Null and void -- hierarchy of governance documents, p. 70; motion contrary is out of order, p. 102. | Null and void -- in case of conflict, constitution of higher body governs, pp. 178, 308. | Null and void implied -- out of order to move anything that conflicts with any laws or rules of the organization, pp. 116, 59-60. |

Appendix A

| No | Issue | Answer | RONR 11th. Ed | § | AIPSC | Cannon | Demeter | Riddick |
|---|---|---|---|---|---|---|---|---|
| 65 | Bylaws provide that EB fills vacancies. Slate elected and president, not present, declined when offered. Recording Secretary elected president. Who fills the vacancy? | The EB Recording Secretary was present and did not decline, so was in office until elected president. Should resign and EB fill vacancy, p. 433. | The EB. Bylaws expressly provide, pp. 467, 575; Recording Secretary took office upon election then vacated office, p. 444. | 47 | The EB. Bylaws expressly provide, p. 184; secretary took office upon election, p. 170. | The EB. Bylaws expressly provide, p. 2; secretary took office upon election, p. 134. | The EB. Bylaws expressly provide, pp. 256, 310; secretary took office upon election, pp. 163, 244. | The EB. Bylaws expressly provid p. 196-7; secretary took office upon election, pp. 92, 101. |
| 66 | The bylaws have been amended to increase dues. Do members who paid for current year before amendment have to pay the additional amount? | No, but should have been clarified at time of vote by proviso, p. 433. | No, bylaws take effect upon adoption absent proviso, p. 597. | 57 | No, bylaws take effect upon adoption absent proviso, p. 240. | No, bylaws take effect upon adoption absent proviso, p. 72. | No, increase in dues does not apply to those who have already paid, absent proviso, p. 190. | No, bylaws take effect upon adoption absent proviso, p. 37. |
| 67 | Bylaws provide: officers serve until successors elected. Officers elected, didn't decline, but resigned before taking office. Do prior officers continue in office? | No, they went out of office when their successors were elected, p. 433. | No, election to office takes effect immediately if candidate is present and does not decline, p. 444. | 46 | No, election to office takes effect immediately if candidate is present and does not decline, p. 170. | No, election to office takes effect on adoption of tellers' report, p. 134. | No, election to office takes effect immediately if candidate is present and does not decline, p. 244. | No, election to office takes effec immediately if candidate is present and doe not decline, pp. 92, 101. |
| 68 | Constitution limits officers to two consecutive terms. Can group elect someone else who resigns after a month then appoint officer to third term? Is that officer eligible for two more terms? | No. Term is charged to one who serves majority. If ineligible at annual meeting, ineligible during following term, p. 434. | No, conflict with constitution is out of order, p. 111; officer serving more than half term is considered to have served the term, p. 448. | 47 | No, conflict with clear intent of constitution, pp. 237-8, 245. | No, conflict with clear intent of constitution, pp. 70, 151. | No, conflict with constitution is out of order, null and void, p. 58, person serving more than half is credited with the term, p. 244. | No, conflict with constitution is ou of order, p. 116, person serving more tha half is credited with the term, p. 193. |

© American Institute of Parliamentarians. All rights reserved.

Appendix A

| No | Issue | Answer | RONR 11th. Ed | § | AIPSC | Cannon | Demeter | Riddick |
|---|---|---|---|---|---|---|---|---|
| 69 | What is previous notice of a bylaw amendment? | Notice at prior meeting or in call giving general purport of amendment, p. 435. | Notice at prior meeting or in call fairly informing members of proposed amendment; becomes general order, p. 596. | 57 | Advance notice of proposed actions stated specifically; where required, can't be waived, pp. 113, 241. | Advance written notice of all substantive motions including complete written text, pp. 100, 71. | Notice at prior meeting of proposed bylaw amendment; at least subject, p. 199, example is entire text, p. 234-5. | Notice at prior meeting with a copy of the proposed amendment should be required, p. 37. |
| 70 | What is ample notice of amendment to constitution? | Each group must decide for itself based on particular circumstances, p. 435. | Notice at prior meeting or in call fairly informing members of proposed amendment; becomes general order, p. 596. | 57 | Advance notice of proposed actions stated specifically, pp. 113, 241. | Advance written notice of all substantive motions including complete written text, pp. 100, 71. | Notice at prior meeting of proposed bylaw amendment, p. 20; at least subject, p. 199, example is entire text, pp. 234-5. | Notice at prior meeting with a copy of the proposed amendment should be required, p. 37. |
| 71 | Can an attempt to amend the bylaws without notice constitute notice of intent to amend the bylaws? | No, not unless everyone understood that the attempt would be treated as notice and the amendments would be considered at the next meeting, p. 436. | No, notice must comply with bylaw specified manner and must be generally understood that it was notice for next meeting, pp. 580-2. Must alert members to timing so that they can be there, p. 581. | 56 | No, requires advance notice of proposed action stated specifically, p. 113. | No, requires advance notice including complete written text, pp. 100, 71. | No, requires notice at prior meeting, p. 20, or in call of meeting, pp. 179, 199; members must know when it will be considered. | No, depends on bylaws but prior notice with copy of proposed amendment should be required, p. 37. |
| 72 | Four years ago, name change referred to EC with power to act. Name was changed and no one questioned but was it legal? | No, procedure violated constitution but referral was unanimous, no one objected and no one injured, so treat as adopted, p. 436. | No, must comply with bylaw requirements, pp. 580-2. | 56 | No, amendment of constitution requires advance notice of proposed action stated specifically, p. 113; point of order not timely -- not a "serious violation" of bylaws, p. 91. | No, requires advance notice including complete written text, pp. 100, 71; but point of order not timely, p. 114. | No, committee must give notice and report and assembly must act, pp. 182-3; null and void even without POO, p. 122. | No, depends on bylaws but prior notice with copy of proposed amendment should be required, p. 37. |

Appendix A

| No | Issue | Answer | RONR 11th. Ed | § | AIPSC | Cannon | Demeter | Riddick |
|---|---|---|---|---|---|---|---|---|
| 73 | At annual meeting, article on bylaw amendments was suspended and bylaws were amended without notice. Was action proper? | No, bylaw provisions can't be suspended and all related actions are null and void, p. 437. | No, bylaw provisions can't be suspended unless they allow their own suspension or are rules of order, pp. 12-3; notice protects absentees, can't be suspended, p. 263. | 2 | No, can't suspend bylaws unless they allow their own suspension or notice requirements, p. 86. | No, bylaws can't be suspended, p. 71. | No, bylaws can't be suspended unless they allow their own suspension, p. 133; notice is a fundamental right, p. 305. | No, bylaws can't be suspended unless they allow their own suspension, p. 188; notice can't be waived or suspended, p. 1. |
| 74 | Bylaws amendment requires notice at a previous meeting. Notice was given, a recess of five minutes was taken and bylaw amendment was adopted. Was post-recess a different meeting? | No, adjournment terminates meeting, recess of a few minutes does not, p. 437. Notice can't be given in one meeting of a convention and acted on within the session either, pp. 437-8. | No, adjournment terminates meeting, recess of a few minutes does not, p. 81-3; notice should be in call for convention, pp. 121, 582. | 8 | No, meeting is not terminated by a recess, pp. 105, 77. | No, adjournment terminates meeting, recess does not, pp. 8, 158, 167; notice should be given in notice of convention, p. 100. | No, adjournment terminates meeting, recess does not, even if it's called "adjournment," pp. 112-3. | No, adjournment terminates meeting, p. 4; recess does not, p. 164. |
| 75 | Bylaws require amendments to be posted for a month. An amendment was posted for three weeks before club season closed. Does it have to be reposted or just posted for a week after season opens again? | It should be posted again for a month, p. 438. | Post again -- purpose of notice is to alert members to proposed amendment so that they can arrange to be there. Posting for "the" month prior is more consistent with purpose, p. 581. | 56 | Post again. Proper notice is that specified in the bylaws, p. 113. Literal adherence is more protective of members' rights in this case. | Post again. Must follow bylaw formalities, p. 71, notice is important -- members don't like surprises, p. 100. | Post again. Follow bylaws strictly -- members must know when it will be considered, pp. 20, 182. | Post again. Must follow bylaws, p. 37. |

© American Institute of Parliamentarians. All rights reserved.

Appendix A

| No | Issue | Answer | RONR 11th. Ed | § | AIPSC | Cannon | Demeter | Riddick |
|----|-------|--------|---------------|---|-------|--------|---------|---------|
| 76 | Bylaws require reading of amendments at previous meeting. Is it compliant to provide printed copies a few days before the ("previous" seems to be implied) meeting? | Yes, although not literally compliant, it carries out the spirit more thoroughly, p. 438. | Yes, as long as copies are provided before the previous meeting so that members have the required advance notice to arrange to be there, p. 581. | 56 | Yes, this complies with the requisite of specificity, p. 113. | Yes, this complies with the recommendation of providing the complete written text, p. 100. | Yes, this provides both the substance, pp. 182, 199, and the entire text, pp. 234-5. | Yes, this provides the recommended copy of the proposed amendment, p. 37. |
| 77 | Bylaws provide that they can be amended at any regular meeting. May they be amended at a special meeting called for that purpose? | No, can only be amended at regular meeting but can adjourn regular meeting to another day, p. 438. | No, special meetings can be called only as authorized in the bylaws, p. 92, but regular meeting could be adjourned to convenient time, pp. 93-4. | 9 | No, special meetings can be called only as authorized in the bylaws, p. 106, but regular meeting could be continued, pp. 107-8. | No, bylaws define authority, pp. 70-1, but could adjourn regular meeting to a specified time, p. 137. | No, bylaws govern what can be done in a special meeting, p. 13, but could set adjourned regular meeting, p. 14. | No, bylaws govern what can be done in a special meeting, p. 183, but could adjourn to a time certain, p. 4-5. |
| 78 | Previous notice provided that new bylaws would be voted on and bylaw committee recommended a general revision. Bylaws were read and adopted but not provided in advance or considered by paragraph. Were they lawfully adopted? | Yes, lawful but careless because recommended procedures for this important document were not followed, pp. 439-40. | Yes, if bylaws complied with, but notice fairly informing members of changes does not appear to have been provided, p. 596. Recommended process also not followed, pp. 593-6. | 57 | Yes, if notice provided as required in bylaws, p. 113, but here a copy of the proposed revision did not accompany notice, as recommended, p. 244. | Yes, if amendment requirements in bylaws complied with, p. 72, which here don't appear to require complete written text of proposed motions, p. 100. | Yes, if bylaws complied with, pp. 179, 199, which here don't appear to require entire text, pp. 234-5. | Yes, if bylaws complied with, p. 36, which here don't appear to require copies to be distributed in advance, as recommended, p. 37. |

© American Institute of Parliamentarians. All rights reserved.

Appendix A

| No | Issue | Answer | RONR 11th. Ed | § | AIPSC | Cannon | Demeter | Riddick |
|---|---|---|---|---|---|---|---|---|
| 79 | Notice was given that amendments would be presented; and they were adopted unanimously. Six months later, can the new president declare them null and void because the bylaws require written notice of proposed bylaw amendments? | No, spirit observed even though a mistake not to submit amendments in writing. Society, not president, should decide whether past action should stand, p. 440. | No, notice was not given in compliance with the bylaws or RONR, p. 596, but objection to procedure not timely, p. 251, and decision should rest with assembly, on appeal if necessary, p. 256. | 57 | No, notice was not proper, pp. 113, 244, but procedural objection may not be timely, p. 91; assembly should decide, on appeal if necessary, p. 83. | No, notice was not proper, pp. 72, 100, but point of order may not be timely and assembly should decide, on appeal if necessary, p. 115. | Yes, notice was not proper, pp. 179, 199, and action in violation of the bylaws is null and void, p. 122. | No, notice was not proper, pp. 36-7, but assembly should decide, on appeal, p. 22. |
| 80 | Bylaws allow bylaw amendment at regular meeting with notice at previous meeting. Notice given but amendment not taken up. Can amendment be adopted at special meeting and ratified at the next regular meeting? | No, assembly can't ratify an action that it could not itself have legally taken, p. 441. | No, assembly can ratify only what it could have approved in advance, and not bylaw violations, p. 125, and special meetings can be called only as provided in the bylaws, p. 92. | 10 | No, motion to ratify for emergencies and where a quorum was lacking, and must be approved by the body with authority; here no authority to violate bylaws, pp. 41-2. | No, no motion to ratify recognized, pp. 98-9; bylaw amendment process must be followed, p. 71. | No, can't ratify unconstitutional or illegal act, p. 168, and bylaws specify what can be done in a special meeting, p. 13. | No, no action can be ratified that is not within the authority of the bylaws, p. 164, and bylaws govern what can be done in a special meeting, p. 183. |
| 81 | State law changed to allow bylaw amendment at any regular meeting. Can amendments be considered at any meeting without notice even if organization rules require notice? | No, bylaws govern notice; state law only affected type of meeting, p. 441. | No, bylaws govern bylaw amendment and required notice, pp. 592, 596, but can be noticed for any regular meeting. | 57 | No, bylaw amendment can't be considered without notice required by bylaws, p. 113, but can be noticed for any regular meeting. | No, must follow bylaw requirements, p. 71, but can be noticed for any regular meeting. | No, bylaws govern amendment procedure, pp. 20, 179, 199, but can be noticed for any regular meeting. | No, bylaws govern process, and notice still required, p. 36, but can be noticed for any regular meeting. |

© American Institute of Parliamentarians. All rights reserved.

Appendix A

| No | Issue | Answer | RONR 11th. Ed | § | AIPSC | Cannon | Demeter | Riddick |
|---|---|---|---|---|---|---|---|---|
| 82 | Amendment to constitution adopted at one annual meeting rescinded at next without notice. (a) Was rescission legal? (b) Is amendment still part of constitution? (c) Was a motion to lay rescind on the table properly ruled out of order? | (a) No, amendment effective immediately so must be rescinded with full process. (b) Yes, rescission null and void. (c) No, motion to rescind is MM and can be laid on the table, pp. 441-2. | (a) No, amendment was effective immediately, p. 597, can only be changed with notice, p. 592. (b) Yes. (c) No, motion to rescind out of order but once made yields to subsidiary motion to table, p. 305. | 57 | (a) No, amendment effective immediately and further change must follow bylaw procedure, p. 240. (b) Yes, rescission was not in order without notice, p. 244. (c) No, table applies to rescind, p. 49, but rescind should have been ruled out of order. | (a) No, amendment effective immediately and further change requires notice, pp. 71-2. (b) Yes, rescind was not in order without notice, p. 71. (c) No, rescind is MM, p. 127, can be postponed, p. 105, not tabled, p. 168. | (a) No, amendment effective immediately p. 178, change requires notice, pp. 179, 199. (b) Yes, rescind in violation of the bylaws is null and void, p. 122. (c) No, rescind yields to subsidiary motion to table, pp. 165, 102. | (a) No, amendment effective immediately, p. 37, notice required for further amendment, p. 36. (b) Yes, rescind was not in order, p. 37, 173. (c) No, rescind is subject to procedural motions, p. 173. |
| 83 | Was it proper to give notice at previous annual convention to amend entire constitution without giving any details? | No, notice must give purport of each amendment. Otherwise move to refer to committee, pp. 442-3. | No, notice must fairly inform members of changes contemplated, p. 596. | 57 | No, notice must be stated specifically, p. 113. | No, notice should be complete written text of all motions, especially bylaw amendments, pp. 71, 100. | No, at least subject of proposed amendments should be given in notice, pp. 199, 182,188. | No, copy of proposed amendment should be required, p. 37. |
| 84 | Bylaw made past presidents advisory committee to board with ability to attend board meetings, make motions, debate and vote. Amendment adopted to change "phrasing" to read "The past presidents shall form an advisory committee to the executive board." Did they lose privileges? | No, if scope of amendment was explained as rephrasing of the first part of the provision, that is all that was adopted, pp. 443-4. | No, bylaw amendment can only be within the scope of the notice, pp. 594-5, so certainly can't extend beyond the language ("phrasing") of the actual motion. | 57 | No, bylaw amendment can only be within the scope of the notice, p. 244, so can't extend beyond the language ("phrasing") of the actual motion. | No, bylaw amendment can only be within the scope of the notice, p. 71, so certainly can't extend beyond the language ("phrasing") of the actual motion. | No, bylaw amendment can only be within the scope of the notice, p. 189, so certainly can't extend beyond the language ("phrasing") of the actual motion. | No, bylaw amendment can only be within the scope of the notice, p. 37, so certainly can't extend beyond the language ("phrasing") of the actual motion. |

© American Institute of Parliamentarians. All rights reserved.

Appendix A

| No | Issue | Answer | RONR 11th. Ed | § | AIPSC | Cannon | Demeter | Riddick |
|---|---|---|---|---|---|---|---|---|
| 85 | Can a motion be made to substitute the bylaws recommended by a committee for the original bylaws? | Yes, that is the proper motion for a revised set of bylaws, p. 444. | Yes, substitution of a new set is called a revision, p. 593. Old set is not open for amendment. | 57 | Yes, complete revision is handled like an amendment and old set is not open to amendment, p. 244-5. | Yes, revision is a free standing MM, p. 71. | Yes, a revision replaces the old bylaws, p. 187. | Yes, revision replaces old bylaws which are not open to amendment during consideration of revision, pp. 37-8. |
| 86 | Should the bylaws be amended section by section before a motion is made to substitute the revision recommended by committee? | No, there is nothing pending; the motion to substitute is considered section by section, p. 444. | No, there is nothing pending; the revision should be moved, considered section by section, then adopted or rejected, pp. 593-4. | 57 | No, there is nothing pending; the motion to substitute is considered section by section, pp. 244-5. | No, there is nothing pending; the motion to substitute is considered section by section, p. 71. | No, there is nothing pending; the motion to substitute is considered section by section, p. 183. | No, there is nothing pending; the motion to substitute is considered section by section, p. 37-8. |
| 87 | When a revision committee brings an entire revision to substitute for old bylaws, what motion should be made? | Motion to substitute, which is a MM because the existing bylaws are not pending, pp. 444-5. | Amend something previously adopted by substitution of revision for existing bylaws, pp. 592-3. | 57 | Amend a previous action by adopting a complete revision to the bylaws, pp. 242, 244. | MM to adopt a complete revision of the bylaws, p. 71. | Incidental MM to revise the bylaws, pp. 171, 187. | Motion to adopt a revision to the bylaws, pp. 37-8. |
| 88 | In offering a substitute for the bylaws, should the old bylaws be read first? | No, but the differences between the old and the new should be explained, p. 445. | No, old bylaws are not open for amendment, pp. 593-6, but differences should be explained. | 57 | No, old bylaws are not open for amendment, but changes should be explained, pp. 244-5. | No, only the new revision is open to consideration and comparison with the old, p. 71. | No, the new revision is considered section by section, p. 183. | No, the revision is read article by article and the changes from the old bylaws are explained, p. 37. |
| 89 | Do the rules governing the amendment of the constitution control the revision of the constitution? | Yes, revision or substitution of a new constitution is still an amendment, p. 445. | Yes, except that assembly is not confined to considering only points of change in the proposed revision, pp. 592-4. | 57 | Yes, presented and considered in the same manner as an amendment, p. 244-5. | Yes, complete revision is just a special case of bylaw amendment, p. 71. | Yes, except that any provision can be changed and in any degree, p. 182. | Yes, but broad scope may require committee consideration and hearings, p. 37. |

© American Institute of Parliamentarians. All rights reserved.

## Appendix A

| No | Issue | Answer | RONR 11th. Ed | § | AIPSC | Cannon | Demeter | Riddick |
|----|-------|--------|---------------|---|-------|--------|---------|---------|
| 90 | Can a society amend a proposed revision of its constitution to any extent it pleases? | Yes, if revision is a new constitution submitted as a substitute, p. 445-6. | Yes, not confined to points of change, open to amendment as fully as if adopting for the first time, p. 593. | 57 | Yes, revision is a new set of bylaws that may considerably affect the structure of the organization, p. 244. | No, not clear that revision is not subject to general notice limitation, pp. 71-2; amendments must be within scope. | Yes, any provision can be changed in any degree, p. 182. | Yes, amendment is limited only to being germane, p. 37-8. |
| 91 | Does the rule limiting amendment of dues to the range provided in the notice also apply to amendment of the number of members? | Yes, p. 446. | Yes, no amendment is in order that increases the modification beyond the scope of the notice, p. 595. | 57 | Yes, out of order to propose a change outside range between the existing provision and the notice, p. 244. | Yes, notice range limitation applies to all bylaw amendments, p. 71-2. | Yes, no change or modification can be made that is outside notice range, pp. 182, 189. | Yes, no amendment is in order that exceeds the scope of the notice, p. 37. |
| 92 | Notice of amendment was to strike out 25 and insert 50 before "members." At the next meeting, it was moved to strike out 50 and insert 100. Was the motion in order? | No, not without notice of the greater change or the whole point of notice could be defeated, p. 446. | No, no amendment is in order that increases the modification beyond the scope of the notice, p. 595. | 57 | No, out of order to propose a change outside range between the existing provision and the notice, p. 244. | No, notice range limitation applies to amendments to membership, p. 71-2. | No, no change or modification can be made that is outside notice range, pp. 182, 189. | No, no amendment is in order that exceeds the scope of the notice, p. 37. |
| 93 | Notice given to strike out the number limit (70) on active members (unlimited). Others wish to increase the number to 150. How can this be done? | Move to substitute "strike out 70 and insert 150." OK because MM, within range of notice, pp. 446-7. | Proposed change diminishes change so within scope of notice, p. 595. | 57 | Move to substitute "strike out 70 and insert 150" -- within range of notice, p. 244. | Move substitute "strike out 70 and insert 150," pp. 71-2; within scope of notice. | Move to substitute "strike out 70 and insert 150" -- within range of notice, pp. 182, 189. | Move to "strike out 70 and insert 150," p. 37. |

© American Institute of Parliamentarians. All rights reserved.

Appendix A

| No | Issue | Answer | RONR 11th. Ed | § | AIPSC | Cannon | Demeter | Riddick |
|---|---|---|---|---|---|---|---|---|
| 94 | Notice given to increase initiation fee from $5 to $10. Amendment adopted also increasing dues. Would it be in order to rescind this change? | No, because increase in dues was without notice and therefore null and void, pp. 447-8. | No, not necessary, the amendment was beyond the scope of notice and not in order, p. 595. Raise POO, p. 250-1. | 57 | No, the amendment was beyond the scope of notice and not in order, p. 244. No need to rescind. | No, the amendment was beyond the scope of notice and not in order, p. 71-2. | No, the amendment was beyond the scope of notice, pp. 182, 189, automatically null and void, p. 122. | No, the amendment was beyond the scope of notice and not in order, p. 37. |
| 95 | Is it out of order to lay proposed bylaw revision on the table or apply subsidiary motions other than amend or close or limit debate? | No, the proposed revision is a MM and subsidiary motions apply as with other MM, p. 448. | No, amendment of bylaws is MM, subject to the same rules as other MM, with limited exceptions (regarding notice, vote, reconsider, etc.), p. 592. | 57 | No, amendment of bylaws is MM, subject to the same rules as other MM, with limited exceptions, pp. 242-4, 41. | No, amendment of bylaws is MM, subject to the same rules as other MM, with limited exceptions, p. 71. | No, amendment of bylaws is an incidental MM, p. 171, subject to the same rules as other MM, with limited exceptions, p. 188. | No, regular amendment process followed, p. 37. |
| 96 | When an amendment to the constitution is tabled in society with meetings at least quarterly, can it be taken from the table at the same or next session and acted on without further notice? | Yes, p. 448. | Yes, special case of amend previous adoption, subject to same rules as other MM, p. 592, subject to all subsidiary motions, p. 305. | 57 | No, if tabled, p. 70; Yes, if postponed -- original notice makes members aware that the MM will be open action, including postponement, pp. 243, 41. | Yes, perfected like any MM without further notice, p. 71, but if postponed, notice should be given when returns, p. 72. | Yes, if same session, like any other incidental MM, p. 171. If next session, notice should be in call, p. 182. | Yes, regular amendment process followed, p. 37. |
| 97 | Committee submits revision to constitution and, after discussion, one article laid on the table. Was that correct procedure? | No, pending question was substitution of revision. Entire question could be tabled but not part, pp. 448-9. | No, pending question was substitution of revision, p. 593, entire question must be tabled, adhering issues can't be tabled alone, p. 211. | 17 | No, pending MM was substitution of revision, p. 244, entire MM must be tabled, adhering motions can't be tabled alone, p. 71. | No, pending MM was substitution of revision, p. 71, entire MM must be postponed, p. 105. | No, pending MM was substitution of revision, p. 171, entire MM must be tabled, p. 98. | No, can't table part of MM, p. 189. |

Appendix A

| No | Issue | Answer | RONR 11th Ed | § | AIPSC | Cannon | Demeter | Riddick |
|---|---|---|---|---|---|---|---|---|
| 98 | Constitution amendment requires 2/3 of those present and entitled to vote. 154 voters present, 99 ayes, 7 noes. Parliamentarian "ruled" that the amendment was adopted. Was the ruling correct? | No, wrong for the parliamentarian to "rule" and constitution clearly required 103 votes for adoption, p. 449. | No, must follow special procedures in bylaws, p. 592, and parliamentarian advises, chair rules, p. 465. | 57 | No, must follow bylaws, p. 244, and parliamentarian only advises chair, p. 181. | No, must follow bylaws, p. 71, and parliamentarian only advises chair, p. 32. | No, must follow bylaws, p. 188, and parliamentarian only advises chair, p. 254. | No, must follow bylaws, p. 36, and parliamentarian only advises chair, pp. 136-7. |
| 99 | Bylaw amendment requires 2/3 of those present. 20 present, 12 ayes, 6 noes, 2 blanks. Club accepted chair's ruling that amendment was adopted. Was this correct? | No, amendment was lost and announcement of adoption was null and void, p. 449. | No, amendment was lost because bylaw procedure was not followed, pp. 592, 580-1, and can't be suspended, pp. 263-4. | 57 | No, amendment was lost because bylaw procedure was not followed, p. 244, and can't be suspended, pp. 86-7. | No, amendment was lost because bylaw procedure was not followed and can't be suspended, p. 71. | No, amendment was lost because bylaw procedure was not followed, p. 188, but if illegal suspension never challenged, never a violation, p. 133. | No, amendment was lost because bylaw procedure was not followed, pp. 36-7, and can't be suspended, pp. 188. |
| 100 | Constitution sets dues at $3 for 30 members or less plus 10c for each additional member. Notice given to strike $3 and insert $6. Adopted and then 10c stricken and 25c inserted. (a) Was second amendment proper? (b) Can proposed amendment never be amended? | (a) No, no notice for second amendment; (b) Can amend proposed amendment while pending but only within scope of notice, p. 450. | (a) No, no notice; (b) Can amend but only within scope of notice, pp. 594-6; can issue new notice. | 57 | (a) No, can amend another provision if reasonably implied but here only implied to 20c, p. 243. (b) Can amend within the scope of the notice and beyond as reasonably implied or to resolve conflicts, or give notice of broader amendment, p. 243. | (a) No, no notice; (b) Can amend but only within scope of notice, pp. 71-2. | (a) No, no notice; (b) Can amend but only within scope of notice, pp. 188-9. | (a) No, no notice; (b) Can amend but only with proper notice, pp. 37. |

© American Institute of Parliamentarians. All rights reserved.

Appendix A

| No | Issue | Answer | RONR 11th. Ed | § | AIPSC | Cannon | Demeter | Riddick |
|---|---|---|---|---|---|---|---|---|
| 101 | (a) May a defeated amendment to the bylaws be reconsidered? (b) What vote is required? | (a) Yes, (b) M vote, p. 450. | (a) Yes, only affirmative vote can't be reconsidered, p. 592, (b) M regardless of vote necessary to adopt bylaw amendment, p. 320. | 57 | (a) Yes, nothing here that can't be undone, p. 45, (b) M, p. 47. | (a) Yes, (b) M same or next day, MN23 later, p. 127. | (a) Yes, defeated amendment can be reconsidered, (b) M even if the amendment requires greater vote, p. 157. | (a) Yes, (b) M, p. 166. |
| 102 | After adoption of a bylaw amendment, can the vote be reconsidered or rescinded at the same convention by 2/3 vote? | No, not even by unanimous vote, p. 450. | No, can't be reconsidered, p. 592. Can't be rescinded; follow bylaw amendment process, p. 598. | 57 | No, goes into effect immediately, p. 240, requires new notice, p. 241. | No, goes into effect immediately, p. 72, requires new notice, p. 71. | No, can't be reconsidered, p. 157; requires another bylaw amendment to reverse, pp. 165, 187. | No, effective immediately so can't be reconsidered or rescinded without following bylaw amendment process, p. 37. |
| 103 | Does president or chair have authority to determine when bylaw amendment goes into effect without the consent of the society? | No, unless a motion is adopted before or concurrently specifying when effective, the bylaw takes effect immediately, p. 451. | No, effective immediately absent prior or concurrent proviso specifying when effective, p. 597; assembly has full and sole power absent rule to the contrary, p. 566. | 57 | No, effective immediately unless motion to adopt delays effectiveness, p. 240; ultimate authority vests in assembly, p. 135. | No, effective immediately unless assembly decided or clearly understands effective date is postponed, p. 72; assembly decides, p. 7. | No, effective immediately unless otherwise agreed at the time or bylaws state otherwise, p. 188; chair leads, assembly decides, pp. 250-1. | No, effective immediately unless it specifies otherwise, p. 37; assembly decides, p. 82. |
| 104 | National organization amended its bylaws to impose requirements on subordinates. A subordinate cannot get required 3/4 vote to amend its bylaws. What can be done? | The bylaws of the superior body govern and the conflicting subordinate bylaw is automatically null and void and is repealed, p. 451. | The bylaws of subordinate body must conform to those of superior body on clearly requisite points, p. 567; superior bylaws supersede subordinate, p. 12n. | 56 | The constituent unit is automatically subject to the bylaws of the parent unit, p. 238. | In case of conflict, superior authority prevails, pp. 69-70. | The bylaws of the higher body supersede those of subordinate, p. 178. | Implied that parent's document supersedes, pp. 89, 92. |

Appendix A

| No | Issue | Answer | RONR 11th. Ed | § | AIPSC | Cannon | Demeter | Riddick |
|---|---|---|---|---|---|---|---|---|
| 105 | Is it legal for a club to require 3/4 vote of membership to amend bylaws? | Yes, but unwise due to difficulty of obtaining necessary attendance, p. 451. | Yes, bylaws should specify vote of at least 2/3 with previous notice, p. 580-1; 2/3 of entire membership rarely present, p. 582. | 56 | Yes, but M vote with prior notice is recommended, p. 244. | Yes, but notice and 2/3 recommended, p. 71. | Yes, but notice and 2/3 or MEM recommended, p. 188. | Yes, but 2/3 vote is typical, p. 37. |
| 106 | President elected for two years at annual meeting in even year. Six months later, bylaw amendment considered to change election of president to odd year. If adopted, will election be necessary one year into two year term? | Yes, because amendment will go into effect immediately unless proviso extends effective date creating a three year transition term, pp. 451-2. | Yes, amendment goes into effect immediately absent proviso, p. 597. | 57 | Yes, effective immediately unless motion to adopt delays effectiveness, p. 240. | Yes, effective immediately unless assembly decided or clearly understands effective date is postponed, p. 72. | Yes, effective immediately unless otherwise agreed at the time, p. 188. | Yes, effective immediately unless assembly specifies otherwise, p. 37. |
| 107 | Bylaws require 3/4 vote of entire membership to amend and impossible to get 3/4 to attend. What can be done? | Provide notice of changing that provision, get 3/4 vote of those present, then get 3/4 mail vote. Not entirely proper but closest method in spirit practicable, p. 452. | Vote by mail if authorized in bylaws, p. 424, but recommends preempting the problem by setting reasonable vote in light of future attendance. Even 2/3 of entire membership "should never be used," p. 582. | 56 | Vote by mail if authorized in bylaws, p. 152, but recommends setting reasonable vote requirement in bylaws to preempt this problem, generally M to avoid giving minority veto power, pp. 137, 244. | Recommends 2/3 vote for bylaw amendment, p. 71. Vote by mail not recognized. | Recommends bylaw provision of 2/3 vote with notice, p. 199. | Recommends 2/3 vote for bylaw amendment, p. 37; use mail ballot if permitted by bylaws, pp. 200-1. |

© American Institute of Parliamentarians. All rights reserved.

Appendix A

| No | Issue | Answer | RONR 11th. Ed | § | AIPSC | Cannon | Demeter | Riddick |
|---|---|---|---|---|---|---|---|---|
| 108 | Officer elected at annual meeting to serve two year term. A month later, a bylaw amendment is adopted that no member can hold office for more than four successive years. (a) Is it retroactive? (b) Is officer legislated out of office? | (a) No, effective upon adoption. (b) Yes, officer for more than four successive years automatically loses office upon adoption, absent proviso, p. 453. | (a) No, effective upon adoption, p. 597. (b) Yes, amendment can affect officers already elected or even abolish office, p. 597. | 57 | (a) No, effective upon adoption, p. 240. (b) Yes, implied but not specifically addressed. | (a) No, but effective upon adoption, p. 72. (b) Yes, amendment can eliminate offices and make other substantial changes, pp. 72, 169. | (a) No, effective upon adoption, p. 188. (b) Yes, amendment can eliminate offices and legislate an officer out of office, p. 180. | (a) No, effective upon adoption, p. 37. (b) Yes, amendment can eliminate offices or terms of office, p. 125. |
| 109 | What is the effect on incumbent officers of a bylaw amendment affecting their offices when nothing is done about protecting them? | The bylaw applies even if it legislates them out of office absent prior or concurrent adoption exempting them, p. 453. | The bylaw applies including abolition of the office unless a protective proviso is adopted before or concurrently, p. 597. | 57 | The bylaw is effective upon adoption unless the amendment contains a proviso delaying effectiveness, p. 240. | The bylaw applies even if it eliminates offices unless assembly decides or obviously understands that effectiveness will be postponed, p. 72. | The bylaw applies immediately unless otherwise agreed upon adoption, p. 188, and can legislate an officer out of office, p. 180. | The bylaw applies immediately unless otherwise specified, p. 37, and can eliminate offices or terms of office, p. 125. |
| 110 | Can a convention amend its constitution to restrict amendments to alternate years? | Yes, provided it is amended in compliance with amendment requirements, pp. 453-4. | Yes, bylaws define the amendment process, pp. 580-2, and bylaws can bind future sessions, pp. 87-8. | 56 | Yes, bylaws define amendment process and can limit time for proposing amendments, to annual meeting, for example, pp. 240-1. | Yes, bylaws define the amendment process, p. 71. | Yes, bylaws define the amendment process, pp. 179, 180, 187. | Yes, bylaws define when and how amendments can be offered, p. 36. |

© American Institute of Parliamentarians. All rights reserved.

Appendix A

| No | Issue | Answer | RONR 11th Ed | § | AIPSC | Cannon | Demeter | Riddick |
|---|---|---|---|---|---|---|---|---|
| 111 | Convention constitution amended with proviso that it will go into effect at the next annual meeting. Can the action be rescinded leaving the article as it was before amendment? | No, there is no way to rescind the amendment except by following the process to amend the constitution, p. 454. | No, even though effective date was delayed, an amendment becomes part of the bylaws immediately, p. 598, and amendment process must be followed to reverse. | 57 | No, even though effective date was delayed, an amendment becomes part of the bylaws immediately, and amendment process must be followed to reverse, pp. 240-4. | No, bylaw amendment provisions would govern, p. 71. | No, bylaw proviso on effectiveness does not open the approval vote to reconsideration (or rescission, by analogy), p. 157, so amendment process should be followed. | No, provisions part of bylaws immediately, p. 37, may not be rescinded, p. 173, so follow amendment procedure. |
| 112 | Bylaw requires a month's notice for amendment. Member proposed amendment, referred to committee, which reported a substitute amendment at the next meeting. (a) Was consideration of the substitute proper? (b) Should substitute have been referred to committee? Deferred for a month? | (a) No, proper notice not given; (b) No, committee had already considered but should have been deferred for a month, p. 455. | (a) No, proper notice of substitute amendment not given, pp. 594-5; (b) No, already been to committee but should be deferred a month, pp. 594-5. | 57 | (a) No, proper notice may not have been given, depending on the scope of the substitute, pp. 241-3; (b) No, already been to committee, but might need to be deferred. | (a) No, proper notice of substitute motion not given, p. 72; (b) No, already been to committee, but consideration should be deferred until notice given. | (a) No, proper notice of substitute motion not given, pp. 182, 189; (b) No, already been to committee, but should be deferred a month. | (a) No, proper notice of substitute motion not given, p. 37; (b) No, already been to committee, but should be deferred a month. |
| 113 | A committee is composed of four members. (a) Can the chair vote? (b) If so, when? | (a) Yes; (b) At any time but has a duty to vote whenever it would affect the result, p. 456. | (a) Yes; (b) At any time, pp. 500, 488, 53. | 50 | (a) Yes; (b) At any time, p. 193. | (a) Yes; (b) At any time -- debate "like any other member" although voting not specified, p. 84 | (a) Yes; (b) At any time, p. 275. | (a) Yes; (b) At any time, unless governing documents provide otherwise, p. 40. |

Appendix A

| No | Issue | Answer | RONR 11th. Ed | § | AIPSC | Cannon | Demeter | Riddick |
|---|---|---|---|---|---|---|---|---|
| 114 | President appoints and is ex officio all committees. (a) Can president call committee meetings? (b) Does president have greater authority than other committee members? | (a) Only committee chairs, or any two members, can call meetings; (b) No, p. 456. | (a) Chair calls meeting, or failing that, any two members, p. 499; (b) No, no distinction, except **not counted in quorum**, pp. 497, 483. | 50 | (a) Chair calls the meeting, or failing that M of committee, p. 193; (b) No, no distinction and is even **counted in the quorum**, p. 190. | (a) Chair has leadership role, p. 84; (b) No, ex officio has same rights and duties as other members, p. 161. | (a) Chair calls meeting, or failing that, any two members, p. 275; (b) No, no distinction, except not counted in quorum, p. 274. | (a) Chair calls the meeting, or failing that M of committee, p. 52; (b) No, no distinction but not counted in the quorum, p. 94. |
| 115 | Should president or executive board name chairs of committees? | No uniform practice; assembly, president, board, but whoever appoints committee has power to appoint chair, p. 456. | As prescribed by bylaws or choice of assembly (election, nominations, motion), chair (nominations, appointment), or committee elects, pp. 492-7. | 50 | Committee chairs can be elected, appointed or elected by committee members, pp. 189-90. | Committee can be selected or elected, pp. 159, 61-3, but no specific mention of naming chairs. | Chair may be selected by vote of the body, by the president, where authorized, or elected by the committee, p. 275. | Chairs may be selected by president, motion committee election, as specified in bylaws, p. 40-1. |
| 116 | Bylaws provide that president appoints certain committees. President appointed the committees then resigned. Does the resignation affect the appointees? | No, when appointed, notified and they do not decline, appointment is complete, p. 457. | No, once appointed and announced to the assembly, appointment is complete, pp. 495-6. | 50 | No, once appointed as directed by the bylaws, the specified process is complete, p. 190. | No, once appointed as directed by the bylaws, the specified process is complete, p. 61. | No, chair's appointment is final if not reconsidered before the end of the meeting, pp. 84-5. | No, chair's appointment is final, p. 50. |

© American Institute of Parliamentarians. All rights reserved.

Appendix A

| No | Issue | Answer | RONR 11th. Ed | § | AIPSC | Cannon | Demeter | Riddick |
|---|---|---|---|---|---|---|---|---|
| 117 | If the chair of a committee resigns, who appoints new chair? | Whoever appointed the original chair. If not done within reasonable time, committee should elect, p. 457. | Whoever appointed the chair -- the power to appoint carries with it the power to fill vacancies, p. 492; committee can elect if committee named by power other than assembly chair, p. 176. | 50 | Whoever appointed the first chair, unless the bylaws provide otherwise, p. 184; if none appointed, committee may select, p. 189. | The authority specified in the bylaws, p. 61. | The appointing authority, pp. 84, 256. | The appointing authority, pp. 50-1. |
| 118 | Committee chair with power to appoint, appoints committee, then resigns. What should be done? | Club could discharge committee and begin again, appoint another chair, or let committee elect its own chair, p. 457. | Could discharge and begin again if special committee, p. 313, appoint another chair, pp. 492, 497. | 50 | Could recall and begin again if special committee, pp. 44, 188, appoint another chair, p. 184, let committee select, p. 189. | Could reconsider referral, pp. 105-6, 126, appoint another chair, p. 61. | Could discharge and begin again if special committee, p. 83, appoint another chair, pp. 84, 256. | Could discharge and begin again if special committee, p. 83, appoint another chair, pp. 50-1. |
| 119 | Committee of three appointed by EC. Chair resigned. (a) Should other two have completed the work? (b) President appointed new chair; was this proper? | (a) Yes, if no additional member appointed; (b) No, EC was appointing power, p. 457. | (a) Yes, if no additional member appointed; (b) No, EC was appointing power, pp. 492, 177. | 50 | (a) Yes, if no additional member appointed; (b) No, EC was appointing power, pp. 184, 189. | (a) Yes, if no additional member appointed; (b) No, EC was appointing power, p. 61. | (a) Yes, if no additional member appointed, p. 269; (b) No, EC was appointing power, pp. 84, 256. | (a) Yes, if no additional member appointed; (b) No, EC was appointing power, p. 50-1. |
| 120 | Society appointed a permanent club-house committee. It now wishes to change the chair. Can this be done? By society or executive board? | Can be done by society, which can remove and replace absent bylaw term of office, pp. 257-8. | Can be done by society, which can remove and replace absent fixed term of office in bylaws, pp. 497, 177. | 50 | Can be done by society, which can remove and replace appointee, p. 185. | Not explicit about removal of chair, but should be society that does so, p. 61. | Can be done by society, pp. 84, 83, 256. | Can be done by society absent bylaw to the contrary, p. 86. |

© American Institute of Parliamentarians. All rights reserved.

Appendix A

| No | Issue | Answer | RONR 11th Ed | § | AIPSC | Cannon | Demeter | Riddick |
|---|---|---|---|---|---|---|---|---|
| 121 | Can a committee chair remove a member for missing meetings without excuse? | No, not unless the chair appointed the committee and must ask appointing authority, p. 458. | No, only the appointing authority has power to remove or replace committee members, p. 177. | 13 | No, must be removed by the authority that appointed them, p. 185. | Not explicit about removal of committee members, but should be done by appointing authority, p. 61. | No, appointing authority removes "disappearing" committee member, p. 257. | No, must be removed by the authority that appointed them, pp. 86, 84. |
| 122 | Is it legal to elect a non-member of a society as chair of a committee? | Yes, society, but not president or board, can decide to have non-member chair, p. 458. | Yes, but assembly must approve unless bylaws or motion allow non-member chair, pp. 174-5, 492. | 13 | Yes, as long as bylaws allow; non-member service is acknowledged at least in ex officio context, p. 190. | Yes, no explicit prohibition, will depend on bylaws, p. 61. | Yes, even assembly president can be non-member, p. 40. | No, only members of the organization may serve on committees, p. 53. |
| 123 | When an officer is authorized to appoint a committee, can the officer appoint a non-member of the local who is a member of the state or national body? | No, the society can approve but the officer does not have that power, p. 458. | No, the assembly must approve unless bylaws or motion allow non-member appointment, pp. 174-5, 492. | 13 | No, not unless authorized in the bylaws, p. 190. | No, not unless authorized in the bylaws, p. 61. | No, not unless authorized by superior law or a vote of the body itself, p. 40. | No, only members of the organization may serve on committees, p. 53. |
| 124 | In a convention, should the committees be appointed from delegates or non-delegate members of local units? | It is the option of the convention; committee tasks may leave little time for delegates to attend convention, p. 459. | Optional, bylaws should provide, p. 602; much committee work occurs before convention so may need to be composed of non-delegates, p. 607. | 58 | Optional, bylaws should provide; may include non-voting advisors, p. 213; work occurs in advance, before delegates are selected, pp. 205-11. | Optional, bylaws should specify committee qualifications, pp. 3, 61, selected well in advance, p. 91. | Optional, conventions and committees are optional topics in bylaws, p. 179. | Optional, bylaws should provide; much work done in advance by "preconvention committees," pp. 60-1, early appointments necessary, p. 64. |

Appendix A

| No | Issue | Answer | RONR 11th. Ed | § | AIPSC | Cannon | Demeter | Riddick |
|---|---|---|---|---|---|---|---|---|
| 125 | What are the duties of the credentials committee? | Examine credentials of delegates and alternates, provide badges, report list to convention and tellers, p. 459. | Distribute registration materials, examine credentials, maintain list, register throughout, report periodically, pp. 610-3. | 59 | Examine credentials, maintain count for quorum, maintain list, register throughout, report periodically, may help with voting and elections. pp. 207-8. | Examine credentials, maintain list, register throughout, report periodically, p. 91. | Determine which delegates are entitled to be seated and to vote, p. 209. | Supervise registration, examine credentials, issue badges, maintain list, register throughout, report periodically, p. 64. |
| 126 | (a) Are the duties of the resolution committee to receive referrals, report amendments, move adoption, and frame resolutions of thanks? (b) Do they have power to take any original action? | (a) Yes; (b) They generally have the power to originate resolutions except where prohibited, p. 459. | (a) Basic purpose is screening of original MM, p. 633; (b) Some types of organizations allow resolutions committee to originate resolutions, p. 635. | 59 | (a) Referral committee generally considers items referred to them, p. 212; (b) Sometimes permitted or expected to originate motions, p. 219. | (a) Resolution committee considers items referred to them, p. 83; (b) But often initiate their own recommendations, p. 83. | (a) Committee on resolutions screens resolutions, p. 295; (b) No explicit bar to origination of resolutions, pp. 295-7. | (a) Screens resolutions for compliance with laws, bylaws and rules, pp. 62-3; (b) May originate resolutions, especially policy statements and courtesy resolutions, p. 63. |
| 127 | Board committee report recommended discharging building committee. Report accepted, followed by vote of confidence. Building committee reports accepted for two years afterwards. New president now rules that building committee was discharged. Is ruling correct? | No, accepting this report did not carry out recommendation. No vote to discharge and subsequent action showed club understanding that committee had not been discharged, pp. 460-1. | No, recommendations may be declarations of intent or authorization of action, so committee report must be clear and recommend action in the form of a resolution, which did not happen here, p. 504. | 51 | No, committee report must be clear and recommend action in the form of a motion or resolution, p. 198. An adopted report is "binding" but here only a statement of intent; discharge was never moved, p. 199. | No, committee report accepted, but specific recommendations apparently not adopted (vote of confidence), pp. 85-6. | No, accepting a committee report adopts recommendations, pp. 18, 281, but here M vote of confidence, p. 259, shows lack of 2/3 support for discharge, p. 83. | No, no motion to adopt discharge recommendation p. 170. Assembly responsible for every word in an adopted report but here only a statement of intent. |

© American Institute of Parliamentarians. All rights reserved.

Appendix A

| No | Issue | Answer | RONR 11th. Ed | § | AIPSC | Cannon | Demeter | Riddick |
|---|---|---|---|---|---|---|---|---|
| 128 | When committee report contains resolutions: (a) Is action on the resolutions the only action necessary?; (b) Must report be adopted first?; (c) Must report be adopted as a whole after action on the resolutions? | (a) Yes; (b) No; (c) No; p. 461. | (a) Yes, receive report, act on recommendations, p. 506; (b) No, pp. 506-8; (c) No, only adopt entire report to publish in the name of entire organization, p. 508. | 51 | (a) Yes, receive report, act on recommendations; (b) No; (c) No, only adopt entire report to publish in the name of entire organization, pp. 198-9. | (a) Yes, only recommendations at issue; (b) No; (c) No, pp. 85-6. | (a) Yes; (b) No; (c) No, normally no action taken where report contains no motion, p. 18. | (a) Yes; (b) No; (c) No, no action should be taken on report itself, p. 170. |
| 129 | (a) If a report includes a recommendation, does accepting the report adopt the recommendation? (b) Is it unnecessary to accept the report and adopt the resolution? (c) If a report does not include a recommendation, is it proper to accept the report? | (a) Yes, if motion is adopted; (b) Yes; (c) Yes, but not necessary, p. 461-2. | (a) Yes, but clearer to receive report, act on recommendations, p. 506; (b) Yes, generally assembly just acts on the recommendations, pp. 506-8; (c) Yes, but should only accept, adopt or agree to report when assembly wants to endorse every word, pp. 507-8. | 51 | (a) Yes, but clearer to receive report, act on recommendations; (b) Yes, generally assembly just acts on the recommendations; (c) Yes, but should only accept when assembly wants to publish report on behalf of entire organization, pp. 198-9. | (a) Yes, if intent is to adopt recommendations; (b) Yes, just act on the recommendations; (c) Yes, pp. 85-6. | (a) Yes; (b) Yes; (c) Yes, but normally no action taken where report contains no motion, p. 18. | (a) Yes; (b) Yes; (c) No, no action should be taken on report containing no recommendations, p. 170. |

© American Institute of Parliamentarians. All rights reserved.

Appendix A

| No | Issue | Answer | RONR 11th Ed | § | AIPSC | Cannon | Demeter | Riddick |
|---|---|---|---|---|---|---|---|---|
| 130 | Motion to donate $10 is referred to committee, which recommends no contribution this year. Motion to adopt committee report is lost. What is the next step? | No motion to adopt committee report should have been made. Motion should be to make donation notwithstanding recommendation of committee, p. 462. | Upon committee report with recommendation on question pending when referred, question becomes pending automatically, pp. 516-7. Put that motion to a vote notwithstanding recommendation. | 51 | Following committee report, vote should be on motion to donate, not on the committee recommendation, p. 203. | Put original motion to vote, p. 85. | Following committee report, referred matters can be acted on immediately, p. 18. | No action should have been taken on the report. Referred motion should now be considered in light of committee recommendation p. 170. |
| 131 | If society adopts an officer's report with recommendations, do they become the recommendations of the society? | Yes, adopted recommendations of the society but not adopted resolutions, p. 462. | Yes, officer report recommendations may be declarations of intent or authorization of action. Here apparently just intent, pp. 355-6, 476. | 48 | No, an adopted report containing recommendations is "binding," p. 199. | No, when report is moved, recommendations are at issue and may be acted upon, pp. 85-6. | Yes, accepting a report adopts all recommendations, p. 18. | Yes, adopted as a statement of intent, p. 170. |
| 132 | At an annual meeting for election of officers, is it proper for an outgoing president to appoint committees for the incoming administration? | No, p. 462. | No, sample bylaws have committee appointments after annual meeting (by new president), p. 587, and one session should not generally interfere with appointments in another, p. 88. | 56 | No, bylaws govern, but would interfere with the function of the president as leader, pp. 190, 173. | No, bylaws govern, but would interfere with the function of the president as leader, pp. 61-2. | No, bylaws govern, but would interfere with the function of the president as leader, pp. 84, 251. | No, bylaws govern, but usually incoming administration, p. 48; otherwise would interfere with the administrative duties of the president, pp. 50, 6, 145-6. |

© American Institute of Parliamentarians. All rights reserved.

Appendix A

| No | Issue | Answer | RONR 11th Ed | § | AIPSC | Cannon | Demeter | Riddick |
|----|-------|--------|--------------|---|-------|--------|---------|---------|
| 133 | What is the best method for appointing a nominating committee? | No one method is best for all. Regional group meeting once a year should have EB appoint a month in advance, p. 462. | Nominating committee should be elected by organization or EB, p. 433, but never appointed by president, pp. 495, 433, who should not even be a member. | 46 | Should be representative, some members elected, some appointed by board, none by president, president-elect or past presidents, pp. 161-2. | Should be selected by board or other governance group, not president, p. 130. | Bylaws should define selection process for nominating committee; should not include president, p. 240. | Bylaws should specify and president should not be a member, pp. 121-2. |
| 134 | Do all standing committees go out of existence at the expirations of their terms? | No, if not provided otherwise in the bylaws, the terms of members expire when successors are elected or appointed, p. 462. | No, committee has continuing function, member terms expire when their successors are elected or appointed, pp. 490-1. | 50 | No, committee must be ready at any time; member terms are usually the same as officers, p. 188. | No, committee continues in existence; member terms are defined in the bylaws, pp. 60-1. | No, committee continues in existence; member terms are defined in the bylaws and are often staggered, p. 277. | No, committee is permanent; member terms usually coincide with administration but as the bylaws specify, p. 48. |
| 135 | (a) Do special committees die with outgoing administration? (b) When they fail to report at the time specified? | (a) No; (b) No, continues until work done unless discharged sooner; except convention committee, p. 463. | (a) No; (b) No, continues until work done unless discharged sooner. Committee of body that ceases to exist ceases with the body, p. 502. | 50 | (a) No; (b) No, continues until work done unless discharged sooner, pp. 188-9. | (a) No; (b) No, continues until work done unless discharged sooner, pp. 60-1. | (a) No; (b) No, continues until work done unless discharged sooner, pp. 269, 277. | (a) No; (b) No, continues until work done unless discharged sooner, p. 48. |
| 136 | When resolutions committee reports substantive and courtesy resolutions, are courtesy resolutions first or last? | It's up to the committee but usually courtesy resolutions are reported last, p. 463. | Resolutions committees generally have the power to arrange resolutions in a logical sequence, p. 635. | 59 | Reference committees generally have the power to group resolutions for orderly presentation, p. 217. | Up to committee, no guidance on resolutions committees. | Committee on resolutions and bylaws will determine order, pp. 295-7. | Courtesy resolutions should be read near the time for adjournment, p. 70. |

Appendix A

| No | Issue | Answer | RONR 11th. Ed | § | AIPSC | Cannon | Demeter | Riddick |
|---|---|---|---|---|---|---|---|---|
| 137 | Is a motion to substitute the minority report for the committee report handled the same was as a motion to substitute a resolution? | Yes, amend committee report, amend minority report, vote on substitution, vote on adoption, p. 463. | Yes, amend committee report, amend minority report, vote on substitution, vote on adoption, pp. 527-9, 156. | 51 | Yes, but different from RONR -- amend minority report, vote on substitution, vote on adoption, pp. 203, 51, 54-5. | Yes, but different from RONR -- amend minority report, vote on substitution, vote on adoption, pp. 85-6, 103-4. | Yes, substitute like RONR or amend -- strike committee report, insert minority report, pp. 283, 79. | Yes, like RONR, amend committee report, amend minority report, vote on substitution, vote on adoption, pp. 112, 14-5. |
| 138 | Does a society have the right to have the EB minutes read to the society? | Yes, by M with notice or 2/3 vote, p. 463. | Yes, by MN23MEM vote, p. 487. | 49 | No, disclosure of sensitive matters could injure society, p. 196. | Yes, no explicit guidance so society decides, pp. 3-4. | Yes, by M vote, p. 23. | Yes, by rule, custom or M vote, p. 28. |
| 139 | May organization go into COTW to discuss the report of a committee? | Yes, p. 464. | Yes, upon receipt and statement of the question, treated like any other MM, 509, 531-2. | 51 | No, but could consider informally, the AIPSC alternative, pp. 133-4, 201. | No, but can use informal procedures to discuss and amend, pp. 85-6. | Yes, COTW can consider any question after statement by chair, pp. 285, 278. | No, but could consider informally, pp. 56-7. |
| 140 | What should happen when emerging from COTW? | President resumes chair, chair of COTW reports to assembly, assembly acts as with any committee report, p. 464. | President resumes chair, chair of COTW reports to assembly, assembly acts as with any committee report, pp. 534-5. | 52 | Informal consideration is automatically ended by making any motion or taking a vote on the question, p. 134. | Informal procedures by consent can be ended at any time by objection, pp. 86, 124-5. | President resumes chair, chair of COTW reports to assembly, assembly acts as with any committee report, pp. 286-9. | Informal consideration ends when members by consensus or M vote determine that question is ready for a vote, p. 57. |
| 141 | What is the difference between a nominating committee and a committee on nominations? | None, either title can be applied to a committee appointed to submit nominations, p. 465. | None, index under committee refers to nominating committee, p. 680, the term used in RONR, p. 433. | 46 | None, no mention of committee on nominations, uses the term nominating committee, p. 161. | None, index under committee refers to nominating committee, p. 172, 130. | None -- terms are synonymous but committee on nominations is more formal and precise, p. 240. | None, index under committee refers to nominating committee, pp. 214, 121. |

© American Institute of Parliamentarians. All rights reserved.

Appendix A

| No | Issue | Answer | RONR 11th. Ed | § | AIPSC | Cannon | Demeter | Riddick |
|---|---|---|---|---|---|---|---|---|
| 142 | Can a member of an organization who is not a delegate make a nomination for office at a convention? | No, a nomination can be made only by someone who can make a motion, p. 465. | No, nomination is a member power, p. 3, and only delegates are voting members of the convention body, p. 600. | 58 | No, nomination is a member power, p. 260; delegates are the voting members of convention, p. 205-6. | No, delegate assemblies, p. 3, represent through delegates only, pp. 91, 160. | No, only those who can make motions can nominate, p. 239, only delegates can do so, p. 209. | No, only delegates may debate and vote, p. 79, only members of anybody can nominate, p. 122. |
| 143 | Can county school directors in nominating superintendents speak against other candidates? | Yes, nominees are not members, decorum rules don't apply, candidates can be freely evaluated, p. 465. | Yes, proposals to fill blanks debatable, pp. 430, 162-5; superintendent analogous to ED, p. 464, not member so decorum not an issue, p. 392. | 46 | Yes, proposals to fill blanks debatable, p. 55; superintendent is employee, pp. 267-8, decorum not an issue, p. 130. | Yes, nominations are debatable, p. 129; superintendent analogous to ED, p. 3. | Yes, nominees not members, p. 239; but should wait for debate, p. 68. | No, can't attack nominees, p. 121; but here non-member, p. 94, decorum not an issue, p. 73. |
| 144 | Are nominations debatable? | Yes, only the method of making nominations is undebatable, p. 465. | Yes, proposals to fill blanks by nomination are debatable, pp. 430, 162-5; motions relating to methods of nomination are not debatable, p. 287. | 46 | Yes, proposals to fill blanks debatable, p. 55; incidental motions not debatable (except appeal), table inside front cover. | Yes, nominations are debatable, p. 129; motions relating to voting are not, p. 98. | No, except for praise of own nominees, pp. 239, 147. | Yes, nominations are debatable, p. 121; motion to choose method is not debatable if election is pending, p. 197. |
| 145 | If constitution requires nomination of officers by ballot, can all officers be nominated on one ballot? | Yes, p. 466. | Yes, same procedure as electing ballot except everyone receiving vote is only nominated, pp. 436-7. | 46 | Yes, nomination by ballot not separately discussed so subject to normal ballot rules, p. 151. | Yes, nomination by ballot not separately discussed; analogy to normal ballot rules, p. 129-34. | Yes, no distinction in method noted for nominating ballot, pp. 241-2. | Yes, no explicit restriction to single office, p. 123. |

© American Institute of Parliamentarians. All rights reserved.

Appendix A

| No | Issue | Answer | RONR 11th. Ed | § | AIPSC | Cannon | Demeter | Riddick |
|---|---|---|---|---|---|---|---|---|
| 146 | Is it necessary for a candidate to be nominated in order to be elected an officer? | No, if qualified and obtains the votes does not need to be nominated, p. 466. | No, can vote for any eligible person whether or not nominated, pp. 431, 439. | 46 | No, can vote for any eligible person whether or not nominated, p. 161. | No, unless bylaws require nomination to ensure eligibility, p. 130. | No, can vote for any eligible person whether or not nominated, p. 209. | No, can vote for any eligible person whether or not nominated, p. 123. |
| 147 | Can a member nominate herself for office? | Yes, but lessens the chance for election, p. 466. | Yes, no explicit exclusion and individual floor nominations do not need a second, p. 432. | 46 | Yes, no explicit exclusion and individual floor nominations do not need a second, p. 160. | No, any member can nominate any **other** member, p. 129. | Yes, a member can nominate himself for office, pp. 239, 347. | Yes, no explicit exclusion and individual floor nominations do not need a second, pp. 122, 198. |
| 148 | (a) Does accepting nomination from a committee preclude floor nomination for another office? (b) Can a candidate appear on the same ballot for two offices? | (a) No; (b) Yes, p. 466. | (a) No; (b) Yes, p. 432. If elected to both on same ballot and bylaws silent, candidate chooses, if present, or assembly decides, p. 440. | 46 | (a) No; (b) Yes, p. 163. If elected to both, must choose if offices are incompatible, p. 163. | (a) No, p. 130; (b) Yes, no prohibition, pp. 131-4. | (a) No, floor nominations always in order after committee report, p. 241; (b) Yes, can be elected to more than one office, p 239. | (a) No, always open to floor nominations, p. 122; (b) Yes, unless bylaws prohibit, p. 121. |
| 149 | One member nominated every other member as director. How many can one member nominate? | One until every other member has had a chance, except by consent, and no more than the places to fill, p. 466. | One until every other member has had a chance, except by consent, and no more than the places to fill, p. 432. | 46 | One at a time implied (example of a single nominee) but no express limitations, p. 160. | One at a time implied (nominate **any** other member, not every) but no express limitations, pp. 129-30. | Only one until every other member has had a chance, p. 239. | Only one -- any member may place **a** name in nomination, p. 122. |
| 150 | If NC has the custom of inviting suggestions, may the committee ignore the suggestions? | Yes, p. 466. | Yes, duty of committee to nominate; suggestions can be repeated from the floor following committee report, pp. 433-5. | 46 | Yes, committee is chosen to use its judgment in selecting nominees, p. 162. | Yes, duty of nominating committee to present its slate, p. 130. | Yes, members can submit suggestions but committee is not bound to follow them, p. 241. | Yes, committee has the responsibility of making selections, p. 121, and suggestions can be repeated from the floor, p. 122. |

© American Institute of Parliamentarians. All rights reserved.

Appendix A

| No | Issue | Answer | RONR 11th. Ed | § | AIPSC | Cannon | Demeter | Riddick |
|---|---|---|---|---|---|---|---|---|
| 151 | Does the NC have the right to nominate its members for office? | Yes, free to nominate anyone except as limited by bylaws, pp. 466-7. | Yes, otherwise service on the committee would be a penalty, p. 433. | 46 | Yes, but nominated members should resign immediately, p. 163. | Yes, no prohibition expressed, p. 130. | Yes, p. 241. | Yes, and need not resign, pp. 121-2. |
| 152 | Is it necessary for NC to ask every nominee whether they will accept before nominating? | No, not unless bylaws require, but desirable if there's any doubt, p. 467. | No, but desirable policy to contact nominees before reporting; bylaws can make mandatory, p. 434. | 46 | No, but listed among the duties usually assigned to nominating committee, p. 162. | No, not specified, p. 130. | No, but generally should make sure that nominees will accept nomination and office, p. 240. | No, but can secure prior consent, p. 121. |
| 153 | Bylaws require NC to prepare two tickets. Can the same name be listed for president on both tickets? | Yes, bylaws should specify if desire is to prevent same name from appearing on both tickets, p. 467. | Yes, committee can nominate more than one but should not be forced to -- can circumvent by naming unelectable candidate, p. 433. | 46 | Yes, multiple slates are not favored; second candidate only if bylaws require -- otherwise results in "throwaway" candidate, p. 164. | Yes, practices vary; second candidate necessary only if bylaws require, p. 130. | Yes, committee instructed to present two slates can nominate the same person for the same office on both slates, p. 240. | Yes, multiple slates are not favored; second candidate only if bylaws require, p. 122. |
| 154 | Motion to nominate by ballot pending. Substitute to nominate by acclamation ruled out of order as negative of original motion. Was ruling correct? | No, those are not the only options. Could also nominate from floor, chair, committee, p. 467. | No, not the only options, p. 431, and acclamation is just a special case of a single nominee, p. 443. | 46 | No, not the only options, pp. 159-61; and general consent not specifically discussed in nomination, p. 148. | No, not the only options, pp. 129-31, and acclamation is just a special case with single nominees, p. 133. | No, not the only options, pp. 240-1, and acclamation is just a special case of unanimity, p. 248. | No, not the only options, pp. 121-2, and acclamation is just a special case of single nominee, p. 3. |

Appendix A

| No | Issue | Answer | RONR 11th Ed | § | AIPSC | Cannon | Demeter | Riddick |
|---|---|---|---|---|---|---|---|---|
| 155 | Bylaws require members to send officer recommendations to NC which selects candidates by majority vote. (a) Are floor nominations allowed? (b) Can NC submit more than one name? (c) Does a tie vote go forward? | (a) No, bylaw procedure governs; (b) Yes, bylaw requires a vote on all submissions; (c) No, tie vote candidacy fails, p. 468. | (a) No, bylaws govern, p. 431; (b) Yes, bylaw requires vote on all submissions and committee can submit more than one, p. 433; (c) No, tie vote candidacy fails, p. 53. | 46 | (a) No, bylaws govern, p. 159; (b) Yes, bylaw requires vote on all submissions, p. 159; (c) No, tie vote candidate is defeated, p. 142. | (a) No, bylaws govern, p. 129; (b) Yes, bylaw requires vote on all submissions, multiple nominations possible, p. 130; (c) No, tie fails, p. 7. | (a) No, bylaws govern, p. 240; (b) Yes, bylaw requires vote on all submissions, multiple nominations possible, p. 240; (c) No, tie fails, p. 35. | (a) No, bylaws govern, p. 120; (b) Yes, bylaw requires vote on all submissions, multiple nominations possible, p. 122; (c) No, tie fails, p. 204. |
| 156 | When a society votes to nominate by ballot, are nominations from the floor also in order? | No, the point of the ballot is secrecy, p. 468. | No, no right to nominate from the floor after ballot unless assembly authorizes by M vote, p. 437. | 46 | Yes, nominations from the floor are always permitted, p. 160. | No, ballot implies secret process, p. 158. | No, ballot nominations are secret, but can still vote for anyone afterwards, p. 241. | No, secret and every member had a chance to nominate through the ballot, p. 123. |
| 157 | Bylaws provide for ballot nomination with two leading candidates being nominees for election. Does this preclude floor nominations? | Yes, but members should be aware that they can elect anyone, not just one of the two, p. 469. | Yes, no right to nominate from the floor, but should not limit election to top two candidates p. 437. | 46 | No, nominations from the floor are always permitted, p. 160. | Yes, ballot implies secret process, p. 158. | Yes, ballot nominations are secret but can vote for anyone, p. 241. | Yes, secret and every member had a chance to nominate through the ballot but can vote for anyone unless bylaws limit, p. 123. |
| 158 | Is it proper for NC to submit two names for the same office? | Yes, sometimes required, otherwise refer back if one desired, p. 469. | Yes, unless bylaws prohibit, p. 433. | 46 | Yes, unless bylaws prohibit, but not recommended, p. 164. | Yes, unless bylaws prohibit, p. 130. | Yes, unless bylaws prohibit, p. 240. | Yes, unless bylaws prohibit, but usually presents one, p. 122. |

© American Institute of Parliamentarians. All rights reserved.

Appendix A

| No | Issue | Answer | RONR 11th. Ed | § | AIPSC | Cannon | Demeter | Riddick |
|---|---|---|---|---|---|---|---|---|
| 159 | What if NC fails to nominate a president and the bylaws don't allow nominations from the floor? | Ballot for president without nominations or ballot for nominations, p. 469. | Ballot for president without nominations or ballot for nominations, pp. 430-1. | 46 | Ballot for president without nominations, p. 161. | Ballot for president without nominations unless bylaws require nomination to ensure eligibility, p. 130. | Ballot for president without nominations, p. 240. | Ballot for president without nominations, p. 123. |
| 160 | If A nominates B and motion to close nominations is carried, can A withdraw nomination? | No, not without reopening nominations, p. 469. | No, not without reopening nominations, pp. 288-9. | 31 | No, not without reopening nominations, p. 160-1. | No, not without reopening nominations, p. 131. | No, not without reopening nominations, pp. 240, 136. | No, not without reopening nominations, p. 123. |
| 161 | Nomination for membership laid on the table by board. Can same name be proposed to a new board? | Yes, even if bylaws preclude repeat nominations because it was tabled and never acted on, p. 470. | Yes, motion to lay on the table merely halts consideration of the question, p. 210. | 17 | Yes, unless bylaws forbid even repeat proposals because motion to table "kills" proposal without discussion or direct vote (i.e., consideration), p. 70. | Yes, only postponements are recognized, so nomination never acted on, p. 105. | Yes, motion to table just removes MM from before the body, p. 98. May also kill if not removed from table, but without consideration, p. 98. | Yes, motion to table "kills" proposal without debate for convenience but contemplates renewal, p. 189. |
| 162 | Is a motion necessary to close nominations? | No, if no further nominations are proposed after prompting, chair can declare nominations closed, p. 470. | No, if no further nominations are proposed after prompting, chair should declare nominations closed, p. 288. | 31 | No, if no further nominations are proposed after prompting, chair may declare nominations closed, p. 160. | No, if no further nominations are proposed after prompting, chair can declare nominations closed, p. 130. | No, nominations can be closed by chair by general consent, by motion or as prescribed in the bylaws, p. 135. | No, if no further nominations are proposed after prompting, chair may declare nominations closed, pp. 122-3. |
| 163 | Can sole nominee move to close nominations? | Yes, after there's been a reasonable time for other nominations, p. 470. | Yes, after there's been a reasonable time for other nominations, p. 288. | 31 | Yes, after there's been ample opportunity for other nominations, p. 160-1. | Yes, after it is certain that there are no other nominations, p. 130. | Yes, after there's been sufficient time for other nominations, p. 135. | Yes, any member may move to close nominations when no more names are presented, p. 123. |

© American Institute of Parliamentarians. All rights reserved.

Appendix A

| No | Issue | Answer | RONR 11th. Ed | § | AIPSC | Cannon | Demeter | Riddick |
|----|-------|--------|---------------|---|-------|--------|---------|---------|
| 164 | Is it reasonable to allow a M to reopen nominations when 2/3 just voted to close? | Yes, closing may deprive someone of a right, reopening does not, p. 470. | Yes, closing deprives members of a basic right, reopening does not, pp. 287-9. | 31 | Yes, closing deprives members of a basic right, reopening does not, pp. 2, 160-1. | No, closing and reopening are M votes, pp. 130-1, 98-9. | Yes, closing removes a right, reopening restores the right, p. 136. | Yes, but closing and reopening are by consent or M votes, p. 123. |
| 165 | If a candidate is rejected for membership, may he be nominated again and again at future meetings? | Yes, at any future session absent a bylaw to the contrary, pp. 470-1. | Yes, can be renewed at any future session absent a bylaw to the contrary, pp. 336-7. | 38 | Yes, can be renewed at any future meeting or convention absent a bylaw to the contrary, p. 25. | Yes, unless bylaws preclude, pp. 95, 126-7. | Yes, can be renewed at any future session absent a bylaw to the contrary, p. 172. | Yes, can be renewed at any future meeting absent a bylaw to the contrary, p. 168. |
| 166 | Two nominees for chair of committee were both elected to the committee but a third received more votes. Who is chair? | Chair apparently not voted for directly, so winner should call committee together and it should elect its own chair, p. 471. | Assembly apparently left chair decision to the committee, pp. 493, 176; nomination irrelevant to outcome of vote, p. 439, but usually first named calls committee meeting to elect chair, p. 176. | 50 | Assembly apparently left chair decision to the committee, p. 189; nomination irrelevant to outcome of vote, p. 161, but usually first named calls committee meeting to elect chair, p. 190. | Committee should decide unless bylaws specify, pp. 3, 129-30. | Assembly apparently left chair decision to the committee, p. 275; nomination not necessary, pp. 209, 241. | Assembly apparently left chair decision to the committee, p. 50; nomination not necessary, p. 123. |
| 167 | To avoid offense, society uses nominating ballot and then declares it to be the election ballot. Is this the best procedure? | No, should simply elect by ballot without nomination, p. 471. | No, should simply elect by ballot without nomination, p. 437, 430. | 46 | No, elect by ballot without nominations -- free to set own election procedure, p. 159; nomination not essential, p. 161. | No, use ballot without nominations -- free to set own election procedure, pp. 129, 99; nomination not essential, p. 130. | No, use ballot without nominations -- free to set own election procedure, p. 242; nomination not essential, p. 241. | No, use ballot without nominations; nomination not essential unless bylaws require, p. 123. |
| 168 | Is it proper to declare the nominating ballot the electing ballot? | No, undermines secrecy, violates bylaw requiring ballot, p. 472. | No, undermines secrecy, violates bylaw requiring ballot election, p. 437. | 46 | No, undermines secrecy, violates bylaw requiring ballot election, p. 151. | No, undermines secrecy, violates bylaw requiring ballot election, p. 158. | No, undermines secrecy, violates bylaw requiring ballot election, pp. 140, 309, 241. | No, undermines secrecy, violates bylaw requiring ballot election, pp. 26-7, 123. |

© American Institute of Parliamentarians. All rights reserved.

Appendix A

| No | Issue | Answer | RONR 11th. Ed | § | AIPSC | Cannon | Demeter | Riddick |
|---|---|---|---|---|---|---|---|---|
| 169 | NC reports, nominee withdraws. (a) Is committee finished? (b) May committee find another nominee? (c) Should withdrawal be shown as blank or withdrawn candidate? | (a) Committee normally finished at report but here didn't confirm acceptance; (b) Yes; (c) Blank, p. 472. | (a) Committee automatically discharged at report but revived if nominee withdraws, p. 435; (b) Yes, p. 435; (c) Blank or replacement, p. 435. | 46 | (a) Committee normally finished at report but here didn't confirm acceptance, p. 162; (b) Yes or nominate from floor, pp. 161-4; (c) Blank or replacement, p. 164-5. | (a) Committee normally finished at report; (b) Yes or nominate from floor; (c) Blank or replacement, p. 130. | (a) Committee automatically expires at report but revived if nominee withdraws; (b) Yes; (c) Blank or replacement, p. 240. | (a) Committee automatically expires at report but can be revived if nominee withdraws, p. 122; (b) Yes, p. 122; (c) Blank or replacement, p. 122. |
| 170 | NC reports. Nominee declines nomination and nominates another candidate. Is nomination proper? | Yes, should be treated as floor nomination not amendment of report, pp. 472-3. | No, committee should nominate if there is time, otherwise treat as floor nomination, p. 435. | 46 | No, committee should nominate if there is time, otherwise treat as floor nomination, pp. 160-2. | Yes, treat as floor nomination, p. 130. | No, committee should nominate if there is time, otherwise floor nomination, p. 240. | No, committee should nominate if there is time, otherwise floor nomination, p. 122. |
| 171 | NC presents ticket at the meeting preceding the annual meeting. (a) When are floor nominations in order? (b) Can members fill gaps in ticket? President appoints some NC members, others elected, which could take longer. (c) Who fills NC vacancy? | (a) In order at both meetings; (b) Yes, at either meeting; (c) The respective appointing power even if this would have the effect of giving president additional power, pp. 473-4. Solution is to elect all. | (a) In order at both meetings, p. 435; (b) Yes, at either meeting, p. 435; (c) The respective appointing power, p. 492. | 46 | (a) In order at both meetings to provide ample opportunity, p. 160; (b) Yes, at either meeting, p. 160; (c) The respective appointing authority, p. 184. | (a) In order at both meetings to provide reasonable time, p. 130; (b) Yes, at either meeting, p. 130; (c) The respective appointing authority or as bylaws provide, p. 61. | (a) In order at both meetings after NC report, p. 241; (b) Yes, at either meeting, p. 241; (c) The respective appointing power or as bylaws provide, p. 276. | (a) In order at both meetings after NC report, p. 122; (b) Yes, at either meeting, p. 122; (c) The respective appointing power or as bylaws provide, p. 197. |
| 172 | Is it democratic to have no nominations? | Yes, p. 474. | Yes, can elect by ballot without nomination but not recommended, pp. 437, 430-1. | 46 | Yes, free to set own election procedure, p. 159; nomination not essential, p. 161. | Yes, can set own election procedure, pp. 129, 99; nomination not essential, p. 130. | Yes, can set own election procedure, p. 242; nomination not essential, p. 241. | Yes, nomination not essential unless bylaws require, p. 123. |

© American Institute of Parliamentarians. All rights reserved.

Appendix A

| No | Issue | Answer | RONR 11th. Ed | § | AIPSC | Cannon | Demeter | Riddick |
|---|---|---|---|---|---|---|---|---|
| 173 | (a) Does "nomination is not necessary when the election is by ballot" mean printed ballot? (b) Does this authorize elections without nominations? | (a) Printed or written ballot; (b) Yes, p. 474. | 46 -- (a) Printed or written slips of paper, p. 412; (b) Yes, p. 430. | 46 | (a) Paper or machine, pp. 151,302; (b) Yes, nominations not essential, p. 161. | (a) Paper or machine, p. 158; (b) Yes, nominations not essential, p. 130. | (a) Any instrument for secret vote, p. 209, generally printed, p. 241; (b) Yes, nominations not essential, p. 241. | (a) Paper, machine or electronic vote, p. 26; (b) Yes, nominations not essential, p. 123. |
| 174 | (a) Should informal ballot results be posted? (b) Is it better to eliminate the number of votes? | (a) Yes, to guide the voters on the formal ballot; (b) No, p. 474. | (a) Yes, purpose of nominating ballot is to show sentiments of voting body; (b) No, p. 436. Compare straw polls (not in order), p. 429. | 46 | (a) Yes, if nominating ballot, p. 159, straw polls improper, p. 158; (b) No, p. 167. | (a) Yes, if bylaws require nominating ballot; (b) No, p. 134. | (a) Yes, purpose of nominating ballot is guidance; (b) No, for the same reason, p. 241. | (a) Yes, purpose of nominating ballot is to show preferences; (b) No, p. 123. |
| 175 | Nominations closed and election postponed for seven months. Should chair call for nominations before election? | Yes, one meeting should not bind the subsequent meeting, p. 474. | Yes, if time has elapsed, read list again and reopen, pp. 435, 289, 87. | 46 | Yes, given passage of time, or M can reopen, p. 161. | Yes, by consent or M, p. 130. | Yes, closure does not carry over to election meeting, p. 240. | Yes, by consent or M, p. 122. |
| 176 | Election held, meeting adjourned, count completed, no majority. (a) Will election come under unfinished business at next meeting? (b) Are nominations in order or must they be reopened? | (a) Yes; (b) Yes, p. 475. | (a) Yes, p. 358; (b) Yes, pp. 435, 289, 87. | 46 | (a) Yes, p. 118; (b) No, must be reopened by M vote, p. 161. | (a) Agendized like any other item, p. 81; (b) No, by consent or M vote, p. 130. | (a) Yes, p. 307; (b) Yes, in order, p. 240. | (a) Yes, p. 30; (b) No, must be reopened by consent or M vote, p. 122. |

© American Institute of Parliamentarians. All rights reserved.

Appendix A

| No | Issue | Answer | RONR 11th. Ed | § | AIPSC | Cannon | Demeter | Riddick |
|---|---|---|---|---|---|---|---|---|
| 177 | May a non-member be elected as an officer? | Yes, p. 475. | Yes, unless bylaws provide otherwise, p. 447. | 47 | No, "officers of an organization are members ... ," p. 173. | No, only eligible members can be nominated for office, p. 129. | Yes, but only nonmember chair explicitly discussed, p. 40. | No, only voting members in good standing may be nominated, p. 121. |
| 178 | May a member hold more than one office at a time? | Yes, unless limited by bylaws, p. 475. Should choose one unless multiple offices approved in advance. | Yes, if intent is clear in advance and bylaws do not prohibit, p. 440. If elected to two offices on same ballot candidate or assembly must choose. | 46 | Yes, except incompatible offices, p. 163. | Yes, no prohibition expressed, pp. 3, 129-34. | Yes, organization has the implied power to consolidate offices, p. 347. | Yes, if bylaws allow, p. 125. |
| 179 | First VP nominated for president. Should she resign at once or retain office until elected president? | Retain office until elected president, p. 475. | Retain office until elected president, pp. 432, 440, 585. | 46 | Retain office until elected president, then choose p. 163. | Retain office until elected president, p. 134. | Retain office until elected and then choose or assume both if permitted, pp. 239, 347. | Retain office until elected, for continuity, p. 125. |
| 180 | Election of officers, ballots collected, member raises parliamentary question. Answer establishes that many members voted under misunderstanding. Was a motion to destroy ballots and vote again proper? | Yes, if members had not yet left. Could be adopted by 2/3 vote even after members had left, p. 476. | Yes, assembly is the judge of questions incidental to voting, p. 409; two-thirds vote protects absentees if members have left, p. 401. | 45 | Yes, members can challenge an election and assembly can declare it void, pp. 170-1. | Yes, assembly decides what to do in case of misunderstanding, p. 134. | Yes, vote by ballot can be reconsidered or rescinded, p. 38. | Yes, assembly can decide to invalidate a challenged vote, p. 205. |

© American Institute of Parliamentarians. All rights reserved.

Appendix A

| No | Issue | Answer | RONR 11th. Ed | § | AIPSC | Cannon | Demeter | Riddick |
|---|---|---|---|---|---|---|---|---|
| 181 | After first ballot resulting in no election, three members arrive before polls close for second ballot. May they vote? | Yes, p. 476. | Yes, right to vote, if in time for subsequent ballot, pp. 252, 286, and can be reopened by M vote if enter after polls close, pp. 286, 415. | 31 | Yes, right to vote if in time for subsequent ballot, p. 146. | Yes, doors are closed on a verification vote not on a new vote, p. 123. | Yes, those inside polling place when polls close entitled to vote, p. 136; can vote on "further voting," p. 137, late arrivals can vote on subsequent ballots, p. 242. | Yes, all members present who wish to vote before polls close may vote, p. 142-3; members who arrive late may vote on subsequent ballot, p. 92. |
| 182 | Can tellers vote? | Yes, p. 476. | Yes, p. 414. | 45 | Yes, all members have a right to vote, p. 146, no express preclusion for tellers. | Yes, no express preclusion, pp. 169, 133-4. | Yes, p. 242. | Yes, no express preclusion, pp. 190-1. |
| 183 | Can a candidate serve as a teller? | Yes, but known candidate for prominent office should not be appointed, p. 476. | Yes, only conflict of interest precludes selection, p. 414, and serving as a teller shouldn't be a penalty (analogy to nomination), p. 433. | 45 | No, by analogy to nominating committee, should resign if nominated, p. 163. | Yes, tellers just report and assembly serves as ultimate authority, pp. 133-4. | No, nominees should not be appointed tellers but can represent candidates or factions, p. 245. | Yes, no express preclusion, pp. 190-1. |
| 184 | Where there is only one ticket and no election procedure specified in the bylaws: (a) Can secretary cast the ballot? (b) Can a member move to make the vote unanimous? | (a) Yes; (b) Yes, but one negative vote defeats the motion, pp. 476-7. | (a) Yes, unless ballot required, p. 413; (b) Yes, by unanimous consent, pp. 410, 54-6, and must be by ballot where ballot required, p. 413. | 45 | (a) Yes; (b) Yes, by general consent, (b) pp. 148, 169. Both are out of order where a ballot is required, p. 151. | (a) Yes; (b) Yes, by unanimous consent, pp. 124-5. Both are out of order where a ballot is required because secrecy is impaired, p. 158. | (a) Yes; (b) Yes, by unanimous consent, bylaws should include both mechanisms, p. 245. Out of order where ballot is required, p. 245. | (a) Yes, p. 203; (b) No, p. 204. |

© American Institute of Parliamentarians. All rights reserved.

Appendix A

| No | Issue | Answer | RONR 11th Ed | § | AIPSC | Cannon | Demeter | Riddick |
|---|---|---|---|---|---|---|---|---|
| 185 | If nominating ballot is unanimous except for one vote, is it necessary to move for secretary to cast one ballot? | Yes, or elect in some other way. Nominating ballots never elect, p. 477. | Yes, results in only nominations, p. 437. Should have electing ballot rather than secretary cast one ballot. | 46 | Yes, results in only nominations, pp. 160, 169. | Yes, nomination is not election, pp. 129-34. | Yes, results in only nominations, p. 241. | Yes, results in only nominations p. 123. |
| 186 | What is the correct procedure for secretary casting ballot? | Assembly directs, secretary actually casts ballot. Not a real ballot and not allowed where ballot required, p. 477. | Not a real ballot and not allowed where ballot required, p. 413. Better to proceed explicitly by unanimous consent, p. 410. | 45 | As bylaws specify, p. 151, but better to proceed explicitly by general consent, p. 169. | Better to proceed explicitly by unanimous consent, pp. 124-5. | Assembly directs secretary to cast ballot if bylaws explicitly provide or bylaws require M of "votes cast," p. 245. | Requires motion and secretary must actually cast ballot and chair announce result p. 203. Not recommended even where bylaws allow. |
| 187 | Where constitution requires election of officers by ballot can secretary cast ballot where there is only one nomination for each office? | No, election must be by ballot, p. 477. | No, must be by ballot and motion to have secretary cast one ballot is out of order, p. 413. | 45 | No, must be by ballot and motion to dispense with ballot is out of order unless specified in bylaws, p. 151. | No, must be by ballot to preserve members' right to secrecy. p. 158. | Depends on language of constitution: Yes, if M of ballots "cast"; No if M of members present unless no objection, p. 245. | No, constitution ballot requirement cannot be suspended even by unanimous vote, p. 203. |
| 188 | Can secretary cast one ballot where balloting is required, there is only one candidate and no objection? | No, one ballot procedure must be in constitution to be used at all, p. 477. | No, bylaw provision requiring ballot can't be suspended unless bylaws so provide, pp. 263, 412. | 25 | No, motion to dispense with ballot is out of order unless also specified in bylaws, p. 151. | No, bylaws can't be suspended, p. 71. | No, not unless bylaws allow ballot by M of "votes cast" or explicitly allow the secretary to cast one ballot, p. 245. | No, constitution ballot requirement cannot be suspended even by unanimous vote, p. 203. |

© American Institute of Parliamentarians. All rights reserved.

Appendix A

| No | Issue | Answer | RONR 11th Ed | § | AIPSC | Cannon | Demeter | Riddick |
|---|---|---|---|---|---|---|---|---|
| 189 | Is it proper for constitution to provide for directed ballot by unanimous consent where there is only one nominee or one person receives a large majority on nominating ballot? | Yes, but "large majority" should be quantified, p. 478. | Yes, any suspension of ballot procedure must be set forth in the bylaws, pp. 263, 413. | 25 | Yes, suspension of ballot procedure must be specified in the bylaws, p. 151. | Yes, bylaws can't be suspended so mechanism must be specified in bylaws themselves, p. 71. | Yes, directed ballot and general consent exceptions may be set forth in bylaws or constitution, p. 245. | Yes, but not recommended, p. 203. |
| 190 | When there are several nominees for the same position, if a member votes by voice for the first and the first is not elected, when the second is voted on may the member vote for the second? | Yes, each question is distinct and a member has a right to vote on each question, p. 478. | Yes, members may vote for each candidate in voice vote, pp. 442-3, can be nominated for several positions, each a separate question, p. 432. | 46 | Yes, members have right to vote on every question, p. 147. | Yes, members have right to vote, p. 52, not limited in voice vote election, p. 133. | Yes, member has duty to vote on every question, p. 37, right to vote on retake, p. 38, assembly votes again when no election, p. 247. | Yes, unless otherwise provided, pp. 92, 202-3. |
| 191 | Does presence of a non-member invalidate the election of officers? | No, not without a bylaw prohibiting non-members at elections, p. 478. | No, not unless the non-members vote and affect the result, p. 445. | 46 | No, guests generally permitted unless excluded by motion, p. 108. | No, guests generally permitted, p. 112. | No, presence of nonmembers who do not vote does not invalidate election, p. 243. | No, not unless nonmembers cast votes and affect result, p. 100. |
| 192 | Person declared elected. After meeting it was discovered that people voted who had not paid their dues and the votes might have affected the results. Does election stand? | Yes, dues don't affect right to vote absent bylaw or custom and even with bylaw no-one objected, p. 479. | Yes, arrears in dues without revocation of membership or disciplinary suspension does not affect right to vote absent bylaw to the contrary, p. 406. | 45 | Yes, member has a right to vote unless bylaws provide otherwise, pp. 260-1. | Yes, no explicit limitation on right to vote in election unless bylaws provide otherwise, p. 131. | Yes, arrears in dues without revocation of membership or disciplinary suspension does not affect right to vote absent bylaw to the contrary, pp. 306, 239. | Yes, member has a right to vote unless bylaws provide otherwise, p. 198. |

© American Institute of Parliamentarians. All rights reserved.

Appendix A

| No | Issue | Answer | RONR 11th Ed | § | AIPSC | Cannon | Demeter | Riddick |
|---|---|---|---|---|---|---|---|---|
| 193 | Is an election invalid if votes are cast by those not entitled to vote but no-one challenges their entitlement? | No, not if the improper votes are insufficient to affect the outcome, pp. 479-80. | No, not if the improper votes are insufficient to affect the result, pp. 445, 250-1. | 46 | No, not if the improper votes are insufficient to affect the result, p. 166. | No, not unless the assembly decides that election should be invalidated, p. 134. | No, not if the improper votes are insufficient to affect the result, pp. 248, 310. | No, not if the improper votes are insufficient to affect the result, p. 100, or not challenged at the time, pp. 141, 205. |
| 194 | What should be done if the ballot is being stuffed? | During balloting, stop, do over and expel those guilty; after, do over only if it could have affected result, p. 480. | Promptly challenge and correct any violations, p. 251; election is invalid only if improper votes are sufficient to affect the result, p. 445. | 23 | Promptly challenge and correct any violations, p. 170; election is invalid only if improper votes are sufficient to affect the result, pp. 166-7. | Promptly challenge and correct fraud; assembly also decides whether completed election should be invalidated, p. 134. | Promptly challenge and correct fraud; election is invalid only if improper votes are sufficient to affect the result, p. 248. | Promptly challenge and correct fraud; election is invalid only if improper votes are sufficient to affect the result, p. 206. |
| 195 | Can tellers omit from their report the fact that a candidate received only one vote? | No, they must give a full report unless the assembly decides otherwise, p. 480. | No, tellers record all votes, p. 415, and report all votes, p. 417. | 45 | No, tellers' report must include number of votes cast for each candidate, p. 168. | No, tellers report results; the assembly controls the election, p. 134. | No, tellers count the ballots and report the results, pp. 245-6. | Tellers' report must be arithmetically correct -- cannot omit any candidates or votes from report, pp. 190-2. |
| 196 | Ballot resulted in A ten votes, B nine votes, Blank one. Was A elected? | Yes, 10/19 is a M; blanks are not votes, p. 480. | Yes, more than half elects and blanks are abstentions, p. 415. | 45 | Yes, blank ballots are ignored and do not affect the number necessary to elect, p. 166. | Yes, a blank is like an abstention which is not a vote at all, p. 95. | Yes, more than half the votes cast elects, p. 246, not counting blanks, p. 247. | Yes, blanks are ignored, pp. 191, 100 ("not always tabulated"). |
| 197 | If a member is nominated but declines, are ballots cast for that member thrown out? | No, they are counted, if M, elected and may accept despite declining nomination, p. 480. | No, all ballots that indicate a preference are counted, p. 415. But if there's time, NC is revived and declining nominee replaced, p. 435. | 45 | No, legal ballots are all counted, pp. 165-6; member receiving the necessary number of votes is elected, p. 161. | No, tellers report all results, p. 134; M of ballots cast vote elects, p. 131. | No, if candidate is elected and does not decline, election effective, p. 244. But remove and replace if time, p. 239. | No, not illegal ballots, pp. 100-1 must be reported pp. 191-2.; M elects unless otherwise provided, p. 92. |

Appendix A

| No | Issue | Answer | RONR 11th. Ed | § | AIPSC | Cannon | Demeter | Riddick |
|---|---|---|---|---|---|---|---|---|
| 198 | Is motion to accept ticket a valid election? | Yes, as long as the bylaws do not require ballot elections in which case the motion is out of order, p. 480. | Yes, voice vote suffices in uncontested election where bylaws do not require a ballot, pp. 442-3. | 46 | Yes, by general consent if uncontested and bylaws do not require ballot, p. 169. | Yes, by consent, voice vote, division, counted vote, if ballot not required, but there are pitfalls, p. 133. | Yes, unchallenged acclamation is legal **even if bylaws require ballot**, p. 248. | Yes, acclamation or motion can be used to elect where uncontested unless bylaws preclude, pp. 92, 3. |
| 199 | What is the difference between reopening the polls and a second ballot? | Polls are reopened before ballots are counted to allow late votes; a second ballot occurs after votes are counted when offices remain unfilled, p. 481. | Polls are reopened before ballots are counted to allow late votes, p. 286; second and subsequent ballots occur after votes are counted when offices remain unfilled, p. 441. | 30 | Balloting procedure has no explicit mechanism for reopening polls, p. 151; repeated voting occur after votes are counted when offices remain unfilled, p. 141. | Polls are reopened before ballots are counted to allow late votes, p. 99; a second (runoff) ballot occurs after votes are counted when offices remain unfilled, p. 131. | Polls are reopened before ballots are counted to allow late votes, p. 137; second and subsequent ballots occur after votes are counted when offices remain unfilled, p. 246. | Polls are reopened before ballots are counted to allow late votes, p. 143; revotes occur after votes are counted when offices remain unfilled, p. 202. |
| 200 | Constitution provides three adverse votes reject a proposed member. Election resulted in three adverse votes but involved minor irregularities that have never been enforced. Can election be declared illegal? | No, there was no timely point of order, p. 481. (Tellers failed to count votes or members present; member voted without paying dues.) | No, there was no timely point of order, pp. 445, 250-1. Also unenforced irregularity may have established a voting custom that would need to be changed by motion, pp. 438-9. | 46 | No, there was no timely challenge, p. 170. | No, there was no timely challenge and this is not a major irregularity, like fraud, that would justify reconsideration, p. 134. | No, there was no timely challenge, pp. 248-9. Unenforced irregularity may have established a voting custom, requiring MN23 vote to change, p. 243. | No, there was no timely challenge, pp. 205, 141. Unenforced irregularity may have established a voting custom, M vote to change, p. 70. |

Appendix A

| No | Issue | Answer | RONR 11th. Ed | § | AIPSC | Cannon | Demeter | Riddick |
|---|---|---|---|---|---|---|---|---|
| 201 | Bylaws changed from annual election of officers to staggered two year terms. First election in even year said nothing about terms. Do those in odd-year positions only serve a single year? | Yes, bylaws require that those offices be filled in odd-years, p. 482. | Yes, bylaw amendment can even affect incumbents absent proviso to the contrary so here clearly affects officers elected after amendment, pp. 597-8. | 57 | Yes, the bylaws govern when offices are filled and hence the terms of office, p. 183. | Yes, the bylaws govern the terms of office, p. 169. | Yes, bylaw amendment can even affect incumbents absent proviso to the contrary so here clearly affects officers elected after amendment, p. 180. | Yes, the bylaws govern the terms of office, pp. 192-3. |
| 202 | Election of secretary by customary ballot resulted in a tie. One candidate moved to elect the other by acclamation. Chair ruled motion out of order, appealed, reversed. Was election proper? | Yes, nomination effectively withdrawn, ballot not required by bylaws, p. 482. | Yes, acclamation possible where only one nominee and ballot not required, pp. 442-3. Customary ballot procedure can be changed by motion, pp. 438-9. | 46 | Yes, alternatives to ballot, including acclamation, may be used where bylaws do not require ballot, p. 169. | Yes, election can be by acclamation and other methods when bylaws do not require ballot, p. 133. | Yes, unchallenged acclamation is legal, p. 248. Nominee may withdraw, p. 239. | Yes, acclamation or motion can be used to elect where uncontested unless bylaws preclude, pp. 92, 3. |
| 203 | Secretary cast ballot for slate according to custom even though bylaws require election by ballot. Was election legal? | Yes, no timely point of order raised, pp. 482-3. But compare answer to question no. 188, p. 477. | No, bylaw provision requiring ballot can't be suspended unless bylaws so provide, pp. 263, 412-3. | 25 | No, motion to dispense with ballot is out of order unless also specified in bylaws, p. 151. | No, bylaws can't be suspended, p. 71. | Yes, unless there was an objection raised at the time vote was taken, p. 245. | No, constitution ballot requirement cannot be suspended even by unanimous vote, p. 203. |
| 204 | Bylaws require election by ballot but secretary was directed to cast single ballot. Was election legal? | Yes, a law ignored for years can't suddenly be enforced, pp. 483-4. | No, bylaw provision requiring ballot can't be suspended unless bylaws so provide, pp. 263, 412. In the absence of bylaw, custom must be changed by motion first, pp. 438-9. | 25 | No, motion to dispense with ballot is out of order unless also specified in bylaws, p. 151. | No, bylaws can't be suspended, p. 71. | Yes, unless there was an objection raised at the time vote was taken, p. 245. | No, bylaw ballot requirement cannot be suspended even by unanimous vote, p. 203. |

© American Institute of Parliamentarians. All rights reserved.

Appendix A

| No | Issue | Answer | RONR 11th. Ed | § | AIPSC | Cannon | Demeter | Riddick |
|---|---|---|---|---|---|---|---|---|
| 205 | Constitution requires election of officers at annual meeting in April. Annual meeting adjourned until November so incumbents could serve during state convention. Was action unconstitutional? | Yes, but impractical to correct so let the action stand, p. 484. | Yes, rules in bylaws can't be suspended, p. 263, and meeting can't be adjourned beyond the next regular meeting, p. 93. | 25 | Yes, election rules in bylaws can't be suspended, pp. 159, 86, 241, and meeting can't be adjourned beyond the next regular meeting, p. 107. | Yes, bylaws can't be suspended, p. 71, and adjournment to a later time is typically a few days later, p. 137. | Yes, bylaws can't be suspended, p. 133, and meeting can't be recessed for more than a short time, such as lunch, p. 112. | Yes, bylaws cannot be suspended, p 188, and meeting can't be adjourned beyond next regularly scheduled meeting, p. 5. |
| 206 | When all officers are elected on a single ballot, is the number of votes cast the total number of votes or the number of votes cast for a particular office? | The number of votes cast for a particular office, p. 485. | The number of votes cast for a particular office; each section is treated like a separate ballot, p. 417. | 45 | The number of votes cast for a particular office, p. 168. | A candidate must receive support from a majority of those present and voting (for that office implied), p. 131. | The number of votes cast for each particular office, p. 242. | A candidate must receive support from a majority of those present and voting (for that office implied), pp. 206-7. |
| 207 | Officers serve two year terms and are ineligible to serve for two years after term expires. Is officer who resigns after three months in office eligible to serve at next election? | Yes, serving more than half a term is considered to be filling a term, p. 485. | Yes, serving more than half a term is considered to be filling a term, p. 448. | 47 | Yes, partial term is not a barrier to election to a full term, p. 183. | Yes, assembly could allow in the absence of bylaw or standing rule, p. 131; no rule in Cannon. | Yes, only serving more than half a term is considered to be filling a term, p. 244. | Yes, serving more than half a term is considered to be filling a term, p. 193. |
| 208 | Bylaws say that election is by ballot but in case of a tie, tellers shall obey instructions of club. Can tie be broken by drawing lots? | Yes, but always better to repeat balloting, p. 485. | Yes, bylaws may define election procedure, p. 573, but preferential or repeat balloting recommended, pp. 428, 441. | 56 | Yes, tie elections are resolved by repeat balloting or method chosen by assembly, p. 142. | Yes, assembly can decide in the absence of bylaw or standing rule, p. 131. | Yes, tie breaking by lot specifically mentioned; method should be in bylaws, p. 246. | Yes, but tie breaking mechanism should be in bylaws, p. 204. |

© American Institute of Parliamentarians. All rights reserved.

Appendix A

| No | Issue | Answer | RONR 11th. Ed | § | AIPSC | Cannon | Demeter | Riddick |
|---|---|---|---|---|---|---|---|---|
| 209 | If voter writes in candidate but doesn't follow directions to erase other candidates or put a cross opposite write-in, is vote illegal? | No, the ballot shows without doubt the selection of the voter, p. 486. | No, the choice of the voter is clear and technical errors do not invalidate, p. 416. | 45 | No, intent of the voter is clear despite technical errors, p. 166. | No, unless bylaw, standing rule or assembly make it illegal, p. 131; no rule in Cannon. | No, intent is obvious when name is written in, p. 211. | No, intent of the voter is clear despite technical errors, pp. 101, 205. |
| 210 | Officer narrowly elected but tellers failed to report two votes they rejected as illegal (one missing teller endorsement, other contained name of voter). Should these two votes have been included in the number of votes cast? | Yes, votes cast must include legal and illegal votes and assembly should decide legality, pp. 486-7. Should have been counted -- legal voters and choice clear. | Yes, votes cast must include legal and illegal votes; doubtful votes must be reported to the chair who asks assembly to decide, pp. 415-6. | 45 | Yes, both legal and illegal ballots must be reported to the assembly, with reasons for rejecting illegal ballots, p. 168. (Requires M of **legal** votes cast) Here intent of voters in clear; should be counted. | Yes, tellers must report to the assembly and let assembly decide how to interpret the results, p. 134. (Requires M of votes) | Yes, tellers report all votes cast, pp. 246, 249. (Requires M of votes cast) | Yes, tellers must report illegal ballots, pp. 191-2 (Requires M of votes cast) |
| 211 | Australian ballot yields: president - A 46, B (write in) 45; director B 67, 100 present and voting. Tellers rejected 3 for A and 6 for B -- lacking X. Who is president? | B is president -- vote for A is clear if single slate ballot unmodified, vote for B is clear if written in, pp. 487-8. | B is president; choice of voters clear and technical errors do not invalidate, p. 416. | 45 | B is president; choice of voters clear and technical errors do not invalidate, p. 166. | B is president; assembly decides but intent of voters is clear, p. 131. | B is president; choice of voters clear (cross not necessary for write-in), p. 211. (Australian ballot -- voters use X to mark their choice, p. 247.) | B is president, intent of voters is clear despite technical errors, p. 101, 205. |
| 212 | Bylaws require ballot, candidate with "highest vote" elected, tellers report only winners. Is this appropriate? | Yes, plurality authorized by bylaws but limited report makes it hard to detect fraud, pp. 488-9. | Yes, plurality authorized by bylaws but repeat or preferential better, pp. 404-5, and tellers should report all results, p. 417. | 44 | Yes, plurality authorized by bylaws but repeat or runoff better, pp. 140-1, and better for tellers to report all results, pp. 167-8. | Yes, plurality authorized by bylaws, p. 131. | Yes, plurality authorized by bylaws, p. 246, but better for tellers to report all results, pp. 245-6. | Yes, plurality authorized by bylaws, p. 140; tellers should report all results, pp. 191-2. |

© American Institute of Parliamentarians. All rights reserved.

Appendix A

| No | Issue | Answer | RONR 11th. Ed | § | AIPSC | Cannon | Demeter | Riddick |
|---|---|---|---|---|---|---|---|---|
| 213 | Bylaws have elaborate nominating process: election, notice, consent. (a) Are write ins counted? (b) If they receive M are they elected? | (a) Yes; (b) Yes, consent requirement does not apply to those not nominated, p. 489. | (a) Yes, pp. 430-1; (b) Yes, pp. 430-1, consent requirement does not apply to those not nominated, p. 434. | 46 | (a) Yes; (b) Yes, p. 161. | (a) Yes; (b) Yes, except where prohibited in bylaws, p. 130. | (a) Yes; (b) Yes, p. 247. | (a) Yes; (b) Yes, except where prohibited in bylaws, p. 205. |
| 214 | Ballot section on officers correct but section on directors has too many votes. Does ballot for officers count? | Yes, p. 489. | Yes, each section treated as separate ballot, pp. 416-7; vote for too many candidates is illegal ballot, p. 416. | 45 | Yes, each section treated as separate ballot; vote for too many candidates is illegal ballot, pp. 168, 166. | Yes, officers received valid vote, p. 131. | Yes, each section treated as separate ballot, p. 242; vote for too many candidates is illegal ballot, pp. 247-8. | Yes, each section treated as separate ballot; vote for too many candidates is illegal ballot, p. 100. |
| 215 | Can voters vote for only one director or delegate when they are entitled to several votes to fill multiple positions? | Yes, p. 489. | Yes, only too many votes is illegal and blanks don't invalidate other sections, pp. 416-7. | 45 | Yes, "bullet" voting allowed unless bylaws prohibit, p. 275. | Yes, absent contrary bylaw or rule, that candidate received valid vote, p. 131. | Yes, "bullet" voting allowed unless bylaws prohibit, p. 247. | Yes, "bullet" voting allowed, p. 199. |
| 216 | President intends to resign. Constitution requires vacancies be filled at regular meeting in same manner as annual meeting -- nominating committee, two weeks' notice. Can president be nominated from the floor and elected the same day? | No, set adjourned meeting and follow nominating process, p. 490. | No, notice of filling vacancy is always required unless bylaws provide otherwise; here must follow procedure in constitution, p. 575. | 56 | No, notice of vacancy should be given, must follow constitution or bylaw procedure, pp. 184-5. | No, must follow constitution, bylaw or standing rule procedure, pp. 2, 130. | No, must follow constitution or bylaw procedure, p. 256. | No, notice of vacancy should be given, must follow constitution or bylaw procedure, pp. 196-7. |

© American Institute of Parliamentarians. All rights reserved.

Appendix A

| No | Issue | Answer | RONR 11th. Ed | § | AIPSC | Cannon | Demeter | Riddick |
|---|---|---|---|---|---|---|---|---|
| 217 | When bylaws make no provision for special election for filling vacancy, can an election be held at any time other than an annual meeting? | Yes, at any regular meeting if notice of the election has been given at a previous meeting, pp. 490-1. | Yes, at any regular meeting with prior notice if filling an office, pp. 445, 291, 575. | 46 | Yes, promptly at regular meeting with prior notice, pp. 184-5. | Yes, should be in bylaws but, if not, assembly decides, p. 134. | Yes, where no bylaw provision, vacancy is filled by special election at any regular or special meeting with notice, pp. 180, 256. | Yes, vacancies should be filled promptly, special election can be called with prior notice, pp. 196-7. |
| 218 | Can the president of a local society call a special meeting in another part of the state? | No, it must be the usual place if possible or a convenient place, p. 492. | No, place of meetings should be specified in a special rule and the rule can be suspended or amended only by the assembly, pp. 575, 89-93. | 56 | No, place of meetings as established by rule or custom can't be changed without notice to all members, p. 105, and can't prevent members attending, p. 260. | No, model bylaws do not give president that power, p. 150; choice of location can't interfere with right of members to attend, p. 52. | No, choice of location can't interfere with right of members to attend, p. 305. | No, place of meetings should be in the standing rules which only the members can change, p. 124, and can't interfere with right to attend, p. 111. |
| 219 | Should the president stand during the transaction of business? | Yes, to put a question, rule or speak on appeal, or whenever speaking in a large assembly, p. 492. | Yes, to put a question, rule or speak on appeal, call to order, adjourn, or whenever speaking in a large assembly, p. 451. | 47 | Yes, when speaking, p. 273, and whenever necessary to maintain control, pp. 174, 273. | Yes, generally at a podium on a raised platform for visibility in large meetings, p. 5. | Yes, to open meeting, introduce, put questions, speak, rule, discuss appeal, adjourn, and when needed, pp. 39, 250. | Yes, whenever good judgment requires, p. 146. |
| 220 | Does the president have control over where members sit? | No, not unless there is a special rule, p. 492. | No, not among president's powers, pp. 449-50. | 47 | No, not among president's powers, pp. 174-6. | No, not among president's powers, pp. 4-5. | No, not among president's powers, pp. 250-2. | No, not among president's powers, p. 126. |
| 221 | When the president is absent, would it be proper to elect the secretary to the chair and elect a secretary pro tem? | Yes, if no VP is present, but usually better to have secretary call for nominations for chair pro tem, pp. 492-3. | Yes, if no VP is present, but usually better to have secretary call for nominations for chair pro tem, p. 459. | 47 | Yes, if officer next in rank is not present, p. 176. | Yes, organization decides its own order of succession of the chair, usually in the bylaws, p. 4. | Yes, in the absence of a VP, assembly can decide, pp. 40, 149. | Yes, if no VP is present, but recommended that secretary call for nominations for chair pro tem, p. 148. |

Appendix A

| No | Issue | Answer | RONR 11th. Ed | § | AIPSC | Cannon | Demeter | Riddick |
|---|---|---|---|---|---|---|---|---|
| 222 | Is it improper for president to ask secretary to take the chair while he addresses the body when a VP is present? | Yes, p. 493. | Yes, sequence is VP, appointed pro tem, elected pro tem, pp. 452-3. | 47 | Yes, sequence is president elect, VP, other neutral officer, p. 176. | Yes, unless bylaws provide otherwise, p. 4. | Yes, sequence is VP, appointed pro tem, elected pro tem, p. 40. | Yes, VPs step in when chair steps down, p. 148. |
| 223 | Should the chair ever read a paper without calling someone else to the chair? | Yes, only needs to step down to debate, when involved or to make report requiring action, p. 493. | Yes, only needs to relinquish the chair to debate, p. 394, when involved, p. 451, or in COTW, p. 530. | 47 | Yes, may present important facts but should leave chair to debate or if involved personally, p. 176. | Yes, as long as impartiality is preserved; step down only when entering debate, p. 23-4. | Yes, chair can inform assembly but to make or second motions or debate should step down, pp. 41-2. | Yes, the chair can clarify and explain but not participate in debate without vacating the chair, p. 147. |
| 224 | When the president makes a report with the VP in the chair, can the president move adoption of his recommendations? | No, p. 493. | No, motions to adopt recommendations of executive officers should be made by a member other than the reporting officer, pp. 476-7. | 48 | Yes, it's the **presiding officer** who should preserve impartiality, p. 176. | Yes, it's the **chair** who should preserve impartiality, pp. 23-4. | Yes, it's the **chair** who should preserve impartiality, pp. 41-2. | Yes, it's the **chair** who should preserve impartiality, p. 40. |
| 225 | Can the chair appoint a secretary pro tem? | Yes, by general consent, p. 493. | Yes, by general consent, but otherwise secretary pro tem is elected, pp. 459-60. | 47 | Yes, secretary usually elected but pro tem could be appointed by consent, pp. 178-9. | Yes, secretary usually elected but pro tem could be appointed by consent, pp. 3, 133. | Yes, secretary usually elected but pro tem could be appointed by consent, pp. 252, 309-10. | Yes, p. 148. |
| 226 | (a) Can president vote once to tie a vote and then cast deciding vote? (b) Can president ever vote twice? | (a) No; (b) No, right to vote comes from membership not office, p. 493. | (a) No; (b) No, chair cannot vote twice, pp. 405-6. | 44 | (a) No; (b) No, chair cannot vote twice, unless bylaws allow two votes to break a deadlock, pp. 142-3. | (a) No; (b) No, chair cannot vote twice, p. 8. | (a) No; (b) No, chair cannot vote twice unless bylaws give 2 votes or by unanimous consent, p. 45. | (a) No; (b) No, chair has only same right to vote as any member, p. 146. |

© American Institute of Parliamentarians. All rights reserved.

Appendix A

| No | Issue | Answer | RONR 11th. Ed | § | AIPSC | Cannon | Demeter | Riddick |
|---|---|---|---|---|---|---|---|---|
| 227 | When ballot result has been announced, may president vote if he has not done so before? | No, not without consent, p. 493. | No, chair can vote on any ballot but only with assembly permission after polls close, p. 414. | 45 | No, chair can vote on any ballot at same time as other members, pp. 142-3. | No, chair can vote on any ballot at same time as other members, p. 8. | No, chair can vote on any ballot at same time as other members, p. 45. | No, chair can vote on any ballot at same time as other members, p. 146. |
| 228 | Should the president cast the deciding vote in case of a tie on a ballot vote? | No, president is entitled to vote before ballots counted not after, p. 494. | No, chair can vote on any ballot but only with assembly permission after polls close, p. 414. | 45 | No, chair can vote on any ballot at same time as other members, pp. 142-3. | No, chair can vote on any ballot at same time as other members, p. 8. | No, chair can vote on any ballot at same time as other members, p. 45. | No, chair can vote on any ballot at same time as other members, p. 146. |
| 229 | Does president have any more authority in the chair than any other presiding officer? | No, can't reverse temporary chair but assembly can reverse either, p. 494. | No, chairman pro tem has same powers as president, pp. 452-3, 448-50, except power to appoint committees, p. 495. | 47 | No, same presiding powers, pp. 174-6. | No, same powers, pp. 4-8. | No, same powers, pp. 40-3. | No, same powers in chair but can't appoint, serve ex officio, speak for organization or make non-procedural rulings, p. 148. |
| 230 | Should president leave chair during annual election in case he's a candidate? | No, not unless he chooses to do so, p. 494. | No, chair should not hesitate to put motion to elect even if he's included, pp. 451-2. | 47 | No, chair presides during election when a candidate, p. 176. | No, chair may preside as long as not entering debate, p. 23. | No, chair may preside as long as bylaws do not require stepping down, p. 243. | No, chair may preside as long as not entering debate, p. 126. |
| 231 | At annual meeting, all officers elected except president. Who should preside at next meeting? | The VP unless bylaws provide that president serves until successor elected, p. 494. | The VP, p. 452, unless bylaws provide that president serves until successor elected, pp. 573-4. | 47 | The VP, p. 177, unless bylaws provide that president serves until successor elected, p. 184. | The VP, p. 4, except as provided in the bylaws, pp. 4, 151. | The VP, p. 255, unless bylaws provide that president serves until successor elected, p. 256. | The VP unless bylaws provide otherwise, p. 127. |

Appendix A

| No | Issue | Answer | RONR 11th. Ed | § | AIPSC | Cannon | Demeter | Riddick |
|---|---|---|---|---|---|---|---|---|
| 232 | (a) Should chair take matters from the table? (b) Should chair announce special or general orders? | (a) No, but may suggest and grant preference; (b) Yes, has duty to bring up orders, p. 494. | (a) No, but may suggest and grant preference over new MM, pp. 359, 300-1; (b) Yes, duty to bring up orders when appropriate, pp. 368-9. | 41 | (a) No, table kills and only assembly may reconsider, p. 71; (b) Yes, has duty to bring up scheduled agenda items, p. 119. | (a) No, postponed item automatically on agenda; only assembly may reconsider postponement, pp. 105, 168; (b) Yes, chair must follow agenda, p. 82. | (a) No, normal motion, p. 169; (b) Yes, has duty to bring up orders, pp. 104-6. | (a) No, table kills and only assembly may reconsider, p. 189; (b) Yes, has duty to bring up orders, pp. 131-2. |
| 233 | The president is ex-officio member of all committees. If he is absent, would VP attend? | No, president only, no obligation to attend and doesn't count towards quorum, p. 494. | No, president (not chair) is ex officio, no obligation to attend and **doesn't count** towards quorum, pp. 456-7, 497. | 47 | No, president (not chair) is ex officio, but is full working member and **counts** toward quorum, p. 190. | No, ex officio is power of office, p. 3. | No, president only, p. 274. | No, president only -- power of office, p. 94. |
| 234 | The bylaws make the president a member ex officio of all committees. Did the NC have a right to fail to notify him of their meetings? | No, president must be notified like any other member, but president should not be made an NC member, p. 495. | No, president ex officio has same rights as other committee members but should not be a member of NC, pp. 456-7. | 47 | No, president ex officio has same rights as other committee members but should not be a member of NC, p. 190. | No, ex officio members serve like any others, p. 3. | No, president ex officio has same rights as other committee members but should not be a member of NC, pp. 274, 240. | No, ex officio members are full-fledged members, p. 94, but president should not be on NC, p. 122. |
| 235 | What is the authority of a chair ex officio? | The same as a chair selected by vote of the assembly, p. 495. | All presiding officers have the same authority, p. 448. | 47 | All presiding officers have the same authority, pp. 174-6. | All presiding officers have the same authority, pp. 4-5. | All presiding officers have the same authority, p. 40. | All presiding officers have the same authority, pp. 40-1. |
| 236 | President elected and resigns before first meeting. Can he be called a past-president? | Yes, election took effect immediately, p. 495. | Yes, election takes effect immediately absent bylaw to the contrary, p. 444. | 46 | Yes, election takes effect immediately absent bylaw to the contrary, p. 170. | Yes, election takes effect immediately absent bylaw to the contrary, p. 134. | Yes, election takes effect immediately absent bylaw or proviso to the contrary, p. 244. | Yes, election takes effect immediately absent bylaw or proviso to the contrary, p. 92. |

© American Institute of Parliamentarians. All rights reserved.

Appendix A

| No | Issue | Answer | RONR 11th Ed | § | AIPSC | Cannon | Demeter | Riddick |
|---|---|---|---|---|---|---|---|---|
| 237 | When president is a working delegate at a convention and reports from podium, how should president refer to herself? | "Your working delegate" and "your president" OK. "The chair" not and "I" only if a report of one delegate, p. 495. | Use official title that will avoid confusion, so "this delegate" or "your president" would be appropriate, pp. 22-4. | 3 | Use impersonal title, so "this delegate" or "your president" would be appropriate, p. 130. | Use formal, impersonal procedure, p. 108. | Use impersonal title, so "this delegate" or "your president" would be appropriate, p. 31. | Use formal, impersonal title, so "this delegate" or "your president" would be appropriate, p. 71. |
| 238 | When president leaves chair, does he lose all but administrative power? | Yes, loses presiding power but retains any other powers, p. 496. | Yes, loses presiding power, pp. 452-3, but retains any other powers, pp. 456-7. | 47 | Yes, loses presiding power, p. 176, but retains any other powers, pp. 173-4. | Yes, loses presiding power, p. 4, but retains any other powers, p. 151. | Yes, loses presiding power, p. 251, but retains any other powers, pp. 250-2. | Yes, loses presiding power, p. 126, but retains any other powers, pp. 125-6. |
| 239 | Does president have authority to decide questions relating to administration of society policy between meetings? | No, but might have to make decisions and have them ratified by the board or the assembly, p. 496. | No, not without bylaw provision, p. 456, but might have to make decisions and have them ratified by the board or the assembly, pp. 124-5. | 47 | No, p. 174, but might have to make decisions and have them ratified by the board or the assembly, pp. 41-3. | No, p. 4. | No, pp. 250-2, but might have to make decisions and have the board or the assembly ratify, p. 168. | No, pp. 145-6, but might have to make decisions and have the board or the assembly ratify, pp. 163-4. |
| 240 | When a chair tenders resignation, does it take effect immediately upon receipt by secretary? | No, a reasonable time is allowed for acceptance by the appointing body, p. 496. | No, a reasonable time is allowed for acceptance by the appointing body, p. 291. | 32 | Yes, unless it has a future effective date, pp. 265-6. | Yes, unless resignation or bylaws provide otherwise. No specific rule in Cannon. | Yes, unless prospective or conditional, p. 205. | Yes, unless it has a future effective date, p. 174. |
| 241 | In organizing a society, is it proper to elect a president who has not yet signed the constitution? | Yes, if he accepts, he should sign and become a member but can preside without doing so, pp. 496-7. | No, election is limited to members, p. 560. | 54 | No, election is limited to members unless otherwise provided in the bylaws, p. 161. | No, election is limited to eligible members, p. 130. | No, election is limited to members, pp. 241, 239. | No, election is limited to members, pp. 121, 123, 92 |

Appendix A

| No | Issue | Answer | RONR 11th. Ed | § | AIPSC | Cannon | Demeter | Riddick |
|---|---|---|---|---|---|---|---|---|
| 242 | Can the chair refuse to recognize a member to make a nominating speech? | No, nominations are debatable, p. 497. | No, nominations are debatable, pp. T18, 435-6. | 46 | No, not if customary to allow nominator to give reasons or if nominating committee gives reasons, p. 160. | No, speeches are contemplated but can be time-limited, pp. 129-30. | No, brief nominating speeches are allowed, p. 300. | No, members have a right to explain their nominations, p. 121. |
| 243 | (a) What can assembly do when chair won't put motions? (b) Can assembly get rid of chair? (c) Can member move to have chair surrendered? (d) Can anyone other than chair put question? | (a) Raise POO, appeal; (b) Yes, if he is not president, move to declare chair vacant; (c)Yes, under certain circumstances; (d) Yes, pp. 497-8. | (a) Raise POO, appeal, p. 650; (b) Yes, at least temporarily, pp. 651-2; (c) Yes, unless bylaws provided fixed term, pp. 653-4; (d) Yes, p. 651. | 62 | (a) Raise POO, appeal, pp. 90-3, 83-5; (b) Yes, for cause, pp. 185-6; (c)Yes, p. 186; (d) No, only presiding officer puts question, p. 306. | (a) Raise POO, appeal, pp. 114-5, 143; (b) and (c) Yes, possibly by motion to reconsider appointment, p. 126-9; (d) No, no explicit authorization. | (a) Raise POO, appeal, pp. 121-4, 126-32, 204; (b) and (c) Yes, for cause, by 2/3 vote, p. 251; (d) Yes, VP, p. 204. | (a) Raise POO, appeal, pp. 140-1, 22-3; (b) Yes, removal for cause, pp. 85-6; (c) Yes, motion to suspend chair, p. 86; (d) Yes, p. 85. |
| 244 | The chair should not end debate but should the chair allow debate to extend beyond the time set for adjournment in the order of business? | No, unless the rules are suspended, the chair declares the meeting adjourned and the item carries over as unfinished business, p. 498 | No, unless assembly reschedules adjournment or extends debate, the chair declares the meeting adjourned and the item carries over as unfinished business, pp. 374-5. | 41 | No, unless assembly reschedules adjournment, the chair interrupts, declares the meeting adjourned and the item carries over as unfinished business, p. 81. | No, unless assembly amends the agenda, the chair declares the meeting adjourned, pp. 31, 82, 136-7. | No, unless assembly changes order of business, p. 19, the chair declares the meeting adjourned and the item carries over as unfinished business, p. 115. | No, unless assembly changes the agenda, pp. 7-8, the chair declares the meeting adjourned, p. 4, and the item carries over as unfinished business, p. 196. |
| 245 | Should chair call for formal motion to adjourn after business meeting before social hour? | No, can adjourn by consent after no response to call for further business, p. 498. | No, can adjourn by consent when scheduled hour arrives or after no response to call for further business, pp. 240-1. | 21 | No, can adjourn by consent when scheduled hour arrives or after no response to call for further business, p. 81. | No, can adjourn by unanimous consent, pp. 124-5. | No, can adjourn by unanimous consent, pp. 116, 309. | No, can adjourn by unanimous consent, pp. 4, 194-5. |

© American Institute of Parliamentarians. All rights reserved.

Appendix A

| No | Issue | Answer | RONR 11th. Ed | § | AIPSC | Cannon | Demeter | Riddick |
|---|---|---|---|---|---|---|---|---|
| 246 | If the chair is authorized to appoint a committee after the meeting adjourns, should the names be given to the secretary for insertion in the minutes? | No, the chair should announce the names at the next meeting and they should go in those minutes, p. 499. | No, the chair should announce the names at the next meeting and they should go in those minutes, p. 496. | 50 | No, the chair should announce the names at the next meeting and they should go in those minutes, pp. 190, 230-1. | No, the chair should announce the names at the next meeting and they should go in those minutes, pp. 135-6. | No, the chair should announce the names at the next meeting and they should go in those minutes, pp. 83, 21. | No, the chair should announce the names at the next meeting and they should go in those minutes, pp. 50, 113-6. |
| 247 | (a) Should minutes be "respectfully submitted"? (b) Can secretary make motions and vote? | (a) No, just name and "Secretary." (b) Yes, same as any member, p. 499. | (a) No, just name and "Secretary," p. 471; (b) Yes, like any member, pp. 3, 458-60 cf. p. 467 (parliamentarian). | 48 | (a) No, just name, signature and "Secretary," pp. 293, 296; (b) Yes, like any member, p. 179. | (a) No, just indicate who prepared them, p. 136; (b) Yes, only chair excepted, p. 7. | (a) Yes, pp. 24-5; (b) Yes, only chair excepted, p. 250. | (a) No, just name signature and title, pp. 115-6; (b) Yes, like any member, p. 180. |
| 248 | Is a motion in order to strike a portion of the minutes? | Yes, but if rules require that portion to be in the minutes a 2/3 vote is required, p. 499. | Yes, the usual rules of amendment apply to approval of the minutes, p. 354. See also, expunge, p. 310. | 41 | Yes, pp. 230-1. | Yes, the usual rules of amendment apply to approval of the minutes, p. 136. | Yes, amend applies to approval of the minutes, pp. 21-2. See also, expunge, p. 167. | Yes, p. 114. See also, expunge, pp. 94-5. |
| 249 | If member requests that his vote be recorded in the minutes, is it proper for the chair to handle by general consent? | Yes, if no objection, chair directs secretary to make the entry, puts to vote otherwise, p. 499. | Yes, if there is no objection, chair directs secretary to make the entry, puts to vote otherwise, pp. 470, 54-6. | 48 | Yes, if there is no objection, chair directs secretary to make the entry, puts to vote otherwise, pp. 230, 148. | Yes, degree of detail is flexible and assembly should control content of minutes, pp. 135, 124-5. | Yes, if there is no objection, chair directs secretary to make the entry, puts to vote otherwise, p. 23. | Yes, if there is no objection, chair directs secretary to make the entry puts to vote otherwise, pp. 114-6, 97. |
| 250 | Are names of makers of motions always entered in the minutes? | Yes, not seconds, but society can decide otherwise, p. 499. | Yes, but not seconds, p. 470. | 48 | No, can be confusing if motion modified, p. 229. | No, not required, but degree of detail is flexible, pp. 8, 135-6. | Yes, but not seconds unless required, p. 24. | No, only if society requires but is usual practice, p. 114. |

Appendix A

| No | Issue | Answer | RONR 11th. Ed | § | AIPSC | Cannon | Demeter | Riddick |
|---|---|---|---|---|---|---|---|---|
| 251 | (a) Are lost and withdrawn motions omitted from minutes? (b) Are only approved motions entered in minutes? (c) When motion is reconsidered and lost, is that recorded in the minutes? | (a) No, MM, POO and appeals are entered even when lost; (b) No, lost MM are entered; (c) Yes, p. 500. | (a) No, lost MM, POO and appeals are entered; **withdrawn only if necessary for clarity**; (b) No, lost MM are entered; (c) Yes, pp. 469-70. | 48 | (a) No, lost MM entered, **withdrawn omitted if not stated by chair**; (b) No, lost MM are entered; (c) Yes, pp. 229-30. | (a) Yes; (b) No, record all actions; (c) Yes, pp. 135-6. | (a) No, lost MM entered, **withdrawn omitted**; (b) No, lost MM are entered; (c) Yes, p. 24. | (a) No, lost MM POO and appeals are entered; **withdrawn omitted unless vote taken**; (b) No, lost MM are entered; (c) Yes, pp. 114-6. |
| 252 | Must counted election vote be entered in the minutes? | Yes, unless rule or vote to suspend rules provides otherwise, p. 500. | Yes, unless rule or vote to suspend rules provides otherwise, p. 470. | 48 | Yes, counted ballot and roll call results must be recorded, p. 230. | Yes, for accuracy, accountability and legal record, pp. 120-2, 135-6. | Yes, all votes taken other than by voice should be recorded, p. 140. | Yes, record all counted votes, pp. 116, 87-8. |
| 253 | What is the preferred form of record for MM? | "On motion of Mr. X, it was resolved that ... "; "The following resolution offered by Mr. X was adopted: ... ", p. 500. | "Mr. X moved that .... The motion was adopted after debate," p. 472. "The resolution was adopted as follows: *Resolved ... "* p. 473. | 48 | "Mr. X moved (that/adoption of the following resolution).... The motion was (action taken)." p. 295. | No format prescribed, but must be accurate legal record of action taken, pp. 135-6. | "On motion of X, duly seconded, it was voted to ... " p. 24. | "Mr. X moved that .... Motion adopted." p. 115. |
| 254 | Is it enough to state who was elected or should report of tellers be recorded? | No, the full report of tellers should be recorded unless assembly orders otherwise, p. 500. | No, the tellers' report is entered in full in the minutes, p. 418. | 45 | No, details of ballot and roll call votes must be included in the minutes, pp. 230, 167-8. | No, tellers' report should be adopted, p. 134, included in minutes, pp. 135-6. | No, all votes taken other than by voice should be recorded, p. 140. | No, all counted votes must be recorded in the minutes, p. 116. |
| 255 | With monthly regular meetings from October to the annual meeting in April, what minutes are read at each meeting? | The minutes of the prior meeting; a committee is recommended to review the April minutes and report in October, pp. 500-1. | The minutes of the prior meeting; a committee is recommended to review and approve the April minutes, pp. 473-5. | 48 | The minutes of the prior meeting; a committee is recommended to review and/or approve the April minutes, pp. 231-3. | The minutes of the prior meeting, p. 8. | The minutes of the last meeting, p. 22, except April meeting which should be approved by a committee or board, p. 23. | The minutes of the previous meeting; a committee may review the April minutes, pp. 113-4. |

© American Institute of Parliamentarians. All rights reserved.

Appendix A

| No | Issue | Answer | RONR 11th. Ed | § | AIPSC | Cannon | Demeter | Riddick |
|---|---|---|---|---|---|---|---|---|
| 256 | Can presiding officer insert in the minutes anything that was not said or read during the meeting? | No, neither the president nor anyone else can do so, p. 501. | No, minutes should generally contain only what was done, p. 468. | 48 | No, minutes should contain only official actions in a meeting, p. 227. | No, minutes should be an accurate record, p. 8, 136. | No, minutes should contain only history of organization's acts, p. 21. | No, minutes should be a record of action taken, p. 113. |
| 257 | Should an annual convention of delegates approve the minutes of the last convention? | No, each convention should approve its own minutes through a committee or board, p. 501. | No, each convention should have a committee or board review and approve its minutes, pp. 474-5. | 48 | No, each convention should have a committee review and/or approve its minutes, p. 232. | Yes, "next meeting of assembly," pp. 8, 135-6. | No, each day approves previous day's minutes and last day approved by committee or board, p. 23. | Yes, but should be reviewed by a committee, p. 114. |
| 258 | May a society authorize its board of managers to approve the minutes? | Yes, p. 501. | Yes, although only recommended where next regular session will not be held within the quarter, pp. 474-5. | 48 | Yes, and recommended where assembly does not meet at least quarterly, p. 232-3. | Yes, no mechanism described but no limit either, pp. 8, 135-6, 70, 151-2. | Yes, explicitly for conventions, possibly for other meetings, pp. 23, 179. | Yes, explicitly provides for review, possibly delegation, pp. 114, 35-6. |
| 259 | Can anyone vote to amend the minutes whether they were present or not? | Yes, p. 501. | Yes, expressly provided, p. 355. | 41 | Yes, no express prohibition, pp. 231-2. | Yes, no express prohibition, pp. 135-6. | Yes, no express prohibition, pp. 21-5. | Yes, p. 1. |
| 260 | Are board minutes open to inspection by a club member who is not on the board? | No, not without board permission or club assembly order, p. 502. | No, not without board permission or a MN23MEM vote of the assembly, p. 487. | 49 | No, and no exception mechanism described, p. 196. | Depends on bylaws, pp. 158-9; no guidance in Cannon. | No, not without rule, vote of the assembly or custom, p. 23. | No, not without vote of the assembly or bylaw, p. 28. |

Appendix A

| No | Issue | Answer | RONR 11th. Ed | § | AIPSC | Cannon | Demeter | Riddick |
|---|---|---|---|---|---|---|---|---|
| 261 | Was it correct to show in the minutes that B moved an amendment to A's motion to which A consented? | No, before the motion is stated, it is a suggestion; after statement, the assembly must consent, p. 502. | No, before the motion is stated, it is a suggestion, not a motion; after statement, the assembly must consent, pp. 295-8; minutes record final wording, p. 469. | 33 | Yes, if not yet stated by the chair, p. 56; AIPSC does not distinguish between motion and suggestion. Minutes record original and final motion, p. 229. | Yes, if not yet stated by the chair, p. 102; Cannon does not distinguish motion from suggestion. Minutes detail is flexible, p. 135. | No, A can consent if not yet stated by the chair, p. 56, 70. Minutes record only MM adopted or lost, p. 24. | No, before the motion is stated, it is a suggestion, not a motion; after statement, the assembly must consent, pp. 12-3. Minutes show MM as moved and as approved, p. 114. |
| 262 | (a) Can a member be elected honorary president if they have never been president? (b) Is this customary? | (a) Yes; (b) No, p. 502. | (a) Yes; (b) No, as provided in bylaws, pp. 463-4. | 47 | (a) Yes; (b) No, as provided in bylaws, p. 181. | No specific guidance, pp. 159, 70. | (a) Yes; (b) No, p. 304. | (a) Yes; (b) No, as provided in bylaws, pp. 99-100. |
| 263 | Can office of honorary presidency be limited to past presidents? | Yes, but it is a title not an office, pp. 502-3. | Yes, but it is a title not an office, p. 463. | 47 | Yes, but it is a title not an office, p. 181. | Yes, can be limited like any bylaw provision, pp. 159, 70. | Yes, by bylaw provision or motion, p. 304. | Yes, but it is a title not an office, pp. 99-100. |
| 264 | Is there any rule against a retiring president being made an honorary president and then later being elected president or committee chair? | No, p. 503. | No, honorary titles in no way conflict with holding a regular office or being assigned a duty, p. 463. | 47 | No, honorary titles do not conflict with holding a regular office or exercising membership rights, p. 181. | No, honorary titles not covered, pp. 159, 70. | No, honorary status does not interfere with regular obligations and privileges, p. 304. | No, pp. 99-100. |
| 265 | Can an honorary president be a board or committee member or serve as a delegate? | Yes, if a member; honorary title does not take away any rights, p. 503. | Yes, if a member; honorary title does not take away any rights, p. 463. | 47 | Yes, if a member; honorary title does not take away any rights, p. 181. | Yes, if a member, p. 3. | Yes, if a member; honorary title does not remove other privileges, p. 304. | Yes, if a member and bylaws do not preclude, pp. 99-100. |

© American Institute of Parliamentarians. All rights reserved.

Appendix A

| No | Issue | Answer | RONR 11th. Ed | § | AIPSC | Cannon | Demeter | Riddick |
|---|---|---|---|---|---|---|---|---|
| 266 | Do honorary presidents have a right to attend and participate in board and committee meetings? | No, p. 503. | No, have only the right to attend and speak at assembly meetings, p. 463. | 47 | No, have only the right to attend and speak at assembly meetings, p. 181. | No, not unless bylaws provide, pp. 159, 70. | No, have only the right to attend and speak at assembly meetings, p. 304. | No, not unless bylaws provide, pp. 99-100. |
| 267 | Do honorary officers or members have the right to make motions or vote? | No, not by virtue of the honorary title, p. 503. | No, not unless a regular member or bylaws confer full membership rights, p. 463. | 47 | No, not by virtue of the honorary title, p. 181. | No, not unless a regular member, p. 3, or bylaws provide, pp. 159, 70. | No, not unless a regular member, p. 304. | No, not unless a regular member or bylaws provide pp. 99-100. |
| 268 | Can a chapter give an honorary regent the power to vote on the board? | No, not unless bylaws provide, p. 503. | No, not unless bylaws provide, p. 463. | 47 | No, not unless bylaws provide, p. 181. | No, not unless bylaws provide, pp. 159, 70. | No, not unless bylaws provide, p. 304. | No, not unless bylaws provide, pp. 99-100. |
| 269 | Can convention give a vote to honorary presidents where bylaws are silent? | No, right to vote belongs to members unless bylaws provide otherwise, p. 504. | No, not unless bylaws provide, p. 463. | 47 | No, not unless bylaws provide, p. 181. | No, not unless bylaws provide, pp. 159, 70. | No, not unless bylaws provide, p. 304. | No, not unless bylaws provide, pp. 99-100. |
| 270 | (a) When an honorary president is elected president, is she both honorary and active president? (b) When an honorary member becomes an active member, is she both honorary and active member? | (a) Yes, and (b) Yes, unless bylaws provide otherwise, p. 504. | (a) Yes, and (b) Yes, unless bylaws provide otherwise, p. 463. | 47 | (a) Yes, and (b) Yes, unless bylaws provide otherwise, p. 181. | (a) Yes, and (b) Yes, unless bylaws provide otherwise, p. 159. | (a) Yes, and (b) Yes, unless bylaws provide otherwise, p. 304. | (a) Yes, and (b) Yes, unless bylaws provide otherwise, pp. 99-100. |

Appendix A

| No | Issue | Answer | RONR 11th. Ed | § | AIPSC | Cannon | Demeter | Riddick |
|---|---|---|---|---|---|---|---|---|
| 271 | (a) If an honorary member becomes an active member does the honorary membership cease? (b) Does an honorary member have to follow the normal procedure for (re)admission to membership? | (a) No, usually a lifetime honor; (b) Yes, p. 504. | (a) No, usually a perpetual honorary title; (b) Yes, pp. 463, 571-2. | 47 | (a) No, the former is just an honorary title; (b) Yes, the latter is a formal relationship, pp. 181, 259. | (a) Not specified; (b) Yes, pp. 159, 70. | (a) No, the former is just an honorary title, p. 304; (b) Yes, the latter is a formal relationship, p. 203. | (a) No, the former is a perpetual honorary title; (b) Yes, the latter is a formal relationship, pp. 99-100, 109-10. |
| 272 | If an honorary title is conferred on a retiring officer, (a) Can that person be later re-elected? (b) Is the honorary title dropped? | (a) Yes; (b) No, p. 504. | (a) Yes; (b) No, honorary titles in no way conflict with holding a regular office, p. 463. | 47 | (a) Yes; (b) No, honorary titles do not conflict with holding a regular office, p. 181. | (a) Yes; (b) Not specified, depends on bylaws, pp. 159, 70. | (a) Yes; (b) No, honorary status does not interfere with regular obligations and privileges, p. 304. | (a) Yes; (b) No, not unless bylaws provide, pp. 99-100. |
| 273 | (a) Does honorary president who holds another office have the right to vote? (b) Can honorary president leave the platform to make motions and vote? | (a) No, voting is a right of membership not office; (b) Yes, if a member, p. 504. | (a) No, voting is a right of membership not office, pp. 3, 463, 447-8; (b) Yes, if a member, pp. 3, 463. | 47 | (a) No, not unless he is a member -- voting is a right of membership not office; (b) Yes, if a member, pp. 181-2, 259-60. | (a) No, not unless he is a member, p. 52; (b) Yes, if a member, pp. 149-52, 52. | (a) No, not unless he is a member, pp. 305, 250-2; (b) Yes, if a member, pp. 305, 304. | (a) No, not unless he is a member; (b) Yes, if a member, pp. 198, 99-100. |
| 274 | If a regent resigns in the middle of her term, can the chapter elect her an honorary regent when there is already an honorary regent? | Yes, it's just an honorary title, p. 505. | Yes, it's just an honorary title, p. 463. | 47 | Yes, it's just an honorary title, p. 181. | Honorary titles not specified, depends on bylaws, p. 70. | Yes, it's just an honorary title, p. 304. | Yes, it's just an honorary title, pp. 99-100. |

© American Institute of Parliamentarians. All rights reserved.

Appendix A

| No | Issue | Answer | RONR 11th. Ed | § | AIPSC | Cannon | Demeter | Riddick |
|---|---|---|---|---|---|---|---|---|
| 275 | If a member is made an honorary officer for life, how can that honor be taken away? | By rescission, p. 505. | By rescission, p. 463. | 47 | By rescission, pp. 181, 48-9. | By reconsideration, p. 126-9. | By rescission, p. 304. | By rescission, p. 100. |
| 276 | Is a roll call necessary to make a meeting legal? | No, unnecessary unless fines levied against absentees or attendance published, p. 506. | No, not required, p. 361. | 41 | No, chair can count or call roll, pp. 124, 2-3, 117. | No, but often done in smaller meetings to determine whether there is a quorum, pp. 91-2, 5. | No, not even mentioned, pp. 13-15. | No, not even mentioned, pp. 38-39, 108-9. |
| 277 | Are there any federal statutes that govern parliamentary law? | No, but each house has its own rules of parliamentary procedure, p. 506. | No, but there is a common law, pp. xxxix, 3, and assemblies are subject to applicable local, state or federal statutes, pp. 3-4. | 1 | No, but local, state or federal statutes may apply to labor unions, non-profits, etc., pp. 2-3. | No, none discussed, pp. 1-8. | No, but there is a common law of procedure, pp. 4-6, 204, and local, state or federal statutes may apply to some organizations, pp. 199-202. | No, none discussed, pp. 179, 89-92. |
| 278 | If a meeting is called to order fifteen minutes after the time specified in the bylaws, even though a quorum was present, is the legality of action taken affected? | No, and the hour should be in standing rules not the bylaws so it can be changed, p. 507. | No, meeting should be called to order promptly, p. 25, but short delay does not impair rights unless it results in absentees, p. 263; time should be in standing rules, p. 575. | 3 | No, meeting should be called to order promptly but short delay does not impair rights, p. 117; time can't be significantly changed without notice, pp. 105-6. | No, meeting should be called to order promptly when a quorum is present but short delay does not impair rights, pp. 5, 142. | No, meetings should be opened reasonably promptly, within ten or fifteen minutes, p. 305. | No, meeting should be called to order promptly when a quorum present; after ten or fifteen minutes elect a presiding officer pro tem, pp. 38-9. |

Appendix A

| No | Issue | Answer | RONR 11th. Ed | § | AIPSC | Cannon | Demeter | Riddick |
|---|---|---|---|---|---|---|---|---|
| 279 | Chair absent 30 minutes after meeting time; another chair is elected, business is done. Chair arrives after meeting is over and claims procedure was illegal. Is she correct? | No, procedure was legal and ten minutes is enough time to wait, p. 507. | No, procedure was legal, pp. 452-3. | 47 | No, procedure was legal, p. 176. | No, procedure was legal, pp. 4-5, 151. | No, procedure was legal, pp. 40, 149. | No, procedure was legal, pp. 147-8. Need wait no more than ten minutes. |
| 280 | If the chair puts a question to vote without a second, and no objection is made at the time, is the vote illegal? | No, p. 507. | No, after debate or a vote it is too late to raise a POO as to lack of a second, and action is valid, p. 37. | 4 | No, after debate has begun by more than one member, there is obvious support for consideration and action is valid, p. 29. | No, after debate has begun there is obvious support for consideration and action is valid, p. 101. | No, once adopted it is valid; time to question lack of a second is while motion is still before body, p. 53. | No, action is valid; time to object is during consideration, pp. 152-3, 158-9. |
| 281 | Motion made, another motion made and seconded, then first motion seconded. Which is the pending motion? | The first, chair should not have recognized another maker before ruling on the first; states, no second, out of order, p. 507. | The first; chair must give adequate chance for motion to be seconded, p. 35; only one MM can be pending and not pending until stated, pp. 102-4, 32-3. | 4 | The first; only one MM can be before an assembly, p. 35, but chair must give adequate chance for motion to be seconded, p. 29. | The first; no absolute need for a second but chair must state motion or rule before allowing another motion, pp. 6, 101-2. | The first; only one MM can be pending, pp. 52, and chair must give adequate chance for motion to be seconded, p. 53. | The first; only one MM can be pending, p. 104; chair must state motion if there is no objection, p. 152. |
| 282 | Can this question be divided: "That we give a whist, the proceeds to go to the French Orphans"? | No, the second phrase makes no sense if the first is lost. Move to strike the second clause to test support, pp. 507-8. | No, each part must present a proper question if no other part is adopted, pp. 272-3; if indivisible, member can move to strike objectionable part, p. 274. | 27 | No, each part must be distinct and independent, pp. 98-99. | No, to divide the question, the parts must be independent, p. 99. | No, must be capable of logical and intelligible separation into independent parts; if part is taken away, a substantive proposition remains, p. 137. | No, each part must be totally independent, presenting a separate question even if no other part is adopted, p. 88. |

© American Institute of Parliamentarians. All rights reserved.

Appendix A

| No | Issue | Answer | RONR 11th. Ed | § | AIPSC | Cannon | Demeter | Riddick |
|---|---|---|---|---|---|---|---|---|
| 283 | Are there any motions that cannot be withdrawn? | No, if renewal is still possible: reconsider can't be withdrawn if too late for someone else to make the motion; notice can't be withdrawn after that meeting, p. 508. | No, but unanimous consent is required to withdraw reconsider and notice when it is too late for renewal, p. 297. | 33 | No, any motion can be withdrawn, p. 97. | No, no exceptions noted, pp. 102-3. | Yes, the following can't be withdrawn: point of no quorum, reconsideration when too late for others to move, and previous notice except during meeting at which it was given, p. 176. | No, no exceptions noted, pp. 208-9. |
| 284 | If a club has adopted a certain hour for adjournment of weekly meetings, can it adjourn before that time without suspending the rules? | No, the rule must be suspended by 2/3 to adjourn early or by M if a standing rule, p. 508. | No, special rules suspension requires 2/3, p. 17; standing rule suspension M, p. 18; see also early adjournment, MM on M vote, pp. 240-1. | 2 | No, rule must be amended for that occasion by 2/3 vote, p. 245. | No, rule must be suspended by 2/3 vote, p. 75. | No, rule must be suspended by 2/3 vote, p. 132. | No, rule must be suspended by 2/3 vote, p. 188. |
| 285 | Can a member be compelled to pay dues if the bylaws do not prescribe a penalty? | No, but after reasonable efforts can be suspended then expelled, p. 508. | No, delinquency dates, suspension and penalties must be provided in bylaws, pp. 571-2; can be suspended, expelled or automatically dropped, depending on bylaws, pp. 584, 571. | 56 | No, can't compel dues, p. 265, but can discipline, suspend or expel for violation of any important duty even if not provided in the bylaws, pp. 263-4; bylaws may provide for loss of good standing, p. 261. | No, but can be terminated if model bylaws are adopted, p. 150. | No, but can be suspended or expelled, p. 306, 266-9. | No, but can be suspended or expelled, pp. 193-4, 34. |
| 286 | Can a member in arrears on dues be deprived of his right to vote if there is no provision for it in the bylaws? | No, not unless suspended from membership, p. 508. | No, not unless bylaws provide for suspension and suspension has occurred, pp. 571-2, 643, 6n. | 56 | No, must be provided in bylaws, pp. 259-61. | No, not unless terminated from membership, p. 150. | No, not unless suspended, p. 306. | No, not unless bylaws remove voting entitlement when in arrears, pp. 111, 198. |

© American Institute of Parliamentarians. All rights reserved.

Appendix A

| No | Issue | Answer | RONR 11th. Ed | § | AIPSC | Cannon | Demeter | Riddick |
|----|-------|--------|---------------|---|-------|--------|---------|---------|
| 287 | If bylaws provide that members in arrears on dues can't vote, can they be counted in the quorum? | No, p. 508. | No, quorum is a specified number of members entitled to full participation, pp. 345, 3. | 40 | No, only members in good standing are counted, pp. 124, 261. | No, members counted must be capable of transacting business, pp. 89-90. | No, suspended members do not count towards a quorum, p. 151. | No, members with disqualifications are not counted, p. 162. |
| 288 | During trial in a discipline case, a member refused to testify and was expelled. Was this proper if the bylaws were silent? | Yes, p. 508. | Yes, a member can be forced to testify on pain of expulsion, p. 655. | 63 | Yes, if failure to testify is found by the assembly to be a violation of an important duty, p. 263. | No, there is no discipline procedure in Cannon so it would have to be in the bylaws, pp. 149-50. | Yes, if the assembly deems the refusal to testify injurious to the association, p. 207. | Yes, if the assembly finds that refusal to testify is cause for expulsion, p. 83. |
| 289 | Is it better for chair to say "opposed" or "contrary" when taking a vote on a motion? | "Opposed" except when chair asks for contrary opinion on the issue of germaneness, pp. 508-9. | "Opposed," pp. 45-6, except "those of the opinion that it is not germane," p. 254. | 4 | "Opposed," p. 32. | "Opposed," p. 42. | "Opposed," p. 34. | "Opposed," pp. 156-7. |
| 290 | What is the difference between a recommendation and a resolution? | A resolution is a motion and a recommendation is not although it can be turned into one by a motion to adopt a recommendation, p. 509. | A resolution is a motion, p. 105, and a recommendation is not although it can be turned into one by a motion to adopt a recommendation, but committees should prepare their own resolutions, p. 504. | 51 | A resolution is a formal motion, p. 307, committees make recommendations to the assembly, usually in the form of formal motions, pp. 198, 203-4. | A resolution is a statement of policy or position, p. 167, recommendations are the specific actions placed at issue by a committee report, p. 85. | A resolution is a MM, typically in writing with a preamble, p. 51, a recommendation of a committee must be moved for adoption, pp. 278-9. | A resolution when moved is a MM, typically in writing with a preamble, pp. 174-6, a recommendation of a committee must be moved for adoption, p. 170. |

© American Institute of Parliamentarians. All rights reserved.

Appendix A

| No | Issue | Answer | RONR 11th. Ed | § | AIPSC | Cannon | Demeter | Riddick |
|---|---|---|---|---|---|---|---|---|
| 291 | What is the difference between a motion and a resolution? | A motion is a proposal for assembly action; a resolution is a formal type of original main motion, p. 509. | A motion is a proposal for assembly action; a resolution is a formal type of original main motion, typically written and with a preamble, pp. 104-6. | 10 | A motion is a proposal to an assembly for consideration and decision, p. 305; a resolution is a formal motion, usually in writing, p. 307. | A motion is a proposal made to obtain a decision, p. 164; a resolution is a statement of policy or direction for action, p. 167. | Both propose a subject to an assembly, p. 50; a resolution is usually in writing and has a preamble, p. 51. | Motions bring business before assembly, p. 116; resolutions when moved become MM, usually longer, more complex and more formal, p. 174. |
| 292 | Is this negative resolution in order: "that the club not accept the offer for the club-house"? | Yes, emphatic but may confuse voters; not like negative amendment, which is out of order, p. 509. | Yes, if it has a different result than no motion but should be stated positively: "that the club **reject** the offer," pp. 104-5. | 10 | Yes, but should be stated in the affirmative ("reject") and presiding officer should request maker to rephrase or consent to rephrase, p. 36. | No, a motion should always be stated in the affirmative to avoid confusion, p. 96; but could "reject." | Yes, negative motions not listed among out-of-order motions, p. 58. | Yes, but a good motion should be affirmative to avoid confusion, p. 105. |
| 293 | Is it proper to ask a proponent for permission to ask a question while he is speaking? | Yes, but request is through the chair, may consent or decline, time charged to speaker, p. 510. | Yes, request for information goes through chair, may consent or decline, time charged to speaker, pp. 294-5. | 33 | Yes, request for information, proper if answer required immediately, speaker must consent, time not charged to speaker, pp. 93-6. | Yes, point of information allowed through chair but not rhetorical questions, p. 113. | Yes, question of information allowed through chair, with permission of speaker, time charged to speaker, pp. 125-6. | Yes, parliamentary inquiry to obtain information, through chair, but interrupts speaker only by unanimous consent, pp. 138-40. |
| 294 | Is it fair to prevent a member from reading an extract as part of his speech? | No, subject to normal time limits and subject to objection if privilege is abused, p. 510. | No, a member has no right to read without assembly permission but custom is to allow short, pertinent quotes, p. 298. | 33 | No, unless the reading violates the rules of member conduct during debate, p. 130. | No, unless the reading violates the rules of member conduct during debate, pp. 108-9. | No, a member has a right to read pertinent material unless objection is made for abuse, pp. 142-3. | No, not brief excerpts, but more extensive reading requires consent, p. 164. |

Appendix A

| No | Issue | Answer | RONR 11th. Ed | § | AIPSC | Cannon | Demeter | Riddick |
|---|---|---|---|---|---|---|---|---|
| 295 | When can a member rise to a point of order? | Whenever the rules are violated, p. 511. | Whenever a member thinks the rules are being violated, p. 247, must be made promptly, p. 250. | 23 | Immediately after a mistake or violation has occurred, p. 91. | When a member believes in good faith that rules are being violated, p. 114. | At the time of a violation or breach of the rules, pp. 121-2. | When a violation or error in the proceedings appears, pp. 140-1. |
| 296 | Show of hands declared tie; doubted; rising vote tie; doubted; roll call carries by one vote, a late arrival. (a) Can members vote later who did not vote on first? (b) Are subsequent votes just recounts? (c) Can late member vote? (d) Can members change their votes on subsequent votes? (e) Can either side bring in other member? | (a) Yes; (b) No, division is a new vote (retake); (c) Yes; (d) Yes; (e) Yes, pp. 511-2. The object of each vote is to obtain the will of the members. | (a) Yes, p. 421; (b) No, division is a new vote (retake), pp. 410, 51; (c) Yes, p. 421; (d) Yes, p. 408; (e) Yes, p. 421. | 45 | (a) Yes, p. 147; (b) No, p. 148;(c) Yes, p. 147;(d) Yes, p. 157 (even current vote); (e) Yes, p. 147. | (a) Yes, (b) Yes, (c) No, (d) Yes, (e) No, pp. 120-4. "General practice is to close the hall's doors" for a counted vote or a roll call vote because it is not a new vote but a "verification of the previous vote," p. 123. | (a) Yes, p. 38; (b) No, doubted votes or verified by retaking by a different method, p. 32; (c) Yes, p. 38; (d) Yes, pp. 37-8; (e) Yes, p. 38. | (a) Yes, pp. 1, 203; (b) No, pp. 202-3; (c) Yes, pp. 1, 203; (d) Yes, p. 198; (e) Yes, pp. 1, 203. |
| 297 | When chair was putting the question to a vote, a member moved to table. Chair ignored the motion. Was he right? | Yes, provided the chair had given ample opportunity for members to debate and make motions before this point, p. 512. | Yes, provided the chair had given ample opportunity for members to debate and make motions before this point, p. 387. | 43 | Yes, only withdraw has clear right to interrupt voting, pp. 19-20, 133, but chair should not begin voting until all members have had a chance to speak, p. 132. | Yes, provided the chair had given ample opportunity for members to debate and make motions before this point, pp. 109-10, 120. | Yes, provided the chair had given members required opportunity to debate and make motions before this point, pp. 25, 100. | Yes, provided the chair had ensured that there was no-one else seeking recognition before the vote began, pp. 156-7. |

© American Institute of Parliamentarians. All rights reserved.

Appendix A

| No | Issue | Answer | RONR 11th. Ed | § | AIPSC | Cannon | Demeter | Riddick |
|---|---|---|---|---|---|---|---|---|
| 298 | In a meeting of delegates to decide which resolutions to bring before convention, motion made to lay a particular resolution on the table. Was this out of order? | Yes, pending motion was adopt order of business; resolution itself was not pending; if opposed, should strike it out of the order of business, pp. 512-3. | Yes, pending motion was adopt order of business, pp. 209-11; resolution itself was not pending; if opposed, should strike it out of the order of business, pp. 147-8. | 17 | Yes, pending MM was adopt order of business; resolution itself was not pending; if opposed, should strike it out of the order of business, p. 50. | Yes, no motion to table, p. 168, postpone only when pending, p. 105, use strike instead, p. 103. | Yes, pending motion was adopt order of business; resolution itself was not pending, p. 98; if opposed, should strike it out of the order of business, p. 76. | Yes, pending motion was adopt order of business resolution itself was not pending, p. 188; if opposed, should strike it out of the order of business, p. 14. |
| 299 | A convention adopted a program that included a set of resolutions. Motion made to lay one of the resolutions on the table, apparently after it was taken up. Ruled out of order as an order of the day. Was this correct? | No, if the resolution had been taken up and was pending it could be laid on the table; orders of the day can't be laid on the table in mass, p. 513. | No, if the resolution had been taken up and was pending it could be laid on the table; orders of the day can't be laid on the table in mass, p. 210. | 17 | No, if the resolution had been taken up and was pending it could be tabled (killed), pp. 70-2. | No, if the resolution had been taken up and was pending it could be postponed (the Cannon preference to table), pp. 105, 168. | No, if the resolution had been taken up and was pending it could be laid on the table, p. 98. | No, if the resolution had been taken up and was pending it could be laid on the table, p. 188. |
| 300 | A resignation of a member is laid on the table and is not taken up. What becomes of it? | If the member is in good standing, it takes effect when the time for taking from the table expires, p. 513. | If the member is in good standing, it takes effect when the time for taking from the table expires, pp. 291-2, 301-2. | 32 | Resignation takes effect immediately unless future time specified in resignation, pp. 265-6. | Resignation takes effect as provided in the bylaws or resignation itself; no guidance on resignation and no motion to table, pp. 2, 168. | If the member is in good standing and acceptance is required, it takes effect when the time for taking from the table expires; otherwise immediate, pp. 206, 98. | Resignation takes effect when time for reconsideration of motion to table expires, pp. 174, 188-9. |

Appendix A

| No | Issue | Answer | RONR 11th. Ed | § | AIPSC | Cannon | Demeter | Riddick |
|---|---|---|---|---|---|---|---|---|
| 301 | When can a question be taken from the table? | Until the close of the next regular meeting if within 3 months; otherwise only until the end of the current session, p. 513. | Until the close of the next regular business session if within quarter; otherwise only until the end of the current session, pp. 301-2. | 34 | The motion to table can be reconsidered before the end of the current meeting or convention, p. 71. | Table should not be used, p. 99; can be taken up at the time of postponement later in the meeting or at a later meeting, p. 105. | Until the close of the next regular business session if within quarter; otherwise only until the end of the current session, p. 169. | The motion to table can be reconsidered before the end of the current meeting or convention, p. 189. |
| 302 | Can lay on the table and previous question be moved at the same time? | No, the combination is useless even if it were allowed, p. 514. | No, lay on the table takes precedence over previous question, p. 210; contradictory purposes -- set aside temporarily, p. 209, vs. put to immediate vote, p. 197. | 17 | No, table takes precedence over close debate, p. 72; different purposes -- kill to avoid action on the motion, p. 70 vs. put motion to immediate vote, p. 69. | No, table should not be used at all and postpone and vote immediately are contradictory, p. 99. | No, lay on the table takes precedence over previous question, p. 98; contradictory purposes -- set aside temporarily, p. 98, vs. put to immediate vote, p. 93. | No, table takes precedence over close debate, p. 188; different purposes -- kill without debate, p. 189 vs. put to immediate vote, p. 44. |
| 303 | Does tabling the MM while objection to consideration is pending kill the objection? | No, the objection is voted on when the MM is taken from the table, p. 514. | No, the objection is voted on when the MM is taken from the table, pp. 210, 213. | 17 | No, table kills the MM, p. 70, and objection to consideration not recognized (table inside front cover). | Both objection to consideration and table are out of order, pp. 98-9. | No, the objection is voted on when the MM is taken from the table, pp. 98, 169. | No, it kills the MM without debate, p. 189; same effect as question of consideration, pp. 158-9. |
| 304 | If a motion to limit debate to one minute per person has carried, is it in order to move the previous question? | Yes, p. 514. | Yes, p. 198. | 15 | Yes, takes precedence and requires 2/3 vote, enough to amend prior action, p. 69. | Yes, pp. 18-9, 109-10, except where time for vote is set, p. 76-7. | Yes, p. 92. | Yes, p.103. |
| 305 | If the previous question is ordered after a motion to limit debate to one minute per person has carried, are the one minute speeches cut off? | Yes, the order closing debate now supersedes the order limiting debate, p. 514. | Yes, previous question supersedes any unexhausted portion of an order limiting debate, pp. 198, 194. | 16 | Yes, takes precedence and requires 2/3 vote, enough to amend prior action, p. 69. | Yes, assembly can decide to end debate before everyone has used their time, pp. 108-10. | Yes, p. 92. | Yes, p.103. |

© American Institute of Parliamentarians. All rights reserved.

Appendix A

| No | Issue | Answer | RONR 11th Ed | § | AIPSC | Cannon | Demeter | Riddick |
|---|---|---|---|---|---|---|---|---|
| 306 | If a special order is interrupted by an earlier special order, is it necessary to lay it on the table? | No, the special order is announced automatically interrupting the pending business, p. 514. | No, special order automatically interrupts except: (1) recess or adjourn, (2) question of privilege, (3) earlier special order, (4) the special order, p. 369. | 41 | No, if an agenda is adopted and items of new business set for a time, they are automatically taken up in the designated sequence, p. 119. | No, no specific guidance but emphasis is on efficient transaction of business, pp. 79-82. | No, special orders are taken up when the time arrives, even if they interrupt the pending question, p. 105. | No, special orders are taken up immediately when the time arrives, even if they interrupt the pending question, pp. 131-2. |
| 307 | When may the orders of the day be called for? | When the order of business is being deviated from without assembly authorization by 2/3 vote, p. 514. | When the order of business is being deviated from without assembly authorization by 2/3 vote, p. 219. | 18 | Orders of the day not recognized but may make a POO when agenda not being followed and no consent of the assembly, pp. 120, 90-3. | Orders of the day not recognized but may make a POO when agenda not being followed and no consent of the assembly, pp. 114-5. | When the order of business is being deviated from without assembly authorization, pp. 104-6. | When the order of business is being deviated from without assembly authorization, p. 132. |
| 308 | When MM and postpone indefinitely are pending, amendment is proposed and carried. Is it now in order to put postpone indefinitely to vote? | Yes, as soon as amendment is voted on, postpone indefinitely becomes immediately pending question, p. 514. | Yes, as soon as amendment is voted on, postpone indefinitely becomes immediately pending question, pp. 60, T4. | 5 | Impossible situation: postpone indefinitely not used: table would have taken precedence over amend, p. 16. | Impossible situation: postpone indefinitely and table not used; after amendment, vote down MM, p. 99. | Yes, as soon as amendment is voted on, postpone indefinitely becomes immediately pending question, pp. 10-1. | Impossible situation: postpone indefinitely takes precedence over amend, pp. 143, 119; principle of precedence applies, p. 118. |
| 309 | Can a member who made a motion, voted for it, and was defeated, offer the same motion at a future session? | Yes, any member can renew the motion, p. 515. | Yes, any member can renew the motion at future session, pp. 336-7. | 38 | Yes, any member can renew the motion at future meeting, p. 25. | Yes, anyone can renew the motion or move to reconsider rejection, pp. 126-9, 95. | Yes, anyone can renew MM at future session, p. 172. | Yes, any member can renew the motion at future meeting, p. 168. |

© American Institute of Parliamentarians. All rights reserved.

Appendix A

| No | Issue | Answer | RONR 11th Ed | § | AIPSC | Cannon | Demeter | Riddick |
|---|---|---|---|---|---|---|---|---|
| 310 | Motion to purchase 40 typewriters rejected. (a) Is motion to purchase 30 in order in same session? (b) Is motion by supporter to rescind rejection in order? | (a) No, too similar; (b) Yes, with 2/3 vote, p. 515. | (a) No, not substantially new question, p. 338; (b) No, rescind can only strike out what was previously adopted, p. 305. | 38 | (a) No, not substantially new question, p. 25; (b) No, can rescind only adopted MM, p. 48; but supporter can move reconsideration, pp. 46. | (a) No, not substantially new question, p. 126; (b) Yes, can rescind or reconsider, pp. 126-9. | (a) No, not material change, p. 172; (b) No, rescind can repeal only what was adopted, p. 165. | (a) No, not substantially different question, p.169; (b) No, rescind action only, p. 173, but supporter can move to reconsider, p. 166. |
| 311 | Quorum present at lunch but not at election following. Was election legal? | No, result must be ratified, p. 515. | No, null and void unless ratified if proof of no quorum, pp. 347-8, 124-5. | 40 | No, not legal without ratification if no quorum timely raised, pp. 122-5. | No, not legal, pp. 89-90. | No, not legal without ratification if no quorum timely raised, p. 148. | No, not legal without ratification if no quorum timely raised, pp. 162-3. |
| 312 | Committee appointed by conference to report at "next conference" reports at **special** meeting of conference and recommendations adopted. (a) Was chair resignation in protest effective? (b) Was adoption illegal? (c) Can it be rescinded and by what vote? | (a) No, committee ceased to exist on report; (b) No, too late to question distinction between "next conference" and "next meeting of conference"; (c) Yes, 2/3 or MN, pp. 515-6. | (a) No, committee ceased to exist on report, p. 502; (b) No, too late to question distinction, pp. 250-1; (c) Yes, 2/3 or MN, p. 306. | 50 | (a) No, committee ceased to exist on report, p. 188; (b) No, too late to question distinction, p. 91; (c) Yes, same vote as adoption, p. 49. | (a) No, ceased to exist on report, p. 61; (b) No, too late to question distinction, pp. 114-5; (c) Yes, reconsider by 2/3 vote, p. 127. | (a) No, committee ceased to exist on report, p. 277; (b) No, too late to question distinction, p. 122; (c) Yes, MN23, pp. 165-6. | (a) No, committee ceased to exist on report, p. 48; (b) Decided by acquiescence that special meeting was consistent with bylaws, p. 38; (c) Yes, same vote as adoption, p. 173. |
| 313 | VP moved away a month ago with no forwarding address. Can board meet and appoint successor? | Yes, if bylaws allow board to fill vacancy. Moving far away is like abandonment, p. 516. | Yes, if bylaws allow board to fill vacancy, p. 467. Moving far away is like abandonment, p. 291. | 47 | Yes, if bylaws allow board to fill vacancy; departure from locality creates a vacancy, p. 184. | Yes, if bylaws authorize; Cannon is silent, pp. 151-2. | Yes, if bylaws allow board to fill vacancy, p. 256. Office abandoned unless contested, p. 207. | Yes, if bylaws allow board to fill vacancy; departure from district creates a vacancy, pp. 196-7. |

© American Institute of Parliamentarians. All rights reserved.

Appendix A

| No | Issue | Answer | RONR 11th. Ed | § | AIPSC | Cannon | Demeter | Riddick |
|---|---|---|---|---|---|---|---|---|
| 314 | Should officers who resign during term report at annual meeting? | No, incumbent reports, prior officers provide data, p. 516. | No, incumbent reports, prior officers provide data, pp. 476, 291. | 48 | No, incumbent reports, prior officers provide data, pp. 117-8, 184. | No, incumbent reports, prior officers provide data, p. 80. | No, incumbent reports, prior officers provide data, pp. 14-5. | No, incumbent reports, prior officers provide data, pp. 10, 196-7. |
| 315 | Bylaws provide that board fills vacancies. Should resignation be sent to board or society? | Board, because it fills the vacancy, p. 517. | Board, because it fills the vacancy, pp. 291, 467-8. | 32 | Board, because it fills the vacancy, pp. 265-6, 184-5. | Board by logic but Cannon silent. | Board, because it fills the vacancy, p. 205. | Board, because it fills the vacancy, pp. 197, 174. |
| 316 | Can a member move to accept his own resignation and vote on the motion? | Yes, he is a member until the resignation is accepted, p. 517. | Yes, the maker of a request can make the motion, pp. 289-92; and can vote, pp. 407-8. | 32 | Yes, if acceptance required, pp. 265-6; not a conflict, pp. 196-7. | Yes, if acceptance required -- no contrary rule. | Yes, if acceptance required, pp. 205-6. | Yes, if acceptance required, p. 174. |
| 317 | Does appoint ever mean elect? | Appoint includes elect, p. 517. | Methods of appointment include election, p. 493. | 50 | No definition but generally distinguishes appointment from election, pp. 184-5. | No definition but generally distinguishes, pp. 61, 131. | No, clearly distinguishes appointment from election, p. 84. | Distinguishes: methods to select committees include appointment and election, pp. 50-1. |
| 318 | To leave a meeting before adjournment, is a motion for personal privilege required? | No, that would be decidedly improper, p. 517. | No, proper uses are rare; examples include correcting minutes, character charges, p. 227. | 19 | No, not an urgent question relating to safety, health, security, comfort or integrity, pp. 73-6. | No, points of personal privilege should be important procedural matters or time is wasted, pp. 44-6, 116-8. | No, not germane to safety, health, integrity or property, pp. 107-8. | No, not related to the character, integrity or comfort of the member, pp. 159-60. |
| 319 | Do questions of personal privilege often arise in ordinary societies? | No, and most that are raised are really requests, p. 517. | No, proper uses are rare, p. 227; compare requests, pp. 292-9. | 19 | No, should only be used for urgent matters, pp. 73-6. | No, should only be used for important procedural issues, pp. 44-6, 116-8. | No, should be limited to issues of safety, health, integrity or property, pp. 107-8. | No, should be limited to issues of character, integrity and comfort, pp. 159-60. |

© American Institute of Parliamentarians. All rights reserved.

Appendix A

| No | Issue | Answer | RONR 11th. Ed | § | AIPSC | Cannon | Demeter | Riddick |
|---|---|---|---|---|---|---|---|---|
| 320 | Are charter members the ones who sign the constitution or are they just the original members? | Originally meant signers of corporate charter but now generally means original members of any society, p. 517. | Persons who sign the roll of initial members or who join before a certain date are charter members, pp. 559-60. | 54 | AIPSC doesn't use the term. | Cannon doesn't use the term. | Complimentary title for those who attend organizational meetings and join proposed organization, p. 315. | Those who adopted original charter; in unincorporated groups, original members, pp. 44, 134. |
| 321 | Does a resolution become null and void when the constitution is revised? | Only if it conflicts with the revised constitution, p. 518. | Only if it conflicts with the amended bylaws, p. 251. | 23 | Only if it violates the amended bylaws, p. 91; repealed by implication, p. 26. | If it conflicts with bylaws, pp. 159, 69, but not specifically addressed. | Only if it conflicts with the amended bylaws, p. 308. | Yes, revised bylaws are effective immediately, pp. 37, 31. |
| 322 | In the absence of a special rule, can an organization assess its members? | No, bylaws must authorize assessments, p. 518. | No, bylaws must authorize assessments, p. 572. | 56 | No, bylaws define all rights, privileges and obligations of membership, p. 259. | No, bylaws define dues and assessments, p. 150. | No, bylaws define dues and assessments, pp. 191, 194. | No, bylaws define dues and assessments, p. 34. |
| 323 | (a) Can a member move that 2/3 shall be necessary for adoption of this motion? (b) Can a majority approve this supermajority vote? | (a) Yes; (b) No, it is in effect a motion to suspend the normal rules, p. 518. | (a) Yes; (b) No, suspend the rules requires 2/3, pp. 260-1. | 25 | (a) Yes; (b) No, suspend the rules requires 2/3, p. 88. | (a) Yes; (b) No, suspend the rules requires 2/3, pp. 98-9. | (a) Yes; (b) No, suspend the rules requires 2/3, p. 132. | (a) Yes; (b) No, suspend the rules requires 2/3, p. 188. |
| 324 | Is a unanimous vote required to require a unanimous vote for a certain election? | No, 2/3 vote to suspend rules is enough; can't declare vote unanimous if one objects, p. 518. | No, suspend rules requires 2/3 vote, pp. 260-1; compare acclamation, p. 443. | 25 | No, suspend the rules requires 2/3 vote, p. 88; requirement of unanimous vote not recommended, pp. 141-2 | No, suspend the rules requires 2/3 vote, pp. 98-9; no election by acclamation if one objection, pp. 133, 124-5. | No, suspend the rules requires 2/3, p. 132; no election by acclamation if one objects, p. 248. | No, suspend the rules requires 2/3, p. 188; no election by acclamation if one objects, p. 3. |

Appendix A

| No | Issue | Answer | RONR 11th. Ed | § | AIPSC | Cannon | Demeter | Riddick |
|---|---|---|---|---|---|---|---|---|
| 325 | Doesn't the organization suffer if the president can vote only when it may affect the result? | No, there can't be a loss if the result is not affected, p. 518. | No, voting rules balance neutral role of chair with rights as a member, pp. 456, 405-6; results not affected. | 47 | No, voting rules balance neutral role of chair with rights as a member, pp. 174-6, 142-3; results not affected. | No, voting rules balance neutral role of chair with rights as a member, pp. 107-10, 7-8; results not affected. | No, voting rules balance neutral role of chair with rights as a member, pp. 41, 43; results not affected. | No, voting rules balance neutral role of chair with rights as a member, pp. 126, 146; results not affected. |
| 326 | Is a motion to declare an office vacant a question of privilege? | Yes, adopted by MN23MEM unless bylaws preclude, pp. 518-9. | Yes, adopted by MN23MEM unless bylaws set terms (removal only for cause), pp. 653-4, 103-4. | 62 | No, removal only for cause; requires notice, hearing and trial, and same vote as appointment, pp. 185-6. | No, no question of privilege and no removal in Cannon; would depend on bylaws, p. 151. | No, removal only for cause; requires notice, hearing and trial, pp. 207, 251, 266-9. | Yes, in extreme cases declare vacancy, p. 196 159; otherwise trial required, pp. 85-6. |
| 327 | What are the privileges of the floor? | Admission to the hall only, p. 519. | Admission to the hall only, p. 29n. | 3 | Not used. | Not used. | Admission to the hall only, p. 311. | Right to speak and recognition, pp. 96-7. |
| 328 | (a) What is a majority vote? (b) Why are illegal votes counted in denominator? | (a) More than half votes cast; (b) The object is the choice of the majority who choose to vote, pp. 519-20. | (a) More than half votes cast by persons entitled to vote, excluding blanks and abstentions at legal meeting, p. 400; (b) The object is the choice of the majority who choose to vote, pp. 415-7. | 44 | (a) More than half **legal** votes cast, p. 305; (b) Illegal votes are not counted, pp. 305, 135, 166. | (a) More than half the votes cast by those present and voting, p. 123; (b) No explicit rule on illegal votes. | (a) More than half the votes cast at a legal meeting with a quorum, p. 246; (b) Determine the majority of those who choose to vote, pp. 247-50. | (a) Over half the **legal** votes cast by members legally entitled to vote, p. 206; (b) Illegal votes are not counted, p. 100. |

© American Institute of Parliamentarians. All rights reserved.

Appendix A

| No | Issue | Answer | RONR 11th Ed | § | AIPSC | Cannon | Demeter | Riddick |
|---|---|---|---|---|---|---|---|---|
| 329 | What is the difference between an adjourned meeting and one held after a recess? | A recess interrupts meetings during a session; adjourned meetings extend to another day sessions that normally are less than a day, p. 520. | A recess is a short break within a meeting, p. 82; an adjourned meeting is a continuation of an incomplete session of the immediately preceding regular or special meeting, p. 93. | 8 | A recess interrupts a meeting; adjournment terminates a meeting, p. 77. Uses "continued meeting" instead of "adjourned meeting" to avoid confusion, p. 303. | Recess interrupts a meeting; Adjourn ends a meeting, pp. 167, 158; "adjourned meeting" is a continuation of the same meeting, p. 137. | Recess interrupts a meeting; Adjournment ends a meeting, pp. 112-3; "adjourned meeting" continues a meeting at another time, pp. 119-20. | Recess interrupts a meeting, p. 164; Adjourn terminates a meeting, p. 4; an adjourned meeting continues business on current agenda, p. 5. |
| 330 | What is the difference between executive session and secret session? | None in common usage, pp. 520-1. | None, "executive session" defined as secret proceedings, pp. 95-6. | 9 | None but "closed meeting" is preferred term, p. 108. | None but "executive session" used, p. 161. | None but "executive session" used, p. 276. | None but "closed session" used, pp. 45-6. |
| 331 | President resigned, motions adopted by majority vote to vacate all offices and committees; President re-elected, new officers elected, new committees appointed. On what authority? | Provided the vote was MEM, authority comes from rescind and discharge committees, p. 521. | Provided terms are not fixed, MEM removes officers, p. 653, rescinds, p. 306, discharges committees, p. 312. | 62 | No authority -- officers and elected committee members can be removed only for cause after trial, pp. 185-6. | No authority for removal in Cannon; would depend on bylaws, p. 151. | No authority -- removal of officers only for cause with notice, hearing and trial, pp. 207, 251, 266-9; committee discharge by NM23, p. 83. | No authority -- declare vacancy only in extreme cases, pp. 196, 159; otherwise trial required, pp. 85-6. |
| 332 | Member sends in resignation, effective immediately. Withdraws resignation before it is acted upon. (a) Did he have that right? (b) Is he still a member? | (a) Yes; (b) Yes, p. 521. | (a) Yes, request to be excused from duty can be withdrawn before stated; (b) Yes, should be acted upon immediately if dues are paid but here not yet acted upon, pp. 289-92. | 32 | (a) No; (b) No, resignation is effective immediately unless future time is specified, no acceptance is necessary unless bylaws specify, and can't be withdrawn, pp. 265-6. | (a) Yes, (b) Yes, based on the terms of the resignation, unless bylaws specify otherwise, pp. 149-50. No rule in Cannon. | (a) No; (b) No, resignation effective immediately if dues paid, no acceptance is necessary unless bylaws specify, pp. 205-6. | (a) No; (b) No, resignation is effective immediately unless future time is specified, p. 110, no acceptance is necessary unless bylaws specify, p. 174. |

© American Institute of Parliamentarians. All rights reserved.

Appendix A

| No | Issue | Answer | RONR 11th. Ed | § | AIPSC | Cannon | Demeter | Riddick |
|---|---|---|---|---|---|---|---|---|
| 333 | Can a member cite another member to appear and answer charges? | No, a member may give notice of intent to prefer charges but only assembly can cite, pp. 521-2. | No, resolution preferring charges is adopted by the assembly and secretary provides notice to the accused, pp. 662-3. | 63 | No, charges are adopted by the assembly and secretary provides notice to the accused, p. 264. | No, discipline not specified but right of assembly not member, pp. 2-3. | No, only the assembly can order trial through adoption of charges, p. 267. | No, only the assembly can order trial through adoption of charges, pp. 193-4. |
| 334 | If a member is expelled, may he be restored to membership? | Yes, by same notice and vote as admission to membership, p. 522. | Yes, not by rescission or amendment but by following bylaw reinstate or admit procedure, p. 308. | 35 | Yes, if organization permits application for readmission, p. 265. | Yes, by reconsideration, p. 127, absent bylaw provision for expulsion and readmission, pp. 149-50. | Yes, but by readmission only, not rescission, p. 175. | Yes, but by readmission only, not rescission, p. 173. |
| 335 | Can a member hold office in national federation and home club? | Yes, p. 522. | Yes, unless bylaws prohibit, pp. 432, 440, 585. | 46 | Yes, can even hold two compatible offices in same organization, p. 163. | Yes, except as provided in bylaws, p. 151. | Yes, except as provided in bylaws, pp. 179, 347. | Yes, except as provided in bylaws, pp. 34-5 125. |
| 336 | (a) Is a motion to limit or extend debate for an entire convention in order? (b) Can the chair grant an extension to a single speaker? | (a) Yes; (b) Yes, if no objection, p. 522. | (a) Yes, p. 192; (b) Yes, if no objection, otherwise 2/3 vote, pp. 197, 387-8. | 15 | (a) Yes, p. 66; (b) Yes, if no objection, otherwise 2/3 vote, pp. 148; 67 (modifies previously adopted limit). | (a) Yes, motion to suspend rules; (b) Yes, if no objection, otherwise 2/3 vote, pp. 75-6. | (a) Yes, pp. 171, 90-2; (b) Yes, if no objection, otherwise reconsider or suspend, p. 92. | (a) Yes; (b) Yes, no objection, otherwise 2/3 vote, pp. 102-3. |
| 337 | (a) Can a rules committee limit debate to one five-minute speech? (b) By suspending the rules? (c) Can a motion still be made to extend debate beyond five minutes? | (a) Yes, Robert's 2x ten minutes can be limited by 2/3 vote; (b) By motion to limit debate; (c) Yes, by 2/3 vote, pp. 522-3. | (a) Yes, Robert's 2x ten minutes can be limited by 2/3 vote; (b) By motion to limit debate; (c) Yes, by 2/3 vote, pp. 191-7, 387-8. | 15 | (a) Yes, no general debate limit in AIPSC, pp. 131-2; (b) By motion to limit debate, pp. 65-7; (c) Yes, by 2/3 vote, pp. 67 (modifies adopted limit). | (a) Yes, accepted rule of ten minutes can be limited by 2/3 vote, pp. 109, 75-6; (b) By motion to suspend rules, pp. 75-6; (c) Yes, by 2/3 vote, pp. 98-9. | (a) Yes, common law rule of ten minutes can be limited by 2/3 vote, pp. 25, 90-2; (b) By motion to limit debate, pp. 90-2; (c) Yes, by reconsideration, pp. 90-2. | (a) Yes, customary rule of ten minutes can be limited by 2/3 vote, pp. 73, 102-3; (b) By motion to limit debate, pp. 102-3; (c) Yes, by 2/3 vote, pp. 102-3. |

Appendix A

| No | Issue | Answer | RONR 11th. Ed | § | AIPSC | Cannon | Demeter | Riddick |
|---|---|---|---|---|---|---|---|---|
| 338 | If it becomes impossible to complete a program, can it be changed by general consent without a formal vote of the assembly? | Yes, anything that can be done by 2/3 vote can be done by general consent of assembly not committee, p. 523. | Yes, change in program after adoption can be done by M of registered delegates, 2/3, MEM or general consent, p. 630. | 59 | Yes, change in program can be made by M or general consent, p. 210. | Yes, change in agenda can be made by 2/3 or unanimous consent, pp. 31, 43, 82, 124-5. | Yes, change in agenda can be made by 2/3 or general consent, pp. 19, 132, 309-10. | Yes, change in program can be made by 2/3 or general consent, pp. 66, 97, 130-1. |
| 339 | (a) Must special meeting business be specified in the call? (b) Can very urgent matter be considered even if not in the call? (c) Can MEM take up urgent matter not in the call? (d) Can call have placeholder for "other business of importance"? | (a) No, not unless bylaws require; (b) No, not if bylaws require notice; act and later ratify; (c) No, but ratification likely; (d) No, not if bylaws require notice, pp. 523-4. | (a) Yes, pp. 91, 93; (b) No, must be ratified later, p. 93; (c) No, but ratification more likely; (d) No, not proper notice, pp. 91-3. | 9 | (a) Yes, p. 106; (b) No, must be ratified later, pp. 106, 41-3; (c) No, but ratification more likely; (d) No, not proper notice, p. 106. | (a) Yes, p. 168; (b) No, and no explicit ratification procedure, p. 168; (c) No; (d) No, not proper notice, pp. 168, 88-9. | (a) No, not unless bylaws require, p. 13; (b) No, not if bylaws require notice; act and later ratify, p. 13, 168; (c) No, but ratification more likely; (d) No, not if bylaws require actual notice, p. 13. | (a) Yes, p. 183; (b) No, must be ratified later, p. 184; (c) No, but ratification more likely; (d) Yes, considered proper notice, pp. 184, 124. |
| 340 | Annual meeting adjourned sine die. Quorum mustered and measures adopted. Was action legal? | No, adjournment sine die ended the meeting and action is null and void, p. 524. | No, adjournment sine die ended the meeting and dissolved the assembly; action is null and void, p. 237. | 21 | No, adjournment sine die ended the meeting and dissolved the assembly, p. 80. | No, adjournment ended the meeting; action is null and void, p. 158. | No, adjournment sine die ended the meeting and dissolved the assembly; action is null and void, p. 118. | No, adjournment sine die ended the meeting and dissolved the assembly; action is null and void, pp. 5-6. |
| 341 | Should any action be taken on president's annual report containing no recommendations? | No, p. 524. | No, p. 525. | 51 | No, just file report, p. 201. | No, only recommendations are at issue, p. 85. | No, pp. 15-6. | No, receive and file, pp. 171-2. |

© American Institute of Parliamentarians. All rights reserved.

Appendix A

| No | Issue | Answer | RONR 11th. Ed | § | AIPSC | Cannon | Demeter | Riddick |
|---|---|---|---|---|---|---|---|---|
| 342 | (a) Should parliamentarian's duties by defined in bylaws? (b) How should they be worded? | (a)Yes; (b) Advise presiding officer, and others on request, on parliamentary law, p. 524. | (a) Yes, under officers, p. 447; (b) See pp. 465-7 (essentially impartial adviser). | 47 | (a) Yes, under officers, p. 181; (b) See pp. 269-71. | (a) Not specified, pp. 165, 151, but professional's duties would be in contract; (b) See pp. 165, 32-3. | (a) Yes, under officers, p. 253 (b) See pp. 253-4. | (a) Yes, in bylaw or regulations, p. 137; (b) See pp. 136-7. |
| 343 | Must an organization abide by the decision of the parliamentarian? | No, parliamentarian doesn't rule or decide, only advises, pp. 524-5. | No, parliamentarian only advises, p. 465. | 47 | No, parliamentarian only advises, pp. 269, 181. | No, parliamentarian only advises, p. 165. | No, parliamentarian only advises, opinion is advice not decision, p. 254. | No, parliamentarian only advises, p. 136. |
| 344 | Should society adopt a rule prohibiting chair from counting abstentions on either side or requiring abstainers to leave the room? | No, chair has no authority to do so, so no need for the rule, p. 525. | No, no need, already in the rules, pp. 407, 415. | 45 | No, no need, pp. 139-40. | No, no need, pp. 120, 123. | No, no need, abstentions not counted, p. 36. | No, no need, p. 2. |
| 345 | Motion is in effect not to fill vacancies created by death. Now wish to fill such a vacancy. What is the correct procedure? | Suspend rule by M, p. 526. | Suspend the standing rule by M, p. 87; only bylaw or special rule can put issue beyond the reach of M. | 8 | Amend or abolish the standing rule by 2/3 vote, p. 245. | Suspend the standing rule by 2/3 vote, p. 73. | Suspend by 2/3 vote or MN, p. 132; standing rules are adopted motions with continuing effect, p. 181. | Suspend the standing order (administrative detail) by M, p. 91; not rule of procedure requiring 2/3 vote, p. 90. |
| 346 | A question is put to a vote; strong "ayes," no "noes," three don't vote. Is this a unanimous vote? | Yes, abstentions are ignored in deciding whether M, 2/3 or unanimous, p. 526. | Yes, unanimous consent does not mean everyone present is in favor, just no objections or votes against, p. 55. | 4 | Yes, unanimous vote does not mean everyone present is in favor, just no votes against, p. 141. | Yes, unanimous consent does not mean everyone present is in favor, just no objections or votes against, pp. 124-5. | Yes, unanimous consent does not mean everyone present is in favor, just no objections or votes against, pp. 35, 309. | No, distinguishes "unanimous consent" (no objection) from "unanimous vote" (every voter in agreement), p. 204. |

Appendix A

| No | Issue | Answer | RONR 11th. Ed | § | AIPSC | Cannon | Demeter | Riddick |
|---|---|---|---|---|---|---|---|---|
| 347 | Is approving a budget the same as approving the bills for the expenditures? | No, budget is approved in advance, bills approved after expenditures, p. 526. | No, a budget is a general financial plan, p. 587; treasurer should still get advance authority to incur expenses, p. 461. | 56 | No, a budget is a general financial plan; treasurer should still get advance authority to incur expenses, p. 251. | No guidance; would depend on bylaws, pp. 150, 152. | No, a budget is a general financial plan; treasurer should get advance authority to incur expenses, p. 253. | No, a budget is a general financial plan; treasurer should still get advance authority to incur expenses, p. 96. |
| 348 | At monthly meeting, treasurer is asked to read condition of the treasury. Should this report be accepted by motion and vote? | No, report is for information; motion would be an endorsement which is the auditor's role, pp. 526-7. | No, report is for information; motion would be an endorsement which is the auditor's role, p. 479. | 48 | No, report is for information and is filed; motion would be an endorsement which is the auditor's role, p. 249. | No, endorsement of report is role of auditors, p. 152. | No, report is for information and is filed, pp. 15, 253. | No, report is for information and is filed; motion would be an endorsement which is the auditor's role, pp. 171-2. |
| 349 | If club has an auditor who makes an annual report, is treasurer's report accepted at monthly meeting or referred to auditor? | Neither, annual report of treasurer is referred to auditor, p. 527. | Neither, monthly report just filed; annual report of treasurer is referred to auditor, pp. 479-80. | 48 | Neither, monthly report just filed; annual report of treasurer is referred to auditor for certification, p. 249. | Neither, filed at monthly meeting and referred to auditor annually, pp. 80, 152. | Neither, monthly report just filed; audits are typically quarterly, semi-annually or annually, p. 253. | Neither, monthly report just filed; auditor's role is typically annual, p. 171. |
| 350 | Motion made to censure treasurer and motion referred. Committee recommends censure of treasurer. Does the adoption of the motion to accept the recommendation of the committee censure the treasurer? | Yes, if report includes a resolution to that effect, p. 527. | Yes, motion was pending when referred and becomes pending automatically after report. Chair states the question and vote is to adopt motion to censure, pp. 516-8. | 51 | Yes, if report includes a resolution to that effect, pp. 203-4; mere reports should not be accepted, p. 201. | Yes, adoption of the report approves any recommendations, p. 85. | Yes, but the motion was pending when referred and becomes pending automatically after report, so Chair states the question as adopt motion to censure, p. 279. | Yes, p. 165. |

© American Institute of Parliamentarians. All rights reserved.

Appendix A

| No | Issue | Answer | RONR 11th. Ed | § | AIPSC | Cannon | Demeter | Riddick |
|---|---|---|---|---|---|---|---|---|
| 351 | Executive board takes action during convention recess. Convention immediately takes opposite action. Does convention prevail? | Yes, board action improper ("between meetings" means when convention not in session) and convention supreme, p. 527. | Yes, board action improper ("between meetings" means when convention not in session) and action in conflict with convention is null and void, pp. 482-3. | 49 | Yes, board action improper ("between meetings" means when convention not in session) and convention can change board action, p. 195; recess suspends meeting, p. 78. | Yes, board action improper ("between meetings" means when convention not in session) and assembly is more powerful, pp. 2-3. | Yes, board action improper ("between meetings" means when convention not in session) and convention can disaffirm, pp. 270-1. | Yes, board action improper ("between meetings" means when convention not in session) and convention can countermand, p. 27. |
| 352 | Does a club have the legal right to refuse to hear board minutes explaining action? | Yes, but discourteous, p. 528. | Yes, board minutes typically available only to board, p. 460, needs assembly agreement to read, p. 298. | 47 | Yes, board minutes typically available only to board, p. 196. | Yes, even assembly's own minutes need not be read, p. 111. | Yes, board minutes are read to the assembly only by rule, vote or custom, p. 23. | Yes, board minutes are read to the assembly only by motion, p. 28. |
| 353 | Do motions adopted by the board and ratified by the club carry over from year to year? | Yes, any resolution of a club continues in force until it is rescinded or amended, p. 528. | Yes, resolution amounts to a standing rule which continues indefinitely, can be suspended by M or changed by MN23MEM, pp. 87, 305-7. | 8 | Yes, standing rule in force until amended or abolished by 2/3 vote, p. 245. | Yes, standing rule in force unless suspended or modified by 2/3 vote, p. 73. | Yes, standing rules are adopted motions with continuing effect, p. 181. | Yes, standing orders that may need frequent change can be amended by M, p. 91; standing rule of procedure requires 2/3, p. 90. |
| 354 | Can society change the action taken by the board? | Yes, unless exclusive power of board or completed action, p. 528. | Yes, unless exclusive power of board or completed action, pp. 482-3. | 49 | Yes, unless exclusive power of board or completed action, p. 195. | Yes, unless bylaws provide otherwise, pp. 2-3, 158-9, 152. | Yes, unless exclusive power of board or completed action, pp. 270-1. | Yes, except completed action, p. 27. |
| 355 | (a) Can board censure? (b) What vote is required for censure? | (a) No, report facts to assembly; (b) M of assembly, p. 528. | (a) No, society itself has power of discipline, p. 643; (b) censure is MM, M vote, p. 125. | 61 | (a) No, society has power of discipline, p. 263; (b) M vote even for "severe discipline", pp. 264-5. | Not specified (Cannon silent on discipline). | (a) No, assembly power, (b) M vote, p. 260. | (a) No, assembly power, (b) M vote, p. 40. |

© American Institute of Parliamentarians. All rights reserved.

Appendix A

| No | Issue | Answer | RONR 11th. Ed | § | AIPSC | Cannon | Demeter | Riddick |
|----|-------|--------|---------------|---|-------|--------|---------|---------|
| 356 | Can the board create an office? | No, p. 528. | No, offices are created by the bylaws, pp. 447, 461. | 47 | No, offices are created by the bylaws, p. 299. | No, offices are created by the bylaws, p. 151. | No, offices are created by the bylaws, p. 194. | No, offices are created by the bylaws, pp. 34-5. |
| 357 | Can the board restore an office that has been dropped from the bylaws? | No, p. 528. | No, offices are created by the bylaws, pp. 447, 461. | 47 | No, offices are created by the bylaws, p. 299. | No, offices are created by the bylaws, p. 151. | No, offices are created by the bylaws, p. 194. | No, offices are created by the bylaws, pp. 34-5, 90. |
| 358 | Bylaws of national society contain a list of names local societies cannot use. Can national board add to the list? | No, the list is presumed to be exclusive; bylaws must be amended to add to it, p. 528-9. | No, bylaw prohibition permits things of the same class that are not mentioned, p. 590; must amend bylaws to add to list. | 56 | No, bylaws should be amended, local groups bound by parent bylaws, p. 238. | No, bylaws define powers and authority, p. 70. | No, change requires amendment, pp. 187-90. | No, change requires amendment, p. 37. |
| 359 | Is 3/11 a big enough quorum for a board and is 5/250 a big enough quorum for a club? | No, board quorum should seldom be less than a third; a club of 250 should have a quorum no less than 12-20, p. 529. (App. 5-10%) | Board quorum default is M; club quorum should the number of members likely to be present except in very bad weather of other exceptional conditions, p. 346. | 40 | Board quorum default is M, p. 123; club quorum should the number of members likely to be present, p. 122. | Quorum default is M; club quorum could be 25 percent of total membership, p. 89. | Each organization is the best judge of its own quorum requirements; can be as little as 10% for large club, p. 151. | Board quorum default is M; club quorum could be 5-25% of large group, p. 162. |
| 360 | Should the roll be called at each meeting to see if a quorum is present? | No, too time consuming; may be self-evident, otherwise use tellers, pp. 529-30. | Chair has duty to determine quorum, subject to challenge and verification by assembly, pp. 348-9. | 40 | Chair has duty to determine quorum, subject to challenge by assembly; can count or call roll, pp. 124-5. | Chair has duty to determine quorum, subject to count if assembly requires, p. 90. | Quorum is presumed but can be challenged at any time by chair or any member, then counted, pp. 148-49. | Chair should check for presence of a quorum at the outset, subject to request for count at any time, p. 162. |

© American Institute of Parliamentarians. All rights reserved.

Appendix A

| No | Issue | Answer | RONR 11th Ed | § | AIPSC | Cannon | Demeter | Riddick |
|---|---|---|---|---|---|---|---|---|
| 361 | An organization with no specified quorum has 100 members credentialed at the first day of a convention, 150 on the second and 75 on the third. What is the quorum each day? | The quorum is M registered even though some have left: 51, 76, 76, p. 530. | The quorum is M registered even though some have left: 51, 76, 76, p. 617. | 59 | The quorum is M registered: 51, 76, 76, pp. 123, 207-9. | The quorum is M registered: 51, 76, 76, p. 91. | The quorum is M registered even though some have left: 51, 76, 76, p. 151. | The quorum is M registered whether present or not: pp. 51, 76, 76, 162. |
| 362 | Exactly a quorum was present but one member refused to vote on a resolution. Was the resolution legally adopted? | Yes, p. 530. | Yes, M is more than half the votes cast, excluding blanks and abstentions, p. 400. | 44 | Yes, M is more than half the **legal** votes cast, p. 139. | Yes, M is more than half the votes cast by those present and voting (not abstaining), p. 123. | Yes, M means more than half the votes cast at a legal meeting with a quorum, p. 246. | Yes, M means over half the legal votes cast by members entitled to vote, p. 206. |
| 363 | Is MEM necessary for a quorum at a special meeting? | No, quorum is the same as at a regular meeting, p. 530. | No, no special quorum required for special meeting, pp. 91-3. | 9 | No, no special quorum required for special meeting, pp. 106-7. | No, no special quorum required for special meeting, pp. 168, 89. | No, no special quorum required for special meeting, p. 13. | No, quorum for special meetings is the same as for a regular meeting, p. 183. |
| 364 | No quorum present but no question raised. Was business transacted legal? | No, may be ratified but should otherwise be stricken from the minutes, p. 530. | No, null and void, pp. 347-8, but may be ratified, pp. 124-5. | 40 | No, any action must be ratified to be legal, p. 122. | No, quorum must be present to conduct business, pp. 89-90. | Yes, quorum presumed and business legal unless challenged before other business taken up, p. 150. | No, any action must be ratified to be legal, p. 163. |
| 365 | Town board with 6 members, quorum of 4, has power to fill vacancies. Two members die without board filling vacancies. If a third dies, could remaining members fill vacancies? | No, board can't reduce quorum by neglecting duty to fill vacancies, pp. 530-1. | No, quorum is necessary for legal transaction of any business, pp. 21, 345, 403n. | 3 | No, quorum is necessary for legal transaction of any business, p. 122. | No, quorum is necessary for transaction of any business, p. 89. | No, quorum is necessary for legal transaction of any business, p. 148. | No, quorum is necessary for valid transaction of any business, pp. 161-2. |

© American Institute of Parliamentarians. All rights reserved.

Appendix A

| No | Issue | Answer | RONR 11th. Ed | § | AIPSC | Cannon | Demeter | Riddick |
|---|---|---|---|---|---|---|---|---|
| 366 | A board of 8 with 5 present votes 3 to 2 to sell property. Absentees, including president and secretary, all opposed. Can president and secretary be forced to sign deed? | Yes, unless 5 opposed rescind action by MN, p. 531. | Yes, M is more than half the votes cast (3/5), p. 400; but could be rescinded by MN (5/8), p. 306. | 44 | Yes, M is more than half the **legal** votes cast (3/5), p. 139; but could be rescinded by same vote and notice (5/8), p. 49. | Yes, M is more than half the votes cast (3/5), p. 123; but could be reconsidered by MN (5/8), p. 127. | Yes, M is more than half the votes cast (3/5), p. 246; but could be rescinded by MN (5/8), p. 165. | Yes, M is over half the legal votes cast (3/5), p. 206; but could be rescinded by M even without notice (5/8), p. 173. |
| 367 | Member leaves early after giving another a memo that he is in favor. Can the rules be suspended to accept the memo as a proxy? | Yes, but only if the bylaws allow proxy voting, p. 531. | Yes, but only if the bylaws allow proxy voting, or state law requires it, p. 428. | 45 | Yes, but only if the bylaws allow proxy voting in that memo form, or state law requires it, pp. 154, 285-6. | Yes, but only if the bylaws allow proxy voting, p. 166. | Yes, but only if the bylaws or rules allow proxy voting, p. 33. | Yes, but only if the bylaws allow proxy voting in that memo form, pp. 155-6. |
| 368 | Can a board delegate power to an executive committee? | No, not unless the bylaws authorize delegation; committees may investigate, report or implement, pp. 531-2. | No, not unless the bylaws authorize delegation; committees must work under board supervision and instructions, pp. 484-5. | 49 | No, not unless the bylaws authorize executive committee, p. 196; committees remain responsible to the board, pp. 182-3. | No, bylaws define powers and duties, p. 152; no general rule on delegation. | No, boards have no powers not expressly provided in the bylaws, pp. 270-1. | No, executive committee must be provided for in the bylaws, pp. 28, 81. |
| 369 | Is it true that delegated authority cannot be delegated? | Yes, but sometimes, for example, committee assignments require subdivision, p. 532. | Yes, except as provided in the bylaws, p. 484. | 49 | Yes, legislative and discretionary powers cannot be delegated, but ministerial powers can with appropriate instructions, pp. 182-3. | No general rule on delegation; bylaws define powers and duties, pp. 149-54. | No general rule on delegation. | Yes, definitive power and duties cannot be delegated and must be conducted by designated individuals, p. 81. |

Appendix A

| No | Issue | Answer | RONR 11th. Ed | § | AIPSC | Cannon | Demeter | Riddick |
|---|---|---|---|---|---|---|---|---|
| 370 | May a convention take action on matters of policy that have not been presented to the constituent organizations? | Yes, if convention bylaws allow, p. 532. | Yes, if convention bylaws allow, p. 601. | 58 | Yes, if convention bylaws allow, p. 205. | Yes, if convention bylaws allow, pp. 3, 160, 150. | Yes, if convention bylaws allow, pp. 291-5. | Yes, if convention bylaws allow, pp. 59, 62. |
| 371 | Bylaws require registrar's books closed 15 days before first day of convention, which is May 5. Should credentials received April 20 be recorded? | Yes, although a less liberal interpretation is possible, p. 532. | Yes, count all calendar days (including weekends and holidays), exclude the day of the meeting, include the day of the notice or other prior event, p. 92. | 9 | Yes, no contrary guidance. | Yes, no contrary guidance. | Yes, no contrary guidance. | Yes, no contrary guidance. |
| 372 | In a meeting of delegates, can the chair allow others to speak if there is no rule to the contrary? | Yes, if no objection: otherwise assembly decides, p. 533. | Yes, if no objection, otherwise assembly decides, pp. 54-6, 601-2. | 4 | Yes, if no objection, otherwise assembly decides, pp. 148, 205-6. | Yes, if no objection, otherwise assembly decides, pp. 124-5, 3. | Yes, if no objection, otherwise assembly decides, pp. 309-10, 291-2. | Yes, if no objection, otherwise assembly decides, pp. 194-5, 58-9. |
| 373 | Can anyone other than delegates offer resolutions at conventions? | No, only members of the convention can offer resolutions, p. 533. | Yes, **members** of the convention can offer resolutions, pp. 633, 600-2, and members may include delegates and officers, p. 603. | 58 | Yes, "delegates (or other voting members)" can conduct business, p. 206. | No, only members of the delegate assembly can conduct business, pp. 3, 160. | No, only members of the convention can conduct business, pp. 291-7. | No, only members of the convention can conduct business, pp. 58-9, 79-81, unless bylaws permit, p. 62. |
| 374 | Has a delegate who is also secretary of a convention a right to two votes? | No, each member has only one vote, p. 533. | No, each member has only one vote, p. 407. | 45 | Membership, not office, carries with it the power to vote, pp. 260, 181-2. | Membership, not office, gives power to vote, pp. 169, 149, 151-2. | Membership, not office, gives power to vote, pp. 305, 33, 252-3, 243. | Membership, not office, gives power to vote, pp. 208, 111. |

Appendix A

| No | Issue | Answer | RONR 11th Ed | § | AIPSC | Cannon | Demeter | Riddick |
|----|-------|--------|--------------|---|-------|--------|---------|---------|
| 375 | Is it necessary to put it in the bylaws that someone at a convention holding two offices is entitled to only one vote? | No, membership, not office, carries with it the right to vote, p. 533. | No, membership, not office, carries with it the right to vote; one person, one vote even if that person has multiple roles each with a vote, p. 407. | 45 | Membership, not office, carries with it the power to vote, pp. 260, 181-2. | Membership, not office, gives power to vote, pp. 169, 149, 151-2. | Membership, not office, gives power to vote, pp. 305, 250-4, 243. | Membership, not office, gives power to vote, pp. 208, 111. |
| 376 | May a club designate an ex-officio member to represent it at a convention? | Yes, ex-officio members have all the privileges of membership, p. 533. | Yes, ex-officio members have all the privileges of membership, pp. 483-4. | 49 | Yes, ex-officio members have all the privileges of membership, p. 190. | Yes, ex-officio members have all the privileges of membership, pp. 161, 3. | Yes, ex-officio members have all the privileges of membership, p. 274. | Yes, ex-officio members have all the privileges of membership, p. 94. |
| 377 | When a delegate is elected president, does his alternate have the right to vote in his place? | No, the president does not lose his right to vote when it would affect the result, p. 533. | No, the president does not lose his right to vote but should refrain except when it would affect the result or when voting by ballot, p. 405. | 44 | No, the president does not lose his right to vote but should refrain except when it would affect the result or when voting by ballot, pp. 142-3. | No, the chair does not lose his right to vote but should refrain except when it would affect the result or when voting by ballot, pp. 7-8. | No, the chair does not lose his right to vote but should refrain except when it would affect the result or when voting by ballot, pp. 45-6. | No, the chair does not lose his right to vote but should refrain except when it would affect the result or when voting by ballot, p. 146. |
| 378 | If the fourth delegate resigns, is the vacancy filled by the fourth alternate? | No, except by special rule, the first vacancy is filled by the first alternate, pp. 533-4. | No, except by special rule, the first vacancy is filled by the first alternate, p. 604. | 58 | Depends on bylaws, no order specified, p. 206. | Depends on bylaws, no order specified, p. 93. | Depends on bylaws, no order specified, pp. 33, 292. | No, except by special rule, the first vacancy is filled by the first alternate, p. 81. |

Appendix A

| No | Issue | Answer | RONR 11th. Ed | § | AIPSC | Cannon | Demeter | Riddick |
|---|---|---|---|---|---|---|---|---|
| 379 | Constitution gives control of admission of members to a council. Annual meeting of society, including quorum of council, unanimously admits member. Was the member legally admitted? | No, power given to council; even unanimous vote can't suspend constitution, p. 534. | No, power given to council; even unanimous vote can't suspend constitution, p. 263. | 25 | No, power given to council; even unanimous vote can't suspend constitution, p. 86. | No, power given to council; even unanimous vote can't suspend constitution, p. 71. | No, power given to council; even unanimous vote can't suspend constitution, but if not challenged, not a violation, p. 133. | No, power given to council; even unanimous vote can't suspend constitution, p. 188. |
| 380 | Can president and M agree by telephone to pay club funds for something? | No, no action of a deliberative body can be taken outside a session; action would have to be ratified, pp. 534-5. | No, no action of a deliberative body can be taken outside a meeting without deliberation; action would have to be ratified in a meeting, pp. 486-7. | 49 | No, no action of a deliberative body can be taken outside a meeting without deliberation; action would have to be approved or ratified in a meeting, pp. 41-3. | No, no action of a deliberative body can be taken outside a meeting, pp. 163, 4-5. | No, no action of a deliberative body can be taken outside a meeting without deliberation; action would have to be ratified in a meeting, pp. 13-4, 168. | No, no action of deliberative body can be taken outside a meeting without deliberation; action would have to be ratified in a meeting, pp. 108-9, 163-4. |
| 381 | An officer, with authority from the society, hired an employee. Officer then resigned and a new officer was appointed. (a) Does resignation cancel the employment contract? (b) Can new officer dismiss the employee and find another? | (a) No, resignation does not affect the contract; (b) New officer has same power as old officer and is bound by the contract terms, p. 535. | (a) No, contracts can't be unilaterally rescinded or reconsidered, pp. 308, 319; (b) contract is binding, pp. 308, 319, so it depends on the termination provision of the contract. | 35 | (a) No, can't rescind action taken (contract) before motion to rescind, p. 48; (b) contract is binding, p. 48, so it depends on the termination provision of the contract. | No relevant guidance, termination depends on terms of the contract. | (a) No, can't rescind executed motion, p. 166; (b) contract is binding, p. 166, so it depends on the termination provision of the contract. | (a) No, can't rescind implemented action, p. 173; (b) contract is binding, p. 173, so it depends on the termination provision of the contract. |

Appendix A

| No | Issue | Answer | RONR 11th. Ed | § | AIPSC | Cannon | Demeter | Riddick |
|----|-------|--------|---------------|---|-------|--------|---------|---------|
| 382 | President elected without the required consent "resigned" upon notification. (a) Was election legal? (b) Does board fill vacancy? | (a) Yes, nomination improper but voting not limited to nominees; (b) No, hold special election; election incomplete: never incumbent so no vacancy, pp. 535-6. | Yes, nomination improper but voting not limited to nominees, pp. 430-1, 439; (b) No, hold special election; election incomplete: never incumbent so no vacancy, p. 444. | 46 | (a) Yes, nomination improper but voting not limited to nominees, pp. 161, 159; (b) No, hold special election; election incomplete: never incumbent so no vacancy, p. 170. | (a) Yes, nomination improper but voting not limited to nominees absent bylaw provision, p. 130; (b) No, never accepted, never vacated, assembly would decide, pp. 129, 134. | Yes, nomination improper but voting not limited to nominees, pp. 240-1; (b) No, hold special election; election incomplete: never incumbent so no vacancy, pp. 241, 244. | (a) Yes, nomination improper but voting not limited to nominees, p. 123; (b) No, consent was required so election is incomplete, p. 92. |
| 383 | Club amends bylaws on 6/2, adjourns to 6/9 to complete unfinished business. On 6/9 no quorum but executive board allowed to conduct unfinished business. Motion to reconsider bylaw amendments adopted and tabled. Are amendments part of the bylaws or not? | Amendments are part of the bylaws effective 6/2. Reconsideration null and void: can't reconsider bylaw amendment, no notice, board exceeded authority, pp. 537-8. | Amendments are part of the bylaws effective 6/2. Reconsideration null and void: can't reconsider bylaw amendment, no notice, board exceeded authority, pp. 597-8, 592, 596. | 57 | Amendments are part of the bylaws effective 6/2. Reconsideration null and void: can't reconsider bylaw amendment, no notice, board exceeded authority, pp. 240-2. | Amendments are part of the bylaws effective 6/2. Reconsideration null and void: no notice of bylaw amendment, board exceeded authority, pp. 71-3, 126-9. | Amendments are part of the bylaws effective 6/2, pp. 188, 178. Reconsideration null and void: can't reconsider bylaw amendment, no notice, board exceeded authority, pp. 157, 188. | Amendments are part of the bylaws effective 6/2, p. 37, reconsideration null and void. Amendment process must be followed by club not board, p. 36. |

© American Institute of Parliamentarians. All rights reserved.

Appendix A

| No | Issue | Answer | RONR 11th. Ed | § | AIPSC | Cannon | Demeter | Riddick |
|---|---|---|---|---|---|---|---|---|
| 384 | Constitution allows special purpose assessments by vote of club but they are not binding unless voted for by M of members in good standing. Favorable vote is M but not M in good standing. Was ruling that motion lost correct? | No, motion passed but assessment not binding -- equivalent to request for voluntary contributions, p. 538. | No, motion passed but assessment not binding -- equivalent to request for voluntary contributions, pp. 588-9, see principles of interpretation 2). | 56 | No, motion passed but assessment not binding -- equivalent to request for voluntary contributions; membership interprets only when ambiguous, p. 245. | No, motion passed but assessment not binding -- request for voluntary contributions; no guidance on bylaw interpretation in Cannon. | No, motion passed but assessment not binding -- equivalent to request for voluntary contributions; give effect to intent of framers, p. 217. | No, motion passed but assessment not binding -- equivalent to request for voluntary contributions; give effect to intent, p. 38. |
| 385 | If an amendment or motion is carried, but should have been ruled out of order when moved, is it null and void? | If it violates the bylaws, is detrimental to someone or could not have been authorized by unanimous vote, it is null and void; if not, the defect is waived by general consent, pp. 538-9. | Points of order must be raised immediately except those relating to actions violating bylaws, MM in force, laws, fundamental principles, rights of absentees, which are null and void and can be challenged at any time, pp. 250-1. | 23 | Points of order must be raised immediately except those relating to actions violating bylaws, laws, and fundamental principles, p. 91. | No, unless it conflicts with bylaws, p. 69, but mistakes can be fixed by general consent or reconsideration, pp. 26, 114-5. | Points of order must be raised immediately except those relating to actions violating bylaws, which are automatically null and void, pp. 121-4. | No, points of order must be raised immediately; mistakes can be fixed by reconsideration or rescission, pp. 140-1, 22-3, 173, 165. |

© American Institute of Parliamentarians. All rights reserved.

Appendix A

| No | Issue | Answer | RONR 11th Ed | § | AIPSC | Cannon | Demeter | Riddick |
|---|---|---|---|---|---|---|---|---|
| 386 | Temporary board, before adoption of constitution and bylaws, voted to make temporary president honorary president and permanent member of board. Bylaws do not provide for honorary president. Can "mistake" be rectified by treating as unfinished business or by rescinding and amending bylaws? | No, the society came into being when its constitution and bylaws were adopted; actions taken before have no effect, p. 539. | No, the society came into being when its constitution and bylaws were adopted; actions taken before have no effect, p. 559. | 54 | No, the society came into being when its constitution and bylaws were adopted and officers elected, p. 255. | No, the society came into being when the contract between the society and its members (constitution and bylaws) was formed, p. 3. | No, the society came into being when its constitution and bylaws were adopted, pp. 177-81. | No, the society came into being when its constitution and bylaws were adopted and members enrolled, p. 134. |
| 387 | If voting is allowed by proxy and each county organization is allowed ten votes, must there be ten ballots or could there be one ballot on which is written "ten votes"? | Each assembly decides for itself but must ensure that no more than the entitled number are cast, p. 539. | Each assembly decides for itself but must ensure that no more than the entitled number are cast, pp. 428-9. | 45 | Each assembly decides for itself but must ensure that no more than the entitled number are cast, pp. 153-5, sample is separate ballot for each proxy, pp. 285-6. | Each assembly decides for itself but must ensure that no more than the entitled number are cast, p. 166. | Each assembly decides for itself but must ensure that no more than the entitled number are cast, p. 33. | Each assembly decides for itself but must ensure that no more than the entitled number are cast, pp. 155, sample is separate ballot for each proxy, p. 156. |
| 388 | What do you suggest as the order of proceedings in a debate with two speakers in the affirmative, two against and also general debate? | Set time limits, opening speeches for and against, general debate, closing speeches for and against, p. 540. | Set time limits, p. 387, opening speeches for and against, general debate, closing speeches for and against, pp. 379-80. | 43 | Set time limits, p. 131, opening speeches for and against, general debate, closing speeches for and against, p. 128. | Set time limits, pp. 108-9, opening speeches for and against, general debate, closing speeches for and against, p. 107. | Set time limits, p. 25, opening speeches for and against, general debate, closing speeches for and against, p. 43. | Set time limits, p. 72-3, opening speeches for and against, general debate, closing speeches for and against, p. 74. |

© American Institute of Parliamentarians. All rights reserved.

Appendix A

| No | Issue | Answer | RONR 11th. Ed | § | AIPSC | Cannon | Demeter | Riddick |
|---|---|---|---|---|---|---|---|---|
| 389 | How should a society disband? | Properly dispose of property and records, give notice of intent to disband, adopt a motion to amend by striking the entire bylaws by 2/3 vote, pp. 540-1. | Properly dispose of property and records, give notice of intent to disband, adopt a motion to amend by striking the entire bylaws by 2/3 vote, pp. 563-4. | 55 | No specified procedure, amend by striking bylaws, with advance notice by M vote, unless bylaws specify otherwise, p. 244. | No specified procedure; could amend by striking bylaws, with advance notice by 2/3 vote, unless bylaws specify otherwise, p. 71. | No specified procedure, amend by striking bylaws, with advance notice by 2/3 vote, unless bylaws specify otherwise, p. 178. | Properly dispose of property and records, give notice of intent to disband, adopt a motion to amend by striking the entire bylaws by M vote, pp. 86-7 |
| 390 | How should two societies unite to form a new society? | Appoint joint committee, draft new bylaws, both make identical reports, adopt motion to consolidate by 2/3 vote, adopt new bylaws by 2/3 vote, elect new officers, pp. 541-3. | Appoint joint committee, draft new bylaws, both make identical reports, adopt motion to consolidate by 2/3 vote, adopt new bylaws by 2/3 vote, elect new officers, p. 562-3. | 55 | No specified procedure but see formation of new entity, pp. 254-5. | No specified procedure, but involves amending existing bylaws and adopting new, pp. 70-1. | No specified procedure, but involves amending existing bylaws and adopting new, p. 178. | Draft new bylaws, adopt motion to consolidate, adopt new bylaws, elect new officers, pp. 57, 111-2. |

© American Institute of Parliamentarians. All rights reserved.

www.ingramcontent.com/pod-product-compliance
Lightning Source LLC
Chambersburg PA
CBHW080433230426
43662CB00015B/2260